African History Archive

Over the past forty years, Zed has established a long and proud tradition of publishing critical work on African issues, offering unique insights into the continent's politics, development, history and culture. The African History Archive draws on this rich backlist, consisting of carefully selected titles that even now have enduring relevance years after their initial publication. Lovingly repackaged, with newly commissioned forewords that reflect on the impact the books have had, these are essential works for anyone interested in the political history of the continent.

Other titles in the archive:

A History of Africa
Hosea Jaffe

No Fist Is Big Enough to Hide the Sky: The
and Cape Verde, 1963–74
Basil Davidson

The Story of an African Working Class: Ghanaian Miners' Struggles
1870–1980
Jeff Crisp

About the author

Baruch Hirson (1921–1999) was a lifelong activist who spent nine-and-a-half years in South African prisons as a result of his opposition to the apartheid regime. Following his release in 1973 he left for England, where he lectured in history at several universities and produced eight finely written, passionately argued books on the history of the left in South Africa. These include *Year of Fire, Year of Ash* (1984), *The Cape Town Intellectuals* (2000) and his autobiography, *Revolutions in my Life* (1995). He also founded the controversial critical journal *Searchlight South Africa*.

Tom Lodge is professor of peace and conflict studies at the University of Limerick, Ireland. He was formerly professor of political studies at the University of the Witwatersrand, South Africa. He is the author of *Mandela: A Critical Life* (2006) and *Politics in South Africa: From Mandela to Mbeki* (2003).

Yours for the Union

Class and Community Struggles in South Africa

Baruch Hirson

With a new Foreword by Tom Lodge

Zed Books

LONDON

Yours for the Union: Class and Community Struggles in South Africa
was first published in 1990 by Zed Books Ltd, The Foundry,
17 Oval Way, London SE11 5RR, UK.

This edition was published in 2017.

www.zedbooks.net

Cover design by Kika Sroka-Miller.

A catalogue record for this book is available from the British Library.

ISBN 978-1-78699-064-8 hb
ISBN 978-1-78360-984-0 pb
ISBN 978-1-78360-983-3 pdf
ISBN 978-1-78360-981-9 epub
ISBN 978-1-78360-982-6 mobi

Contents

Photographs and Illustrations

Foreword by Tom Lodge

Written nearly fifty years after the story it tells, *Yours for the Union* focuses on South Africa's black working class in its making. At the outset of his analysis, Baruch Hirson points to parallels between the status and treatment of workers in Czarist Russia and the experiences of many black South Africans. Both were first-generation migrants to the cities, often leaving their families behind in the countryside and retaining other kinds of affective connections with rural life. They were both without rights in their new settings and they would find their most natural solidarities and camaraderie around kinship ties, preserved through hometown associations. But in new workplaces and in the places in which they lived, these ties would assume fresh significance in defensive and sometimes assertive struggles against the treatment they received from employers and officials. Sometimes the associations and networks derived from clan and kinship performed bridging functions enabling workers to embrace wider kinds of collective action. This was most likely when leaders appeared who were able to combine ideas drawn from a moral order reinforced by 'direct experience and oral tradition' and fresh notions 'based on structured ideas learned from others'.

This book's narrative is centred on the Witwatersrand – home, more or less, to half a million Africans, mostly workers, though their numbers included a small 'petty bourgeoisie' of traders, teachers and other white-collar workers, as well as a tiny elite of professionals. Aside from those who worked on the mines and who as mineworkers lived in strictly controlled compounds, most African workers were 'casual' – that is, often employed in insecure temporary jobs, and almost always unskilled: 'employed simply to lift, carry, clean and dig'. Mineworkers were different, their contribution to the economy was of fundamental importance; hence the restrictions and controls that regulated their existence.

Efforts to organise South African workers remained focused on whites; in the early 1930s even revolutionary socialist groups believed that 'natives' were only 'workers of the first generation', not really proletarianised, and too vulnerable and too inexperienced to undertake their own assertive class action. Certainly it was true that workers without legal rights were very difficult to organise, and people whose worldview was shaped by their rural upbringing remained very susceptible to prophetic charlatans.

But between 1932 and 1945, the period that supplies the setting for Hirson's narrative, fresh opportunities existed for this African workforce to make gains as a class. Devaluation after South Africa abandoned the gold standard created the conditions for an industrial boom, and a consequent rise in urban employment for Africans. South Africa's declaration of war in 1939 supplied a second prompt in expanding manufacturing. In replacing

200,000 whites recruited into the army, Africans began to undertake semi-skilled or skilled work in factories for the first time. The declaration of war on Germany was politically divisive for white South Africans and opposed by Afrikaner nationalists; in this context, government was keen to secure the loyalty of its African subjects. In fact, a key reform had been enacted just two years before the war, when legislation extended wage boards to black workers; as Hirson notes, a springboard for efforts to build trade unions amongst them.

So, this was an unusually promising time for black South African workers, notwithstanding their recent assembly. For their numbers were growing in a political setting in which government was unusually predisposed towards conciliation and incorporation rather than direct repression, at least until the tide of warfare turned in favour of the Allies in 1944. And, as Hirson notes, there were a few activists, mainly though not only whites, 'who had self-consciously crossed the colour line'; who, taking their dictum from Trotsky's essay on unions in the 'epoch of imperialist decay', began to build effective organisations, step by step, around local wage struggles.

Not that the agency of external revolutionaries was indispensable to successful class assertions by black workers. Hirson's analysis of the Vereeniging protests against police raids of September 1937 and their aftermath supplies impressive evidence of the speed and effectiveness of communal self-mobilisation. Such actions were enabled, he thinks, through the communicative networks supplied by hometown organisations. Despite the violence of the riots and the repression that followed them, Vereeniging householders won concessions, and in forthcoming years a series of trade unions under local leadership undertook successful strike actions.

Too often, though, workers were misled or badly led by external agencies. A key theme in Baruch Hirson's work is 'the enthusiasm, courage and weakness of the workers'. In his view, this courage and enthusiasm was squandered. From 1940 onwards, the Communist Party of South Africa began seriously competing with the Trotskyites for influence over the nascent African trade union movement. From mid-1941, after Germany's attack on the Soviet Union, the Communist Party tended to oppose or at least discourage strike actions that might disrupt the war effort. The turnaround in the party's position, from being an opponent of an imperialist war to being patriotically supportive, coincided with the beginning of a wave of spontaneous strike action. Under more militant and determined national leadership, arguably, a much stronger organisational base for black labour might have emerged. In particular, communist trade unionists dissuaded key groups of workers, in power stations, collieries, and indeed on the gold mines from striking in that key period, before 1944, when government and management might have conceded wage gains and organisational rights.

Expansion of the party's following amongst 'middle class whites', as well as the influence of the American communist Earl Browder's call for class collaboration, helped to explain why communists were so ready to eschew militancy. On the Witwatersrand and elsewhere, Baruch Hirson thinks, the party's preoccupation with obtaining short-lived white electoral support distracted them from supplying leadership and resources to a range of different kinds of struggles, not just in the factories and other workplaces, but in the countryside and in the townships, even in locations in which their own activists were strategically placed. So, for example, despite the existence of a party group in Orlando, where the shanty town movement began, the arena of 'the biggest social and political upheaval of the war years', the party remained aloof. It was even perceived as an adversary by the squatters' leader, James Mpanza.

Only in 1946, two years too late, were communists ready to put themselves at the helm of militant working-class protest, in the massive mineworkers strike of that year. Baruch Hirson is insistent, though, that the party and its trade unionists deserve little credit for the networks that underpinned this extraordinary event. He draws on ethnographic research amongst surviving participants to show the salience of the elected *izibonda*, as well as hometown groups, in supplying the communicative under-webbing of mineworker mobilisation: few mineworkers, he thinks, had heard of the communist-sponsored union before the protest. The union's activities during the war had been desultory enough, and in 1946 its leadership failed to prepare for the confrontation forced upon it by its rank and file. In circumstances in which African industrial employment was falling and government had abandoned conciliation of African workers, any strike call was unrealistic; the mineworkers defeat presaged a more wholescale evisceration of African working-class organisation. As Hirson concludes, 'for this failure of leadership, African workers were to pay dearly'.

Baruch Hirson wrote *Yours for the Union* towards the end of the 1980s, after another decade in which black working-class struggles had successfully built up their own political organisations and were poised to secure political reforms. Originally written as a doctoral dissertation, *Yours for the Union* was directed at a readership that might recognise the contemporary salience of its message. Though Hirson resisted the suggestion of his academic mentors that he should write autobiography, the story he tells in this book is one in which he himself played a part, initially as a novice organiser with power-station workers in 1944.

In 1989 and in the years that followed he found himself observing from a distance, in exile in London, a partial re-enactment of the history he had so painstakingly reconstructed in *Yours for the Union*. In this re-enactment, what was at this time Africa's mightiest industrial working class once again 'surrendered its class role'. In so doing, the space was created in which members of the African 'petty bourgeoisie' would impose 'their own distinct view of the world' on South Africa's national settlement. South Africa's working-class communities are still paying the price for that abdication and Baruch Hirson's tragic history is still their story.

Tom Lodge
November 2016

Abbreviations

AAC	All African Convention
ACDWU	African Commercial and Distributive Workers Union
AMWU	African Mine Workers Union
ANC	African National Congress
ADP	African Democratic Party
CNETU	Council of Non-European Trade Unions
CPSA	Communist Party of South Africa
DPC	District Party Committee
FAATU	Federal Association of African Trade Unions
FIOSA	Fourth International of South Africa
IC	Industrial Conciliation (Act)
ICU	Industrial and Commercial Workers Union
IDU	Industrial Development Corporation
ILO	International Labour Organisation
MRC	Member of Native Representative Council
NEUF	Non-European United Party
NAD	Native Affairs Department
NMC	Native Military Corporation
NRC	Natives Representative Council
NUDW	National Union of Distributive Workers
PTU	Progressive Trade Union Group
SATALC	South African Trades and Labour Council
SAIRR	South African Institute of Race Relations
SAYL	South African Youth League
SP	Socialist Party
TAC	Transvaal African Congress
TATA	Transvaal African Teachers Association
TCNETU	Transvaal Council of Non-European Trade Unions
VFP	Victoria Falls and Transvaal Power Company (Gas and Power Workers Union)
Wenela	Witwatersrand Native Labour Association
WIL	Workers International League
WP	Workers Party of South Africa
ZBA	Zoutpansberg Associations
ZCA	Zoutpansberg Cultural Association

Preface

In this study of the making of the African working class in South Africa, the concentration is on the southern Transvaal between 1930 and 1947. The period was not chosen arbitrarily, although it saw little change in the social fabric of South Africa or in the country's political configuration despite the removal of Cape African males from the voters' roll in 1936. Furthermore, the division of the land into white-owned farmlands and black Reserves had long since been accomplished, and the new land regulations following the passage of the Native Trust and Land Act of 1936, though they might have quickened the movement from the country to the towns, did not alter the basic process. Nevertheless, this was the period during which South Africa emerged from the depression of 1929—32, and money flowed into the country to finance a boom in construction, manufacture and commerce.

The concentration on the Transvaal, and particularly the Witwatersrand, also recognises the continued domination of the country's economy by the gold mines. Indeed, it was gold that shielded South Africa from the worst ravages of the depression. The Witwatersrand then, as now, was also the area of greatest population density in South Africa, containing just over half of all urban Africans in the mid-1930s — 517,000 out of a total urban African population of just over one million in 1936. It was here, therefore, that the African working class was concentrated, and the first major industrial organisation of the black proletariat developed. The increase of population was not matched by a corresponding expansion in housing and transport, and when steps were taken to remove Africans to locations on the outskirts of the towns, the stage was set for a housing crisis. The war brought the issue of accommodation to the fore, and this triggered off broad popular movements for more housing and better transport facilities.

The African trade unions published neither newspapers nor journals. Except for Naboth Mokgatle's account (1971)* of his participation in the trade unions and the Communist Party of South Africa (CPSA), and an interview with J.B. Marks (President of the African Mine Workers Union) by T. Karis, there are few accounts of black trade unionists of this period (the records of most unions seem to have been lost or destroyed). To supplement the available sources, I have interviewed former trade unionists and members of political organisations. Some spoke of the unions, or events during the war, and on the state of the black working class. All assisted me in reconstructing the history of which they had been part.

---

* Bracketed references to sources used are given in the text, full citations in the bibliography. Longer notes are at the end of each chapter.

It is not only the trade unions that have been neglected by historians. There are few accounts of the impact of the major events of the 1930s and 1940s on African workers: the depression (1929–32) has been largely ignored; the *voortrekker* celebrations and the 'shirt movements' with their fascist programmes have rarely been mentioned; and the impact of war — in Ethiopia, Asia, and Europe — has only recently been investigated. These are discussed in this volume as events that helped shape black workers' consciousness.

Even more remarkable has been the neglect until recently of events in the locations or townships, hostels or compounds — miserable slums where the workers lived, alone or with their families, and spent their leisure time. It was here that an increasing number were reared and went to school, joined a church, played or watched sport, drank and danced, sought entertainment in shebeens, and belonged to political movements or to 'hometown' associations; these were centres, too, of gangland warfare, mugging, rape, and murder. I found invaluable accounts of location life in the auto-biographies of Ezekiel Mphahlele (1962) and Bloke Modisane (1963), in Modikwe Dikobe's novel (1973) and in studies of the early slum yards of Johannesburg by Ellen Hellmann (1948) and Eddie Koch (1981).

The locations were also arenas of bitter struggles — against passes, lodger permits and beer raids; against poor transport or high fares; housing shortages or high rentals. Each conflict had its own pattern of leadership and of grassroot support. Three are described in this work: the bus boycotts and the squatters' (or shantytown) movements in Johannesburg, led by local committees or by charismatic leaders; and the riot in Vereeniging, in the wake of police provocation, where there was no overt leadership. There were other struggles, such as those involving lodger permits in 1945 in Heidelberg; the protest against the dismissal of David Bopape, teacher and ANC leader, in Brakpan in 1944 (Sapire, 1987); and so on. Some have been the subject of recent researches, but most still require investigation.

There is a dearth of research on location struggles and, in part, this coincides with the paucity of writing on the position of women in the towns — their fight to stay there, and their campaigns against discriminatory regulations. Being excluded from manufacture, commerce, and clerical work, they brewed beer, became domestic servants or took in washing, and this had a direct bearing on their involvement in riots, bus boycotts and shanty towns. Research on urban struggles and on the position of women in towns must proceed in tandem to understand events in the locations.

If the working class, or more precisely, its consciousness, is 'made' through its struggles, as E.P. Thompson argues (1968 and 1978), these take place in the yard, the street and the neighbourhood as well as the workplace. The differences between struggles at the workplace and those in the townships are obvious. There were different class configurations: an all-male working class confronted the employers at work, and a cross-section of the community — men, women, and children — confronted the authorities in the locations.

Prior to the organisation of industrial unions in the 1930s (following the revival of the economy), the struggle for higher wages and better living conditions centred on the townships. After unions were built there were two foci of struggle which seldom overlapped. If the two had converged, the nature of the workers' struggle would have changed qualitatively, yet, despite calls on the trade unions to assist in the township (see the Alexandra bus boycott below), the labour and community struggles remained apart, and this inevitably weakened the working class movement.

The history of the towns tells only one part of the story. The vast majority of African people lived in the rural areas, and a discussion of the ideas nurtured there must contribute to our understanding of the proletariat. The consciousness of urban workers was derived from their rural perceptions and the new experiences to which they were subjected. There was the same 'lack of harmony' between urban and rural experience in the towns of South Africa as has been noted among Russian peasants in the factories in the late nineteenth century (Zelnik, 1968; Rudé, 1980). There were also tensions between artisans and labourers (in South Africa, read white workers and black) similar to those that had been experienced in Britain. Yet a syncretic understanding of social needs was achieved which allowed the workers to confront their everyday problems and find the necessary solutions.

The history of urban organisation has its own complexity and awaits further research. Some associations were taken by people from the Reserves to the towns, and there adapted to meet the new problems they confronted; others, like the ubiquitous *stokvel* (based on the rotating kitty), or the hometown groups, were fashioned to meet the new conditions in mine compounds or locations. Inevitably, class interests led to new organisations in the locations as stand holders, artisans, bus owners, businessmen and others formed their own local bodies. Workers also banded together in the factories, forming self-help groups that resembled the *stokvel* or joining trade unions.

In the organisation of industrial unions and cultural clubs the initiative often came from whites who had self-consciously crossed the colour line. Their ranks included individuals (like lawyers and politicians) but they were more frequently churchmen and missionaries, members of liberal bodies (like the Joint Councils of Europeans and Natives, the Institute of Race Relations and the Society of Friends of Africa), trade unionists and activists from left-wing parties. The histories of some of these people and associations appear in this volume; others are mentioned only when they impinge on the black working class.

The nationalist movements appear in the context of ongoing campaigns and struggles. The most important movement in the Transvaal was undoubtedly the African National Congress (ANC): its intervention (or inaction) is analysed in the many episodes discussed in these chapters. Other bodies like the Non-European United Front, the All African Convention (AAC), and those representing the Indian and Coloured communities were all present. Where these bodies affected the development of the African working class, they appear in this history.

Some of the events described below are covered in Roux (1949) and Simons and Simons (1969), but I have often found myself in disagreement with them over both matters of fact and interpretation. In addition, events to which I attach some importance have been omitted from their work. I have avoided extensive polemic in the belief that the facts speak for themselves. Finalising these pages in August 1987 I am only too aware of the importance of writing the pre-history of contemporary unions and their struggles. What happened during the war years has been left untold for too long, and the lessons that should have been learnt then still have relevance for the working class of South Africa today. That is the most important justification for publishing this work. The gulf between my interpretations and those of Roux and the Simonses marks the difference in our perspectives of the role of the working class and its party in the struggle for control of the South African state.

In completing this book, I did not have direct access to archives in South Africa, although friends sent me important documents. I can claim certain advantages in writing about the war years, having participated in some of the events during 1940−46, and having known some of the main actors. I witnessed the long walk from Alexandra, and spoke with Lilian Tshabalala about the women in the struggle. I had the misfortune (or was it the honour?) to be arrested with her on a visit to a location. I interviewed James Mpanza, the shantytown leader; assisted Dick Mfifi in reorganising the Gas and Power Workers (VFP) Union; visited many of the trade union offices as an organiser of the Workers International League; observed some of the meetings called by the Mine Workers Union; attended the conference of African trade unions in 1945 and then the report back meeting of the Progressive Trade Union group. I have not relied on my memory and only record what is available in documents. But, in so doing, I have found it invaluable to have a picture of people, of places and of events in my mind's eye.

I described these events in *Socialist Action, Revolutionary Communist* and the *Internal Bulletin* of the Workers International League in 1944−46, and have checked what I wrote then against documents (some on microfilm, photocopies or fiche) from private or public collections of papers. I have rejected or amended earlier views in the light of the material now available to me. At the time, we had an incomplete view of what other people or groups were saying or doing. I have quoted the sources from which the material is taken, first in my PhD thesis and now, with some abbreviation, in this volume. Copies of papers in my possession will be lodged at the Institute of Commonwealth Studies, or are available in libraries in Britain or South Africa.

I am grateful to those who agreed to be interviewed (and lent or gave me documents) — they are listed in the bibliography; to the staffs of libraries at the Institute of Commonwealth Studies, the School of Oriental and African Studies, the Royal Commonwealth Society, the

University of the Witwatersrand, the Documentation Centre of the University of South Africa (and particularly Annica van Gylswyk) and the South African Library, Cape Town. I am particularly grateful to those who allowed me to read documents or found them for me: to Marian Lacey, Brian Willan, Tom Lodge, Tony Southall, Karel Roskam, Bob Edgar, Michael and Margaret Hathorn, Neville Rubin, Charles van Onselen, Tim Couzens, Debby Gaitskell, Debby Posel, Brian Bunting, Nachum Sneh, Miriam Basner, Millie Levy, Ike Horvich, David Hemson, Mark Stein; to Dunbar Moodie for showing me his unpublished typescripts; and to Helen Bradford who so generously sent documents, notes and information.

My thanks to students at the Middlesex Polytechnic who extracted information from newspapers at Colindale; to Allen Hirson and Jane Starfield who read chapters and suggested corrections; to Hillel Ticktin and Paul Trewhela for discussions that proved invaluable; and to Shula Marks for the careful reading of many drafts, and her encouragement in getting the work on which this volume is based completed for presentation as a doctoral thesis. I alone am responsible for errors of fact or interpretation in the text.

Among those who gave me every assistance was Jenny Curtis Schoon, one-time archivist at the South African Institute of Race Relations (SAIRR). Although we had not previously met, Jenny informed me on sources, sent me copies of documents and, on her last visit to London, urged the completion of this work. A few months later she and her daughter Katryn were killed by a letter bomb at their home in Angola. To their memory I dedicate this book.

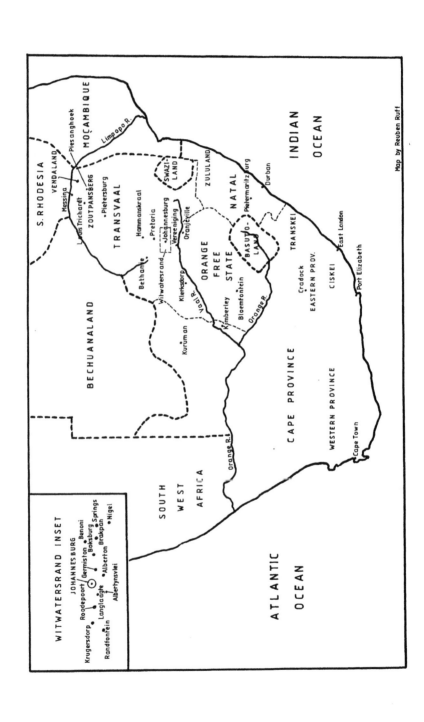

WITWATERSRAND INSET

JOHANNESBURG

Krugersdorp   Roodepoort / Germiston • Benoni
                              • Boksburg Springs
Randfontein Langlaagte • Alberton Brakpan
                    Albertynsvlei   • Nigel

S. RHODESIA

VENDALAND

MOÇAMBIQUE

Piesanghoek

Limpopo R.

Messina

Louis Trichardt

ZOUTPANSBERG

Pietersburg

TRANSVAAL

Hammanskraal

Pretoria

Johannesburg

Vereeniging

Witwatersrand

Bethanie

SWAZI-
LAND

ZULULAND

NATAL

Pietermaritzburg

Durban

INDIAN
OCEAN

Klerksdorp

Oranjeville

ORANGE
FREE
STATE

BASUTO-
LAND

Vaal R.

Kimberley

Bloemfontein

Orange R.

Kuruman

BECHUANALAND

TRANSKEI

Cradock

EASTERN PROV.

CISKEI

East London

Port Elizabeth

CAPE PROVINCE

WESTERN PROVINCE

Cape Town

Orange R.

SOUTH
WEST
AFRICA

ATLANTIC
OCEAN

Map by Reuben Ruff

1. The African Worker:
Class and Community

Driven to the city originally by the necessity of supplementing their inadequate earnings . . . a part of them were seasonal workers who . . . regularly returned to their land. . . . Another part continued to work in the cities the year round . . . and left behind their families, who cultivated the family allotment in their absence. While it is true that a genuine working class permanently cut off from the land was becoming more and more numerous . . . the overwhelming majority of the workers were peasants, still strongly tied to the land, who came to the cities reluctantly to round out a subsistence which could not be adequately provided by tilling the soil alone.
Jacob Walkin[1]

His tastes and appetites were those of the village, but his outward life was that of the factory. There was no harmony between the two.
Theodore von Laue[2]

The growth of an urban community

There are striking similarities between the recruitment and working conditions of workers in Czarist Russia and those of many black workers in Southern Africa until at least 1939 — further evidence of the widespread use of repressive methods in the early stages of industrialisation. Some came voluntarily (or even eagerly) to the towns, seeking employment and also the opportunity of building a better life; others came because of economic pressure or administrative fiat and returned home seasonally or at the end of a contract. They left their wives and families in the village or on the farms, and they lived either in single-sex hostels subject to tight controls, or where they could in the towns. Trade union organisation was forbidden (in Russia) or denied recognition (in South Africa) because, it was said, they were peasants (or 'tribal') and not workers.

A large section of the work force in South Africa came from the three High Commission territories — Swaziland, Basutoland and Bechuanaland — and were considered part of South Africa's labour force; others came from territories north of the Limpopo. Most were recruited on limited contracts for the mines; an unknown number entered the country illegally to work on the farms and in the towns. What they contributed to the growth of working class organisation through their own unique initiatives is not known — despite the lengthy survey conducted by First (1983) of the men from Mozambique. There is also little information about the men who illegally crossed borders and stopped at farmsteads on their way down to the towns. They avoided prying eyes, leaving few accounts of what they endured in their quest for jobs. Yet it is obvious from the agitation (by Africans) for their removal that there were unresolved problems that kept these 'strangers' away from fellow blacks.

In 1928 the Transvaal African Congress (TAC) spearheaded by Selby Msimang pressed for a petition to the government to have all Nyasas (Malawians) deported, arguing that these men, who often worked as domestic servants, deprived the women of the northern Transvaal of employment, 'exploiting' and then deserting them.[3] It is not known what precipitated that particular agitation, nor what occurred in 1941 when clashes involving large numbers of Africans from 'northern territories' were reported. Requests from Senator Rheinallt Jones, the Native Representative, for information on the latter event were refused.[4]

There can be little doubt about the importance of the migrants — both in terms of the country's economy and also as a consequence of their contact, or conflict, with the local inhabitants. But they obviously represented a minority group (or groups) inside the larger black community and they only entered certain areas of the country. In the mid-1930s the Africans of South Africa lived mainly in the rural areas: some 2 million in the Reserves, 2.2 million on farms (almost all white-owned), and 1.4 million in the towns. Ten years later the numbers had increased by 300,000, 260,000 and 660,000 respectively, marking the continued movement to the towns, particularly on the Witwatersrand. Those with roots in the Reserves returned home periodically, while those who came from the farms stayed permanently.

There was a continuous movement from the white farmlands to the towns and the Urban Areas Acts of 1924 and 1930 both aimed to limit the number of Africans entering towns and villages, while several other measures were aimed at converting labour tenants into wage labourers. Trade unionism was forbidden on the farms and labour was controlled by Masters and Servants Acts which made desertion a criminal offence. Furthermore, the Native Services Contract Act of 1932 forbade the employment of labour tenants or their children in towns (Horwitz, 1967, pp.203—4). This did not stop men and women absconding, and the youth in particular sought to escape the poorly paid labour to which they were subjected. But this left them at the mercy of employers in villages and towns en route to their urban destinations when they stopped (as did the migrants from the north) to earn money for the journey.

The transition from countryside to town was slow and the process of proletarianisation uneven: some became permanent town dwellers, others travelled backwards and forwards, making painful adjustments at both ends. The factors that led different sectors of African society to work in the towns varied. Some men came willingly or were sent by their chiefs to secure money for arms and ammunition; others found that spells of labour in towns allowed them to obtain the money (though wages were so low) to buy cattle or increase production. But there was also reluctance to leave the land, particularly when the crops were good, because the towns — with their squalid slums or compounds, their unrewarding or dangerous work — held few attractions.[5] Ultimately, decisions had to be made on whether to stay or return to the land. The multiple factors that determined their length of stay included the conditions inside the towns, the outcome of struggles (whether sharp or muted) for better conditions, and the struggles within the ruling classes over the disposal of their labour power.

This continued link with the land distinguished these African workers (like their Russian counterparts) from those of western Europe who had been 'freed' from the countryside (Brenner, 1977, p.35). In the end, however, the mines and the towns would 'swallow people' and an increasing number of men and women left the land.[6] There was too little land, and eroded land at that, to sustain an increasing population: drought and disease only speeded the exodus. Whether they came permanently or as migrant labourers (many of whom went home for little more than an unpaid 'vacation' before returning to work), these were the new proletariat of South Africa.

Yet even those who had left the land retained links with their kinsmen, either directly or through contact with those who poured into the towns, and they imbibed or were absorbed by the cultures of both town and Reserve. Kinship ties were reinforced in hometown associations, and these were conditioned in turn by the system of segregated housing and reinforced through language, folklore and age group loyalties.

There were inevitably new conflicts, both in the towns and in the Reserves, as the workers confronted new problems. These struggles brought new organisations into being, fashioned by newly emergent leaders and by conditions in the towns that they entered. Because so many workers were unskilled, and worked in small shops, organisations first appeared in the locations or townships alongside, and not always separate from, church groups, youth clubs and organisations of stand holders, craftsmen, herbalists and tenants. It was these groups, bound in loose alliances, that took up the struggle for better living conditions.

In the workshops men grouped together, joining trade unions and political groups; in the rural areas, the same men belonged to clan associations or formed new groups, joined in 'traditional' pursuits and clashed with their own elders. They adjusted to different conditions as they moved between town and village, adapting the organisations of one 'culture' to meet the needs of a' new environment or building unique groups to cope with new situations. It was this use of traditional forms to cloak associations of a new type that led to clashes, when ethnicity and class were joined to become the basis of workers' solidarity. Thus, men determined on a strike would ascribe scabbing to ethnic differences, and picketing gave way to factional (or so-called tribal) fighting.

By 1936 census returns showed the appreciable growth of the population on the Witwatersrand. There were now some 570,726 Africans in the region, out of a total population that just topped the one million mark. But the inflow was dominated by men, the sex ratio badly skewed. In Johannesburg, the largest town, it was still 2.6:1, due in part to the official policy as formulated by Colonel Stallard (*Local Government Commission of Inquiry*, 1922, p.241):

natives — men, women and children — should only be permitted within municipal areas in so far and for so long as their presence is demanded by the wants of the white population. . . .
    [T]he town is a European area . . . [with] no place for the redundant native, who neither works nor serves his or her [sic] people but forms the class from which the professional agitators, the slum landlords, the liquor sellers, the prostitutes, and other undesirables spring.

New legislation, including the Urban Areas Act of 1923, together with pre-industrial regulations, controlled or excluded Africans from the towns. Vagrancy laws, Masters and Servants Acts and so on were used as weapons against the unemployed or those on strike, and the liquor laws under which home brewing was controlled were used to deny women an economic base in the towns (B. Hepple, 1960, pp.760–813). Africans were also squeezed off the land, or white farms, under the Land Acts of 1913 and 1936, and although regulations excluded their entry to the towns (Lacey, 1981, pp.268–9), men and women squatted on farms and fields and sought casual labour in neighbouring urban suburbs.

Over 300,000 men lived in compounds (on the mines and railways, in municipal and hospital services, as members of road gangs and sometimes as industrial workers). Other workers lived in 'slum yards', hostels, locations and townships, all of which lacked modern amenities and few of which had medical, educational or leisure facilities. During the 1930s the slum yards and some townships were closed by the authorities and their residents moved, by regulation and by force, to segregated areas.[7]

Residents' or tenants' associations opposed the evictions through the law courts[8] but there were no campaigns against residential segregation. The residents demanded better housing, more transport, cheaper fares and improvements to the townships; and they campaigned against removal. This degree of acquiescence in the existence of racial ghettoes was an admission of powerlessness and an indication that those who came to the towns did not aim to undermine the system: they wanted integration into society. When the townships erupted, it was against the background threat of expropriation (Alexandra and Vereeniging), for lower bus fares (Alexandra and Pretoria), after serious traffic accidents (Sophiatown, 1944), for more houses (Orlando, 1946), for the right to trading stalls (Moroka, 1947), in protest against attacks on beer brewing (Springs, 1945), in support of demands for the reinstatement of a teacher (Brakpan, 1944), against lodger permits (Heidelberg, 1945) or to call for an end to police harassment (Vereeniging, 1937).

Community, identity, class struggle

The centralising tendency of manufacture, argued Engels (1976, p.55), led to a concentration of people, firstly at the place of work and then in residence. On the gold mines, black labourers were doubly concentrated — in the mine compounds and underground. Consequently, work and social activities tended to merge. Informal associations, originally based on clan organisations, helped determine work companions, dormitory associates and the dance groups that participated in the weekly displays run by the mine management.

But life on the mines was hard and the men took their complaints to management. These concerned food shortages, constraints on beer brewing, maltreatment by compound officials, safety conditions underground, wages and work conditions. Significantly, mineworkers presented their complaints over work and living conditions through their *izibonda*, or dormitory leaders — men who did not belong to the newly organised trade union, nor necessarily to ethnic associations. The *izibonda* represented the workers and called them out, independently of the African Mine Workers Union (AMWU), when there was a strike call in 1946.

Mineworkers did not link all their complaints together, nor did complaints inevitably lead to strikes. Nor were all miners of like mind; some protested over perceived injustice, others acquiesced; some were still rooted in their rural societies, others were said to have 'deserted' their kinsmen because they did not return to their former homes. The latter were as 'urbanised' as men who worked in industry, distanced themselves from ethnic associations and were amongst the firmest adherents of the AMWU.

There is little information available about hometown associations, or direct workers' representation, in industrial and municipal compounds, and nothing is known about relations between such organisations and either management or the trade unions. Ethnic associations existed and they planned their own leisure activities, including inter-ethnic dance competitions. In the power works, (migrant) workers organised and established contacts between compounds in several towns, and called a strike in 1942 without being mobilised in a formal union (see Chapter 13).

The workers in towns (in locations or slum yards) lived in less homogeneous communities than those in the compounds, their fellow residents including workers from other industries, the young and the old who were not employed, and the women who, in addition to household work, took in washing, brewed, or occasionally engaged in hawking. They also lived alongside small independent craftsmen, hawkers and traders, stand holders, churchmen, shebeen keepers, teachers, nurses, and so on.

This latter group, a petty bourgeoisie barely distinguishable from workers in living standards, and sometimes taking labouring jobs, nevertheless tended to adopt their own distinct views of the world. Some were fiercely traditionalist, supporters of the chiefs; all were keen to assimilate to the culture of the ruling class, seeking advancement through education or turning to the more orthodox religions. Mkele (1961, pp.12–13) mentions their attachment to the 'more respectable denominations' (Anglicans, Presbyterians, the American-based A.M.E. Church and the Methodists) and the 'best schools' (St Peters — the 'Eton of South Africa' — Adams, Lovedale and Healdtown). Some cultivated 'Western' values, and 'took considerable pains to behave in the proper and correct manner', earning themselves the appellation 'Scuse-me-please' (ibid., p.9). They welcomed the entertainment, the plays and the tennis that became possible at the Bantu Men's Social Club, or the lectures and debates provided by the Gamma Sigma (Know Thyself) clubs.[9]

Yet most of these men and women were tied by a thousand threads to the larger black community, through colour and language, and through kin, friends and clansmen. Those involved in politics usually alternated between a benign liberalism and an exclusive black nationalism, but they were torn between their liberal mentors and their anger at the inferior position to which they were relegated. Such was the path of the petty bourgeoisie — uncertain and unsafe, keen to advance in an alien world, and not always able to identify with their uneducated fellows in the townships.[10] Yet it was also from amongst this class that some of the most advanced and militant activists were to emerge — but only when they had learnt to identify with the needs of the proletariat or, as Amilcar Cabral put it years later, learnt to 'commit class suicide'.

As distinct from struggles at the workplace, where workers were organised into trade unions and confronted their (white) employers on class lines, conflicts that were based in the community affected all sections of society: class demands were usually submerged in wider struggles in which the petty bourgeoisie also participated. The distinction between people's and workers' struggles is not always obvious because the fight over bus fares (for example) was as much part of the workers' struggle as was a strike for higher wages, and was as important to the teacher as to the washerwoman or the township artisan.

It was in action that differences between the petty bourgeoisie and the workers became apparent. The former would hesitate before extending a struggle, or retreat as did the leaders of the African Democratic Party in the shantytown struggles, or the leaders of the African National Congress (ANC) and the Alexandra Workers (Artisans) Union in the bus boycott. Although not every worker was a resolute fighter, it was from their ranks (and most particularly from the washerwomen and other workers who occupied marginal positions in the economy) that the more militant action came.

Consequently, the petty bourgeoisie played a secondary role in many township struggles. In the shantytown movement — the largest of the wartime community struggles — they were absent, the more prominent leaders being drawn from lumpen elements. James Mpanza, the major figure and initiator of the movement, served time for fraud and murder. He was a clerk, an interpreter and a teacher; a felon, a bible-puncher and a petty trader; and he was venerated as a saviour, a procurer of land and houses, and as a man who could defy and beat the city council. Mpanza and other shantytown leaders are not unlike Hobsbawm's 'social bandits' (1972, pp.18-19), coming from kinship societies 'absorbed into larger economies resting on class conflict'. They were not peasant leaders (the origin of Hobsbawm's social bandits) and yet they often acted as if they were 'chiefs', had praise-singers, kept court and had their strong-arm retainers.

Mpanza was a 'figure of social protest and rebellion' (ibid.), and belonged to an urban community in which there were still strong links with rural societies. Family relations, rites of passage, leisure activities, beer brewing, dancing, religious life, age group sub-cultures and even herdboy stick fighting were adapted in the towns from their original rural forms. Marriages and funerals were often performed twice: first in traditional form, and then in 'Western' style. *Lobola* was almost always paid. Youths with formal classroom schooling were sent away for circumcision ceremonies; the herbalist and the doctor were both consulted in the event of illness; social functions might begin with 'tribal' dancing and end with ballroom performances.

Changes there were, of course, but these were uneven. Those who aspired to integration, particularly among the new petty bourgeoisie, sang in church choirs or turned to ballroom dancing; others in the slum yards of Johannesburg danced *Marabi* style (which owed much to Ragtime) at beer brewing parties. Singing, too, played an important role in the townships — extending from mission style choirs, through glee club performances, to popular songs accompanied by the accordion and protest songs that were sung in the streets. Commenting on the many concerts he attended in 1937, Ralph Bunche noted on one occasion that 'these people surely go in for singing in a big way. The kids are rehearsing every day for their choir contests', and elsewhere, that 'These people *must* sing more than any people in the world, but it's not a happy kind of singing. . . .'

Inevitably the instrumentalists engaged for *Marabi* dances could command a fee that exceeded factory wages, and troupes were organised to sing at concerts and raise money. Describing a concert at the Wenela (Witwatersrand Native Labour Association) hall, Bunche noted in his diary:

> Two troupes, one of men, and one of two girls and two boys, sang Zulu songs, weird and with shuffling steps as they sang. Money was being paid to 'buy' dances and to 'buy' singers not to sing. . . .
> In the hall there was a chairman . . . to announce items and also to receive cash either for the request of a choir to sing or stop singing. . . . Small sums of even a penny are accepted. If, however, one is tired or not interested in the singing of a group, one can go up and 'buy' the choir 'off' with a slightly higher sum than the person who has bought them. . . . There are cases where bidding in this fashion has been very keen and of course the highest bidder wins.

The problems faced by the urban population were manifold. They had to find the money with which to survive and, with average wages too low to meet the costs of rent, clothes and food, they sang and danced for money, they begged, or they pilfered. It was widely known in the townships that stolen goods could be bought 'through the back door'. Clothes, furniture, fuel, accessories like watches or stationery, gramophones and records, and even large items like stoves and pianos could be obtained at prices township residents could 'afford'.

The pilferers were themselves the victims of gangs who preyed on the township populations. Between the pilferers and the gangsters there was a yawning gap. The latter left behind a trail of destruction — maiming, raping, mugging and murdering.[11] This was publicised and condemned by the press when white communities were affected, but little was said about the mayhem engendered by gangs on the mines who did not hesitate to kill their victims; nor about mobsters who controlled the locations, filling hospitals and morgues each weekend with their victims.

Gangs differed, in origin and in approach: the *Isitshozi*, for example, must be distinguished from the *Amalaitas*. The former were organised along army lines, with Generals and Captains whose men imposed their control both inside and outside mine compounds, robbing and killing their victims; while the *Amalaitas*, condemned by whites in the 1920s and 1930s, 'represent[ed] an attempt by young Africans to organise on their own account sport and diversion according to tribal tradition. They frequently turn[ed] to crime, although this aspect has been over emphasised' (Simons, 1936, p.60). The *Amalaitas* were young men who brought the herdsmen's traditional stick fighting into the towns. In the country the contests were organised to determine the 'pecking order' among herdboys, with the conquered paying tribute to the conqueror; the same sticks were used to defend one's cattle against rustlers. In towns fighting with sticks was organised as a sport, and clubs were set up by some local authorities (including Pretoria) to control the contests. The stick fighting, sometimes violent and cruel even in the countryside, was all too often transformed in the towns, giving rise to marauding criminal gangs and generating 'inter-tribal' clashes.[12]

Violence and criminality in the locations was not a phenomenon unique to South Africa — although it can be said that particular features of the country provided 'ideal' conditions for the emergence of gangs. There was little schooling and few amenities for sport or leisure activities. Few jobs were available for young men — and none for young women. Left to their own devices, and often abandoned by their parents, youths from the age of seven years begged, smoked *dagga* (cannabis), resorted to petty theft, gambled, and then moved on to robbery, housebreaking, rape and murder.

Confronted by these criminal gangs, the location residents could not (and did not) turn to the police and administrators for protection. These officials often inspired more fear than criminals. Residents were subjected to harassment and cruelty, arbitrary arrest, and violence in the 'black marias' (police vans) and police cells (see Chapter 6). Justice in the courts was as arbitrary as the laws were discriminatory. Dr Xuma (1943) wrote that the number of (black) convictions numbered 588,329 in 1938 and 663,079 in 1939. Of these, 90 per cent were for illegal possession of liquor, pass and tax offences, contraventions of municipal labour and location rules, and trespass. These laws, he said:

> restrict the movement of the African, limit his bargaining powers, doom him as a racial group to unskilled employment, and to the lowest wage level. He may not show individuality, personality and initiative according to his ability beyond the

limited sphere outlined for him by our Native legislation. He must remain a 'Native', act like a 'Native', and think like a 'Native', at least outwardly, to satisfy the rulers.

On the Witwatersrand alone it was estimated that in 1938 the number of convictions of Africans (210,632) was slightly greater than the total number of men, women and youth employed in the towns in the region (Phillips, 1940). Some 80 per cent of those convicted were sentenced to less than four months' imprisonment and from 1932 these prisoners were offered to farmers as labourers at 6*d* per day. Reports of cruelty on the farms did not stop the traffic. In July 1946 the superintendent of one gaol told the Penal Reform Commission that he could not keep pace with the demand for labour (Wilson and Perrot, 1973, p.447).

It is not always possible to show a connection between the endemic violence in the locations and the reactions of the residents, but under conditions of severe harassment this tension could lead to rioting. This was not unlike eighteenth century Europe when a dissatisfied peasantry and disgruntled urban crowds exploded in riots (Rudé, 1980). The riots against police harassment in Vereeniging and against the allocation of stalls in Moroka described later are examples of only two of the many disturbances of the period. What needs to be stressed is that these were moments in the assertion by men and women of their humanity and that they bound the community together in confronting authority.

Men sought refuge from the tensions of the alien town in places where they could 'feel at home'. Churches, and particularly the independent sects, offered an identity that allowed an escape from white officialdom. Women domestic servants, attired in their blue uniforms, gathered in fields every Sunday with their Zionist priest; congregations crowded into small rooms where they prayed devoutly. Many sects were syncretic, following traditional practices inside a Christian framework. Dance and music used in worship had ethnic roots and the message from the Bible offered delivery from colonial masters (Coplan, p.369). Biblical references to Ethiopia gave the texts an immediate relevance during the invasion of that country by the Italians.

The Church was only one of many refuges for the urban population. The intimacy of rural communities, whether real or imagined, was recreated in hometown (or 'homeboy') associations. These bodies acted as mutual aid societies, maintained links with families in the rural areas, reinforced traditional cultures, and even sought control of specific jobs on the mines and in the towns: the Zulu were predominant as policemen and 'bossboys', the Sotho were used on the mines as shaft-sinkers, and even night-soil removal was the monopoly of one ethnic group.[13]

Other hometown groups were involved in political activity and introduced their members to political and industrial organisations. The Zoutpansberg Cultural Association (ZCA) engaged in a struggle against the implementation of the Land Act of 1936 in the northern Transvaal. Its leader and spokesman was Alpheus Maliba, a member of the CPSA, who criticised hometown groups that were concerned only with mutual aid issues. He brought recruits to the CPSA in Johannesburg and organised the first May Day demonstration in Pietersburg. The ZCA in Johannesburg differed from all other hometown organisations in having an office in Progress Building, headquarters of the CPSA and the Garment Workers Union, and all ZCA statements were carried in the Communist press.

The story of the African working class would be one-dimensional if it excluded their mobilisation in hometown organisations, churches, clubs (sports and otherwise), but ultimately the making of the African working class on the Witwatersrand required the organisation of trade unions, achieved in Johannesburg and Pretoria in the 1930s. This development is the central theme of the present study. These unions need to be placed in their historical setting: in the era between the depression and the onset of war. And it was this war which shaped the responses of workers, employers and government to new industrial relations.

More is known about some (but by no means all) of the leaders than about the rank and file; and the interaction between socialist and liberal bodies and the unions is better documented than internal union activities. More research is needed into workers' responses, union activities, and the interaction of leaders and rank and file. Furthermore, because of the difficulty in finding material on hometown organisations, and their effect on workers' organisations, an important dimension has been omitted in some of the following chapters. Except for the miners and the power workers, we know little about the role hometown groups played in encouraging or obstructing trade unionism, and even in the exceptional cases the information is still fragmentary.

The hometown groups were ubiquitous — among servants, in the mines and workshops and townships — and yet there is little evidence of their combining during urban struggles. This was in line with the overall position in the towns where there were separate foci of struggle: at the workplace, and in the townships (or locations). But they were not necessarily independent: the struggles of the working class for higher wages and better living conditions were complementary and, if the campaigns did not converge, that was at least partly the fault of existing movements — industrial and political — who stood aloof from the people's struggles. That failure was ultimately disastrous because figurehead leaders lacked the support of a mobilised work force when the government moved to suppress them.

The search for an African working class

From their inception, socialist groups in South Africa were equivocal in their appraisal of the African working class. This was a failure compounded of theoretical poverty, an inability to analyse the nature of capitalist development in the country, and a difficulty in understanding the problems of the newly formed or forming African proletariat. Socialists also faced an insuperable task in their attempts at recruiting white workers. The frustration of socialists was summed up by the Workers Party of South Africa (WP) in their journal *Spark* in March 1935:

Here in South Africa, Capitalism has succeeded, more completely perhaps than elsewhere, in dividing the working class, utilising in full the strong racial prejudices. It is not only skilled against unskilled, higher paid than lower paid, as in other countries, but it is also White against Black. The miserable wage (if it can be called a wage) paid to the unskilled, the Native and the tremendous profits and super profits derived from the enormous exploitation, made it possible for Capitalism here to bribe the skilled worker, the white worker, with a higher wage, a much higher standard of living, than in the countries of Europe. The white worker has as a general rule become an aristocrat of Labour, and by ceaseless capitalist propaganda carried on by the Church, the Press, the Schools, and 'public opinion', has been kept separate, economically, culturally, and socially, from his black fellow-workers. Indirectly he has become the supporter of Capitalism, the supporter of Segregation, the supporter of the Colour Bar. . . .

The perspective on black workers was still far from clear. Many socialists in the 1930s maintained that the black labourers were not yet a proletariat: in the struggle for socialism they could not fulfil the task ascribed by Marx because they were still rooted in the soil and not divorced, as a 'true' proletariat should be, from the means of production. In their draft thesis on 'The Native Question' (c. 1934) the WP argued that 'it must be made clear to the [white?] workers and intelligentsia of South Africa that the Native Problem, the Agrarian Problem, is *their* problem, and the liberation of the Native is *their* liberation'. Obviously the Africans were producers, said the editors of *Spark*: 'they were the direct producers in agriculture and the mines, and also, though to a less[er] degree, in industry generally'. But the WP did not believe that Africans were possible recruits for their movement:

The Native worker, usually a worker only of the first generation, coming from the Reserve or the *Kraal*, backward, downtrodden, uneducated, could not at once shake off his tribal way of life, his barbaric naivety, and his suspicion of the white man, who he could not imagine in any other role than that of an oppressor. Marxism was too much for him as a start (ibid.).

Nonetheless, comparing the situation to that of Russia in 1917, where they said there was the same 'backwardness, illiteracy, division on racial grounds', they found a parallel with conditions in South Africa, and believed that a revolutionary party (as in Russia) could overcome these obstacles.

Yet there were objective problems confronting socialists in their appraisal of the African worker in the 1930s. Many of the men (the work force at the time was almost exclusively male) thought of themselves as temporary sojourners in the town, looking forward to the time when they could return home. Or, if they had left the rural areas, they maintained contacts with kin, sending their children, by necessity, to live in the country with their grandparents during the first six (or more) years of their lives. This was interpreted by socialists, white and black, as demonstrating the backwardness of the African worker.[14] Many found the attachment to the land anachronistic or, at best, irrelevant and little attention was paid to the rural areas.

Even those who looked to urban organisation seemed beset by doubts and there was some scepticism about the nature of the African working class. The vast majority were unskilled manual labourers or employed in 'unproductive' labour. The largest occupational group (outside of mining) was in domestic service and even those in factories or shops were often employed in such menial tasks as cleaning, delivering, tea making or carrying the white man's tools. This surely was not the material that would create the hoped-for socialist revolution.

The CPSA was also concerned about the black working class but, in a period of opportunism in which it was trying to forge an alliance with the Labour Party and the white trade unions (an exercise known at the time as 'popular frontism'), it jettisoned all revolutionary theory to become condescending and insulting. In a pamphlet entitled *Communism and the Native Question: The White Worker, and his Duty on the Race Issue*, the CPSA said that it took 'no sentimental view of the Native Question. It fights hard for the native's interests because he is a worker, and it fights for the true interests of the european worker in the same way.' Declaring that ultimately 'the workers' interests were necessarily identical', the pamphlet continued:

> Further the Party does not try to blink the facts or pander to mistaken beliefs. To many [white] workers the barbarity, uncouthness and backwardness of the native is a serious deterrent. The individual worker may object to the native's colour or his smell (*sic*) and may start by shuddering at the idea of being his 'comrade', but the Communist Party knows that economic struggle is not a parlour game. It is a grim battle to be fought only by the working class as a whole — a battle for survival. . . . The Native does not want to oust the white man in industry. . . . He wants the european to help him and to lead him.
>
> Workers! Do not let the Government persuade you or frighten you out of doing this.
>
> It is absolutely necessary for your own preservation and for the maintenance of any Standard of Decency (*sic*) in South Africa.

There was a minority that thought differently and they proceeded with the work of building African trade unions. Their importance lay in their ability to mobilise significant sections of the newly urbanised working class in towns throughout the country. I have concentrated on events on the Witwatersrand because this was the region with the largest industries (including the mines) in the country, and with the greatest concentration of workers. But workers in other regions of South Africa responded just as readily when unions were formed. This was made evident in 1941 when Max Gordon, the main exponent of unionisation in Johannesburg, was invited to visit Port Elizabeth to organise African trade unions. In a short visit of ten weeks, Gordon established seven unions, made contact with workers in three other trades, and set up workers' committees and a trade union centre (Hirson, 1977).

Without Gordon, the development of trade unions might have been less successful: it would undoubtedly have been different. But the emergent unions were shaped by factors independent of the volition of Gordon and his co-workers: the development of the economy; the steps taken by the ruling class to control the work force; worker resistance to the repressive system erected by the employers and the state; and the emergence of organisation, both formal and informal, in the countryside, in locations and in factories.

The war and the working class

In reading through the diaries of Ralph Bunche, I was struck by the lack of reference to the growth of the 'shirt movements' and the imminence of war. Evidence of the coming conflict was immediately apparent in the *Voortrekker* centenary celebrations, the increased racial attacks on blacks, and the growth of the local fascist movements. Yet Bunche recorded conversations with many politically active members of the ANC, the AAC, the CPSA and the trade unions, all of whom would have been thoroughly aware of the tensions in South Africa and the wider world. Future events were to show that, after the failure of the Ethiopians to stop the Italians, blacks showed little interest in the approaching conflict. This was not for lack of political interest or out of ignorance of world events — even if some of the complexities of the time remained unexplained. When an event did attract attention, few failed to follow what was happening — as reactions to the news of fighting in North Africa, and more particularly in Asia, made abundantly clear.

Nonetheless, it is not possible to understand the attitudes of socialists in the 1930s without following the course of conflict in China after 1931, and the rise of fascism in Europe. This was the prelude to the conflagration of 1939—45 which altered the nature of South African politics. In this respect attention must be focused on the declaration of hostilities and the polarisation of the white population; the recruitment of the army; the progress of the war in North Africa, Europe and Asia; the call for a 'second front'; and the rift in the Allied forces when Churchill warned against the threat of Communism in his Fulton speech.

The attitude of government to the workers also altered. In the first years of war, a conciliatory approach provided the space within which industrial organisation could grow. Even more remarkably, after the invasion of the USSR by Germany a minister in the Cabinet (Colin Steyn) became patron of the Medical Aid for Russia campaign and the leader of the CPSA, Bill Andrews, addressed the nation on radio. But, by the end of 1943 when the danger of defeat disappeared, it became harder for the black working class to win any concessions from capital. Although more needs to be said about the events surrounding the war, I have sketched in its bearing on the changing conditions in which these first industrial unions found themselves. The development of war industries also led to new strains in living conditions. Little or no new housing was built during the war, despite a massive influx of Africans to the towns where they took up positions in the factories — both to replace whites who joined the armed forces, and to man the new wartime industries. Living conditions became unbearable, which gave rise to the illegal occupation of land and the erection of giant shantytowns. There was a shortage of buses and trains to get the men to work and fares were raised. The campaigns against increased fares, together with the fight for more houses, were part of the development of black consciousness and of working-class action. The struggles they undertook were to become part of the mythology of the coming generation — but their story has either not been told or bowdlerised. We need to tell it now, not only to clear the record of the past, but also to help explain the course of subsequent events.

Notes

1. Walkin, 1954, pp.163-84. In the excerpt I exclude phrases that identify the country as being Russia. As well as parallels with South Africa there are differences, some of which are explored below.
2. A reference to the 'peasant-come-to-the-factory' in Russia, *c*. 1900, quoted by Zelnik, 1968, p.158.
3. *Umteteli wa Bantu*, 18 February and 31 March 1928. This was rejected by both Richard Msimang and Sol Plaatje in subsequent issues. See also *The Times* (London), 2 February 1928, on a petition being drafted by the TAC for their removal.
4. A confidential record of discussions between Rheinallt Jones and a representative of the governments of Northern Rhodesia and Nyasaland. Jones could obtain no information on what had happened. Nothing was found at the Public Records Office, London on the events.
5. See 'Introduction' to Marks and Rathbone, 1982, pp.15–25, for an elaboration of some of these problems.
6. In Britain, after the early enclosures, it was said that sheep ate people. In South Africa dispossession, a crueller form of enclosures, left people at the mercy of the labour recruiter.
7. The move to segregated locations took several decades. Only servants could live legally in the white suburbs.
8. Saura Woolf informed me of the work of Dr Max Joffe, her late husband, in the tenants' associations (see Chapter 11). Josie Palmer (interviewed by Julia Wells) said they were formed on her initiative. Little is known of their activities.
9. Phillips, 1930, p.118, describes the origin of these clubs, the provision of lectures and debates, and the opportunity 'to improve their English'.
10. This is a composite picture that encapsulates the experiences (as reflected in their own accounts) of D.D.T. Jabavu, Selope Thema and Selby Msimang.
11. See Modisane, 1963, pp.26–7, on the gangs who controlled Sophiatown and their destructive impact on families.
12. A fight, in which rocks as well as sticks were used, is described by Jingoes, 1975, pp.42–3. See also *Conference on Urban Juvenile Native Deliquency*, 1938, contributions by Dan Twala, W.G. Ballinger, and Ray Phillips; and La Hausse, 1984, p.37, who describes the *Amalaitas* of Durban as 'a vivid expression of how a rural people adapted to punishing conditions of proletarianisation and probably, in many instances, landlessness'.

13. See also Van Onselen, Vol. 2, 1982, on '*Amawasha*: the Zulu washermen's guild of the Witwatersrand, 1890–1914', pp.74–110.
14. Bunche in his diary records E.S. (Solly) Sachs as saying in 1937: 'Native mine workers are not really proletarianised. They retain *kraal* and peasant psychology. This is deliberate policy of Chamber of Mines — to keep them from organising. Tendency is for natives not to trust European organisers . . . .' And Edwin Mofutsanyana, interviewed in the 1980s, said: 'The miners are the most backward people from the countryside who know only the voice of the chief and nothing else.'

2. Desperately Lean Times: The Socio-economic Background

A people trapped in depression

In June 1930, at the height of the depression, a government commission was appointed to inquire into the

> social and economic conditions of Natives especially in the larger towns . . . to report on laws regulating wages, conditions of employment and methods of dealing with industrial disputes; and on measures to be adopted to deal with surplus Natives in, and to prevent the increasing immigration of Natives to such areas. (Native Economic Commission, 1932, p.1.)

There was no mention of the depression in the terms of reference, despite the marked growth of unemployment and poverty in the recent past. As the Inquiry was to show, economic depression had affected blacks long before the world slump hit South Africa.

The commissioners found that the steady drift of Africans to the towns in recent years was the result of conditions in the Reserves which were deteriorating due to 'denudation, donga-erosion, deleterious plant succession, destruction of woods, drying up of spruits [and] robbing the soil of its reproductive properties' (para. 16). They believed this was caused by a 'primitive people' who persisted in overstocking the land, but argued that not even better farming methods could provide much improvement unless congestion on the land was relieved and more land provided for African settlement (paras 73, 192).

In fact, by 1930 the Reserves were already beyond redemption. In the Transkei, a comparatively fertile Reserve, a family of five produced an estimated annual surplus of £2 12s 6d. This was insufficient for a family paying taxes and needing such staples as sugar, tea, wheaten meal, coffee, condensed milk, paraffin and soap, as well as 'luxury' items like tobacco. Men therefore had to work on the mines to supplement the family income (pp.277–8).[1]

The commissioners found conditions in the towns little better. In Johannesburg the 'common wage' was £3 10s per month, leaving £1 16s 8d for food, clothing, education and so on, after rent, transport and poll tax had been paid. Yet the medical director of Rand Mines advised that food for a family 'consistent with reasonable maintenance of health' cost a minimum of £3 per month. In the light of these conditions and despite evidence 'that the present conditions of depression make any wage regulation specially difficult and dangerous and that the fall of commodity prices has effected a general rise in real Native wages which makes any present raising of their money wages unnecessary' (para. 1037), the Commission ruled that existing wage levels were 'too low for a decent standard of living for a Native with a family' (para. 1039).

Thus by 1930 an impoverished people, moving out of overpopulated and overstocked Reserves, was flooding the urban labour markets where an ever-enlarging pool of unskilled labour kept wages low. The situation grew even worse as the impact of the world economic depression began to be felt in South Africa in the form of unemployment for blacks and whites. It was said that gold had a stabilising effect on the economy and protected the country from the worst effects of the depression (Simons and Simons, 1969, p.462; Kaplan, 1977, pp.80 and 150). This was the case for capital (in general), the mine owners and the government, but, as the Commission report indicated, blacks were not insulated from the depression. Many found themselves being replaced in government service by so-called 'poor whites' and the only industry that always had vacancies for men was the gold mines.

South Africa during the depression

Economists who wrote of the 'relative mildness' of the depression in South Africa noted that '[b]ecause South Africa was largely an agricultural country, the depression brought widespread economic distress (Katzen, 1964, p.79). That is, 'stability' and 'mildness' did not apply to the overwhelming majority of the population,[2] already afflicted by the global fall in agricultural prices in late 1928, a year before the crash on Wall Street (Heaton, 1948, p.694). Prices for wool, hides, maize and other produce had dropped sharply and did not revive through the 1930s. Income from wool (then the main agricultural export) fell by over £5 million in 1928 and the value of exports fell by 65 per cent in 1929–32, despite an increase in the clip of nearly 50 per cent; farming and fishery exports fell by 40 per cent. Farmers in the Reserves were also affected, and their annual 'surplus' (*sic*), previously estimated as £2 12*s* 6*d*, fell even lower.[3]

A nation-wide drought, starting as early as 1930 in some regions and extending to 1934–35, killed thousands of livestock (F. Wilson, 1971, p.142) and forced many whites and blacks off the land. In the towns they competed for jobs at depressed wages. Distress was endemic in a country where the subsistence wages paid by employers on mines and farms set the standard for all other remuneration.

Gold production expanded during 1929–32 by some 25 per cent and for (gold) mining capital there were immense benefits. For shareholders the depression was indeed 'mild'. This new-found prosperity rode on the back of world-wide misery, from which emerged the fascist governments of Europe, the civil war in Spain and ultimately the Second World War. One revolutionary journal said of the situation:

> Accompanying the world depression and the disintegration of markets, the international financial crisis which brought about unprecedented gold prices has thereby led to the recent boom on the Rand. Increased gold-mining activity with its

stimulus to secondary industry, building, etc., has produced an appreciable acceleration of industrial tempo, and this is hailed by bourgeois economists and publishers as 'returning prosperity'. This 'prosperity', founded as it is upon international crisis and collapse, is the prosperity of undertakers in a plague. . . . (*Spark*, March 1935).

The government proceeded with its fiscal programme (half its revenue coming from gold) and saved (white) farmers from bankruptcy by subsidising their exports, but many farm labourers were discharged during the long fallow period (Neumark, 1934). The number of mineworkers increased by 11 per cent from 203,527 to 226,628 during 1929–32, while the average annual wage stayed almost constant at £33 6s (Tinley, 1942, p.269). If falling food prices led to savings (as stated in the Native Economic Commission), these accrued to the mines, which provided the rations.

Unemployed . . . and unemployable

. . . the average number of Natives seeking work, mostly coming from outside Johannesburg [being] 5,000, and the average wastage estimated at about 4,000. The excess of those offering their labour over the jobs vacant allows of a reasonable selection by employers (G. Ballenden, 1934).[4]

They go from gate to gate in the Johannesburg suburbs, touching their aged hats and saying — what is often their one word of English — 'job'. . . (Sarah Gertrude Millin, 1934, p.94).

The number out of work during the depression is not known. Statistics were first compiled for whites in 1929, for Africans only in the 1950s. Estimates, presumably taken from pass office records of men with permits to seek work, show 14,000 seeking jobs in Johannesburg in 1932, but there are no figures for women who, officially, were 'unemployable' (Simons and Simons, 1969, p.454).

In the absence of the men most women were trapped in the Reserves, tending small allotments. Others moved between Reserve and town, trying to build a life for the family, but always caught in an impossible 'African tragedy' (Ntantala, 1957). The story of Mrs Sahluko was typical of that life of frustration, grief and blighted hopes. She saw little of her husband after her marriage in 1932 in Engcobo at the age of nineteen. He returned from his place of work in Cape Town, and she bore his children, but neither they nor the livestock survived the drought, famine and privation. She eventually joined her husband in Cape Town, staying with two other families in one room and living, she said, no better than animals. Conditions improved when she became a domestic servant, but that was terminated by pregnancy. Only when the child was sent back to Engcobo did she get another job. The couple later returned to their allotment, but the yield was too low and the husband sought work in town again, where he died. His widow remarried and was in Cape Town when she told her story.

The accounts of men who entered the towns in the 1920s and 1930s were not dissimilar. Naboth Mokgatle (1971), a future trade union organiser and political activist, arrived in Pretoria in 1930 at the age of 20. Kinsmen helped him find work and then he moved from job to job, seeking better conditions and higher wages. He delivered meat for a butcher, and learnt how to make sausages; delivered parcels for a department store; carried tools for a white worker; made tea for the (white) office staff; ran errands, or just cleaned and polished floors. He wrote that:

> Nineteen-thirty was a year of depression. Many Africans were out of work . . . [some were dismissed] . . . to make room for European workers. Hard manual jobs like working on the railways, road making, digging trenches and sweeping streets, which [ordinarily] were considered suitable for Africans only, were taken away from them and given to Europeans. In cities like Pretoria . . . the authorities were even inciting European families to boycott factories, bakeries, butcher shops, laundries and others which kept on employing African labour. . . . Notices appeared in the windows . . . stating that the work done there was only by white labour (p.176).

Mokgatle earned 12s per week and slept with others in a room in a yard. There was no bed and no furniture. After a year in Pretoria he earned 15s per week which he regarded as a 'big advance'. Despite low wages and uncongenial work, he was at least employed during the depression, when structural changes in manufacturing and commerce led to the closure of firms and the retrenchment of workers. The diamond fields closed in 1929 and, though some men went to the alluvial diggings, more were thrown on the labour market. The few new industries which provided import substitution or serviced the mines could not absorb all the unemployed.

Table 2.1
Gains and losses in employment, 1929–1932

Sector	Whites	Africans	Coloureds	Indians
Males				
Net gains				
Gold mines	1,500	———	23,900	———
Net losses				
Diamond mines	7,000	———	32,000	———
Coal mines	300	———	11,200	———
Railways	5,600	10,300	2,900	230
Govt. manufacture	3,000	———	2,200	———
Pvt. manufacture	4,000	14,400	3,700	1,200
Females				
Net gains				
Pvt. manufacture	3,500	–	–	–
Net losses				
Pvt. manufacture	–	120	300	–
All mining	–	———	600	———

Source: *Union Statistics for Fifty Years: 1910–1960*, 1960.

The situation was worsened by the restructuring of the work force on racial grounds, primarily by the government but also by some private companies. This had been fostered by the government since at least 1924 and was used to particular effect on the railways, where the number of white workers had increased from 4,760 in 1924 to 10,750 in 1925 and reached

16,248 in 1929. In the same period (1924–29), the African labour force declined from 37,564 to 31,600 and the Indian from 2,113 to 1,002, though Coloured workers increased from 5,628 to 7,669.[5] There was a drop in freight traffic during the depression years, particularly from some country areas, resulting in cuts to the black work force, but for whites numbers increased from 28.7 per cent in 1929 to 38.75 per cent of the total work force in 1934. Railway wages fell by between five and twenty per cent in 1929, and then again in 1932, until some Africans were receiving as little as 2s for a full working day. When the cuts were restored in 1935, African wages remained unaltered, because, said the Minister, there had been a 'reorganisation of the scale of pay'.[6]

The 'golden' road to recovery

Britain went off the gold standard on 21 September 1931 and the consequent rise in the gold price effectively devalued the pound sterling. This stemmed the outward flight of British capital because goods were now cheaper and exports increased. But South Africa suffered; the capital flow was reversed and for the next fifteen months there was an outward flight.

Initially N.C. Havenga, J.H. Hofmeyr and John Martin, speaking for the government, the opposition and the Chamber of Mines respectively, claimed that going off the gold standard would only benefit the economy temporarily, and would be negated by inflation and rising prices (De Kiewiet, 1950, p.173). Furthermore, the devaluation of sterling was advantageous to South Africa. Gold, taken mainly to Britain, fetched a handsome premium from the devalued pound and the cost of British goods, including mining equipment, was lowered. With gold effectively revalued, mining shares boomed in South Africa and Britain as investors cashed in on the depression (Hocking, 1973, p.157).

On 13 December 1931 John Martin called for a reversal of policy, claiming that the increased revenue from gold would more than offset inflationary costs and that devaluation would extend the life of mines otherwise near to exhaustion. The government was unmoved. The British 'recovery' was limited, and Australia and Canada, which had both devalued, were still in considerable economic difficulty (Katzen, 1944, p.79). The cabinet imposed currency controls to stop the flight of capital; offered a bounty of first 10 and then 20 per cent to exporters to meet foreign competition; increased levies on imports; and cut the wages of public servants and railwaymen (Simons and Simons, 1969, p.462).

The government's economic policy revealed the tensions between nationalist objectives, and (mainly foreign) shareholders' interests. The government could maintain its balance of payments surplus, and also increase the balance held by South African banks abroad, allowing freer lending and lower interest rates by 1932. By August 1932 there was an upturn in the economy but nonetheless, on 27 December, the country went off the gold standard.

The effect of the turnabout was dramatic. Capital flowed into the country as gold shares boomed, gold mining profits soared and, as a spin-off, local industry mushroomed. Commentators wrote about a return of prosperity for the gold industry, for finance houses, property speculators and some industrialists. Government receipts from the gold mines crept upwards from £3.2m in 1929 to £3.5m in 1931 and £4.3m in 1932, and then zoomed to £14.5m in 1933 (Jacobsson, 1936, Appendix B).

But the Reserves, white farms and factories did not share this prosperity. Nor did the men in the mine compounds. Wages remained at subsistence level and Peter Abrahams (1954), writing retrospectively about the 1930s, spoke for all blacks: 'The long depression that was lifting all over the world seemed permanent in Vrededorp [a Johannesburg mixed-race slum]. Desperately lean times had come to stay in our lean world' (p.163).

Devaluation and the new inflow of capital also led to a restructuring of political forces. The majority of the National Party joined with the South African Party to form the South African National United Party (United Party) in 1934, regrouping mine owners with farmers who anticipated a new prosperity, traders who despaired of old policies, and sections of the white working class who wanted their old pay packets restored. The Nationalists were split, the inevitable consequence of falling support from erstwhile followers — farmers and workers in transport and light industry. More importantly, this represented a recognition by northern Nationalists that the economy of the country was tied to the gold mines and that politicians associated with the mining houses had to be in the government.[7]

Boom time — boom town
On the fiftieth anniversary of the founding of Johannesburg, D. Jacobsson (1936), mining editor of the *Star*, enthused about the transformation of South Africa after 1933. The 'indefinite extension of the life of the mining industry', he wrote (referring to the mining of even lower grade ore than previously), had strengthened credit because the future looked secure. State revenue from the mines had quadrupled between 1932 and 1936 while dividends to shareholders almost doubled, bringing a new Johannesburg into being:

> Into three short years the city had crowded the building progress of three decades; from a general level of from four to five storeys . . . the building skyline had been raised . . . to the impressive standard of buildings of ten, twelve storeys and more, imposing evidence of the spectacular increase in land values.
> . . . Johannesburg has been rebuilding at the rate of between half a million and three quarters of a million pounds a month . . . and there is little sign yet that the movement has spent itself. Nor has it . . . been restricted to the mother city for, particularly on the Far East Rand, the field of the greatest mining expansion, young towns have grown out of all recognition and new towns have appeared almost, as it were, overnight (pp.185–6).

One effect not noted by Jacobsson was the sale of buildings and slum yards in and near the centre of the town as property values rose. Many old buildings, now demolished, had provided housing for Africans. This displacement, and the rates paid on the new buildings, provided the city council with the funds to expropriate regions, clear the slum yards, and move Africans to locations (Koch, 1984).

By 1936, there were over one million people on the Witwatersrand: 400,000 whites, 45,000 Coloureds and Indians, and over 500,000 Africans. In Johannesburg alone there were some 200,000 Africans,[8] but none could live in those 'towering blocks of flats', except for servants in roof-top quarters. There were few places where blacks could own property in Johannesburg or the new towns that had 'appeared . . . almost overnight' and, in mid-1938, Africans were said to hold title deeds to no more than 65 unimproved stands worth £3,060 and 271 improved stands valued at £70,900 (Hellmann, 1963, quoting from 1938 census).

Most Africans in towns were searching not for property, but for employment. The new prosperity demanded the existence of a large reserve army of labour: many blacks remained underemployed or unemployed. The number of jobs created in the period 1933—39 has been estimated at 100,000 for whites and 400,000 for blacks (Houghton, 1971, p.34), but this seems to be inflated. Available figures suggest that only 230,000 jobs were created for Africans, 20,000 for Coloureds and 5,000 for Indians. Rounded figures for the sectors involved are shown in Table 2.2.

One significant item excluded from these figures is domestic service. Officials, assuming an average of one servant per white family on farms and in the towns, estimated that in 1921 there were 162,905 women and 88,953 men in domestic service; by 1936 this had increased to 242,405 women and 114,502 men (*Union Statistics for Fifty Years: 1910—1960*, 1960, A-33). If all the expansion was in the towns, the increase in the period 1933—39 could not have exceeded 50,000, bringing the total increase in jobs to just under 300,000.

Table 2.2
Increase in jobs for Africans, 1933—39 (000)

Sector	No. employed 1933	No. employed 1939	Increase 1933-39	Comments
Mining	295	409	114	Some 40—50% drawn from outside South Africa
Pte. industry	55	130	75	
Railways and harbours		47	22	Estimated to include casual labour
Construction		23	17	Figures only available for all blacks
Electricity and power		10	5	
Distribution*		26	10	Guesstimate
Total			**243**	

Source: *Union Statistics for Fifty Years: 1910—1960*, 1960, G—4, 6, 7, 13, 15.
* Van der Horst, 1942, p.258.

Consequently, for Africans streaming into the towns, the mines and domestic service provided the largest number of openings, and some

130,000 new jobs were created in the boom period before the war. Few if any required skills and few offered wages above subsistence level.

The 'casualness' of urban employment
Economists investigating urban employment for 1936–44 examined records at the Johannesburg pass office and concluded that:

1. An extremely high proportion of African males were engaged in domestic labour.
2. An extremely small proportion of African workers received a wage sufficient to maintain a family, even on a 'minimal scale of urban life'.
3. There was a high turnover of labour, which had little to do with country–town migration but was due to 'the casualness of urban employment itself' (Richards et al., 1948, p.vii).

The prevalence of domestic servants in South Africa was one indication of the unequal distribution of wealth which was exacerbated by depression. In 1938, 43,792 Africans were employed as servants in Johannesburg: that is, 25–32 per cent of all Africans over eighteen listed as resident in Johannesburg and Alexandra Township.[9] Nearly half (21,027) were men, but the economists believed that there would be a rise in wages which would end the 'luxury' of employing male domestic servants (ibid., p.6). Wages did not rise appreciably, however, and in 1946 the number of male servants in the country had increased by one third over the number in 1936: 151,803 as against 114,502 (*Union Statistics for Fifty Years, 1910–1960*, 1960, A–33).

The 'casualness' referred to in the employment study was not quite the word that African workers would have used, there being nothing casual about the work or about securing a job. In 1934 the plight of 10,000 unemployed in Johannesburg was described as follows:

> A *Reuter* message describes the streets immediately surrounding the offices of the Native Affairs Department as being packed, in such a fashion as to disorganise traffic, by Natives seeking a renewal of their permits to remain in the area after seven days of fruitless searching for work (Wilson and Perrot, 1973, p.410).

For academics, 'casualness' referred to the high turnover of workers at any one plant, and this they ascribed to the 'sort of work which is customarily set aside for Native performance' (Richards et al., 1948, p.6). That is, the unskilled worker was often employed simply to lift, carry, clean or dig; moving from one firm or industry to another provided the only avenue to improvement. The annual turnover rates of workers, excluding losses due to illness or death, were: 157 per cent in transport, 155 per cent in the building trade, 136 per cent for cleaners in flats and buildings, 101 per cent in the steel industry and 94 per cent in distribution. Other rates were also high: in the 90 per cent range in food industries, chemicals, timber industry and rubber. The rate dropped to 57 per cent in textiles, 51 per cent in paper, 56 per cent in leather and 40 per cent in the furniture industry: these industries paid significantly higher wages. Even in the more stable occupations, however, less than 15 per cent of workers stayed with a firm for three or more years — furniture alone recording 18 per cent (ibid., pp.694 and 818—22). The 'casualness' of labour was closely related to the wages offered in the 1930s: 48.5 per cent of African males earned 15—20s per week in industry and the median wage was 19s; 16 per cent earned less than 15s and only 10.6 per cent earned over 27s per week. This is not the whole story. Some employers made deductions for 'board and lodging' or 'food'; or there was underpayment which left very little in the weekly pay packet. Max Gordon, a trade union organiser, described practices in some industries:

> *Liquor and Catering Trade*: . . . their wages are covered by a Wage Determination, in which is laid down £1 per week for a seventy hour week, allowing a deduction of 7s per week for board and lodging; in spite of this we have had to refer cases of underpayment to the Department of Labour for attention. . . .
> *Restaurants and Tea Rooms*: . . . unskilled employees are entitled to receive £3 10s per month for a sixty hour week, plus meals during working hours. The employer, however, is allowed to deduct £1 10s per month for lodging. About fifty cases of underpayment have been reported. . . . Very often as many as nine Native employees are forced to sleep in one small room, and each is charged £1 10s per month. . . .
> *Dairy Trade*: . . . The usual working week is seven days per week, two shifts in 24 hours for each employee, and a working day of from 14 to 18 hours per day. . . .[10]

Few occupations were mechanised, most industries being labour intensive until 1939, and machines were 'extremely primitive' according to A.J. Norval (1962), a former Chairman of the Board of Trade and Industries. 'Engineering works' were usually repair shops and foundries were exclusively man-operated because only the mining houses financed industries. No other capital (local or foreign) was available for manufacture, the return from which was too low. Furthermore there was little international investment in the 1930s, the 'creditor countries' recording a net inflow of capital in the pre-war years (Lewis, 1957, p.71).

Norval noted that local investors preferred gold shares: capital for manufacture had to be raised from friends, legal firms and trust companies. This accords with an independent observation by Hyman Basner, a young (and impecunious) lawyer. In the early 1930s he was asked for a loan to float a company for the manufacture of nails. 'Why nails?' he asked, 'Surely there are plenty of them made in South Africa?' and was told: '*Nothing* is made here — not a pin, not a shovel, not a pick. I'm not starting with bigger things, because the mines mightn't buy them, but there'll be customers for my nails.' Basner, knowing that the banks opposed the manufacture of articles made in Britain, referred the man to another attorney.[11]

During the period 1932—39 an average of £37.5 million per year was set aside for private and public net investment. This was about 11.5 per cent of national income and well below the amount required to raise real income.[12] Manufacturing firms were starved of capital: the average fixed capital per establishment grew from £7,000 in 1934/35 to only £9,000 in 1939/40 (Norval, 1962, p.3) during a period described as one of 'increasing prosperity'. Instead of machinery, more labour was employed: to carry, dig and haul or to cut and bend. Instead of cranes, gangs of men moved steel girders, carried railway lines, raised building materials. It was slow and primitive, wasteful of time and labour power; but capital was sparse, the price of labour was low, and the rate of profit was kept high. This was a period in which the accumulation of local capital was rapid and industrialisation was proceeding apace — but with little technology, and not much machinery!

War, industry and the economy

When war was declared in September 1939, the government had to obtain armaments for mechanised warfare, clothes and equipment for an army which topped 300,000 men, and consumer goods for the population that would now be cut off from the trade routes. The army was undermanned and its equipment largely obsolete (Smuts, 1952, p.381). The navy and the air force required refitting. Everything from rifles to tanks, airplanes and minesweepers had to be found or produced. Some was obtained from the United States; the rest had to be manufactured in South Africa.

The United States was prepared to bend rules to provide war materials, including bomber aircraft, and transport them to South Africa in her supposedly neutral ships. This was ascribed by Smuts to 'our good name and credit' (p.183) but that misses the main point: gold was crucial in the financing of the Allied war effort and South Africa, almost uniquely, could pay with bullion. Goods came to South Africa and gold went back to the USA in the same ships.

Gold played a remarkable part in the economy throughout the war years and a vast labour force was involved in its production. The gold mines were described in 1941 as the 'economic fly wheel of all our economic activities' and dependent 'on the continuance of cheap Native labour'.[13] At the same time these mines provided 20 per cent of the nation's net income, over 40 per cent of annual state revenue, and over 70 per cent of total yearly exports.[14] In the years 1936–41 the gold mines were able to extend production, partly because of the increased inflow of African labour which reached a record 384,000 in 1941,[15] and partly because it became profitable to exploit ever lower grades of ore when the price of gold moved upwards from £7.103 per fine ounce in 1936 to £7.035 in 1937, £7.765 in 1939 and £8.840 in 1940 (Horwitz, 1967, p.236).

Capital was available for the gold mines but not for manufacturing, and this led to the formation in 1940 of the Industrial Development Corporation (IDC) by Act of Parliament. The IDC acted as an industrial bank and promoted industries to supply the armed forces, its first loan being for the manufacture of blankets with wool which was not exported for lack of shipping. The IDC was more effective in the post-war period, but during the war the first priority was import substitution. To achieve this contracts were signed on a 'cost plus' basis and these were 'highly remunerative' (Norval,

1962, p.53). Some contracts went to established firms; others to new workshops, undercapitalised and often using sweated labour, set up to profit from wartime needs.

A feature of some wartime production was the growth in mechanisation. The facilities of the mint were used for precision engineering and, although the process was uneven, new technology was introduced on a wider scale. Nonetheless, the rate of net capital investment in industry dropped slightly over the war years (Franklin, 1948, p.69).

There were structural changes in the labour process to cope with war demands and fill the places left by the men who joined the army. The work force was reduced in sectors such as municipal and railway construction, furniture making and printing, and the diamond fields at Kimberley were closed. There was little or no building work during the war and the construction of arterial roads was carried out by Italian prisoners of war. Employment soared in food processing, leather and textiles, engineering and chemicals, but the largest expansion was in the gold mines, where the labour force peaked in 1941 and then dropped slightly. Altogether there were 18,000 new positions for whites in industry and just under 100,000 for all blacks in the war years 1939–45.[16]

Some African workers were employed in semi-skilled and skilled work, replacing servicemen or working in new plants; most still did the menial work. Where conditions improved it was mainly due to trade union militancy. Although some wages were raised, particularly for semi-skilled or skilled work, the standard of living of African workers declined. Between 1940 and 1944 the average wage, including the compulsory cost of living allowance, rose by 22 per cent while the cost of foodstuffs on the Rand and Pretoria rose by 58 per cent, plus 15 per cent because of gross profiteering in shops frequented by Africans.[17]

While wages lagged behind rising costs, living conditions in the townships deteriorated. There were no new houses to accommodate the expanded work force; transport worsened and became more expensive. On each issue there was confrontation and struggle during the war years as well as complaints over food shortages, higher taxes (particularly from the Sotho), pass raids and so on. Each grievance became a focus of demonstration, boycott or strike: it was these struggles that made the African working class during those crucial years of industrial development.

Notes

1. This evidence was given by Mr S.G. Butler, principal of Tsolo Agricultural School, Umtata, 14 November 1930.
2. O'Meara, 1983, p.35, states that 'for some, the mildness was more relative than for others'; he refers to extensive unemployment, but does not elaborate.
3. See Katzen, 1964, pp.48 and 77, and Houghton and Walton, 1952, p.4 for the place of wool in this region's exports.

4. Report of the Manager of Native Affairs Department, November 1934, quoted by Proctor, 1979, p.65.
5. 'Native wages and the cost of living', mimeo, 1938, p.12, *Ballinger Papers*.
6. Letter from C.R. Goodlatte, Secretary of the Cape Peninsula Joint Council of Europeans and Bantu, 21 June 1933, to Rheinallt Jones, reporting on her interview with Oswald Pirow, Minister of Railways, *Rheinallt Jones Papers*.
7. O'Meara, 1983, who discusses the split in Nationalist circles on a north/south axis, does not link this with the powerful influence exerted by gold on the economy.
8. Annual *Report of the Manager of the Non-European and Native Affairs Department*, Johannesburg, 30 June 1939, citing local census of 12 July 1938 (159,135 in the city and 21,843 in Alexandra Township, on the outskirts of the city). Many preferred not to be enumerated and Hellmann, 1963, gave the African population in 1939 as 244,000.
9. Ibid.
10. Report to the Trustees, Bantu Welfare Trust, 20 December 1938, mimeo, *Saffery Papers*, No. 1, A4. On 2 June 1941, *South African Outlook* reported that these workers received £3 10s for an 84 hour week, plus food valued at £1.
11. I owe this to Miriam Basner, who is completing the unfinished autobiography of Hyman Basner.
12. Planning Council Report of 1944, quoted by Franklin, 1948, p.69.
13. Quoted from the Native Economic Commission by Donald Molteno, *Parliamentary Debates*, 17 March 1942.
14. *Third Interim Report of the Industrial and Agricultural Requirements Commission, 1941*, UG 40-1941, extracts of which are reprinted in Houghton and Dagut, 1973, Vol. 3, p.149.
15. Katzen, 1964, p.19. Recruitment on this scale was not to be repeated until 1959.
16. *Social and Economic Planning Council Report No. 1: Re-employment, Reconstruction and the Council's Status*, UG 9, 1943. See Norval, 1962, facing p.12.
17. *Race Relation News*, Vol. 6, No. 1, January 1944. The obligatory cost of living allowance gave all workers, excluding domestic servants, agricultural labourers and mine workers an increase of 20 per cent between 1941 and 1943, and a further 10 per cent in September 1944.

3. Industrial Legislation and Minimum Wages

'Civilised' labour

Civilised labour is the labour rendered by persons whose standard of living conforms to the standard generally recognised as tolerable from the usual European [white] standpoint.

General Hertzog[1]

The term 'poor white' could hardly have come into common usage except in a country inhabited by an inferior non-European population as well as by Europeans. The term 'poor white' itself implies that traditionally the European inhabitants have a higher standard of living.

Carnegie Report on the Poor White Problem (Vol. 1, pp.xviii, xix)

The main characteristic of the South African economic system . . . is the exceptionally low level of the wages of the unskilled and semi-skilled workers. . . . In England the average rate [ratio?] of the skilled to the unskilled wage is 15:11, in Germany, before 1933, the rate was even more favourable to the unskilled worker. Over the whole range of South African industry the rate of the skilled to the unskilled wage is 6 to 1. On the Witwatersrand, taking all types of employment, the rate is 7 to 1, but taking the mining industry only, the rate averages 10 to 1, in spite of the arduous and dangerous nature of the toil involved.

Max Gordon (c. 1938).

Industrial legislation in South Africa was shaped by the complex needs of capital, first in the mines and then in industry, and by the outcome of struggles between employers and their workers. Capital demanded a plentiful work force and meant to keep it cheap and compliant. The essential precondition for this had been largely achieved before the opening of the mines through the conquest and dispossession of the African peoples.[2] The process was accelerated in the late nineteenth century when regulations in the Cape forced Africans off the land and into the labour market. At the same time skilled labour was drawn from abroad by the relatively high wages offered by the mines and by manufacturing firms.

The black work force was controlled from the inception of the mining 'revolution' by confinement to barracks (or compounds), body searches (on the diamond mines) and restrictions on movement. Workers were also subject to pass regulations and tax laws, required to return to the rural areas after completing a term of duty, denied access to alcohol, and so on. Similar attempts to control white miners led to bloody clashes between workers and company police over body searches in Kimberley, after which the practice was curtailed. Black workers supported the whites, but with little or no reciprocation (Turrell, 1982, pp.45-66). Clashes between white labour and management continued and intensified on the Witwatersrand, and for about

30 years the unions (the first of which was formed in 1881) fought some of the bitterest strikes in the history of South Africa. The issues involved working conditions, occupational hazards and the maintenance of the white/black ratio within the work force: these were struggles which set black and white labour apart.

Mineworkers constituted a special case owing to their numbers and the centrality of the new gold fields, but other workers also organised and were involved in clashes with employers. In this turbulent era policemen wielding pickhandles confronted workers on picket lines, angry crowds burnt down buildings and placed detonators on tramway lines, and the government abducted working-class leaders and shipped them abroad in order to stifle the nascent working-class movement (Cope, 1943, pp.117–23; Simons and Simons, 1969, pp.74ff.; Haysom, *passim*).

In 1924 the Smuts government introduced the Industrial Conciliation Act (IC Act) with its two distinct but connected provisions: employees could form trade unions which would be approved, recognised and registered; and, with an employers' association, could form an Industrial Council in any industry (farming excepted). All disputes were to be mediated by this Council, and then through conciliation, before a strike was permissible. African men (as pass bearers) were excluded from registered unions because by definition they were not employees. They could form their own segregated unions but these bodies had no legal standing.

The IC Act was meant to accommodate and control the semi-skilled and skilled workers; the unskilled were excluded from the Act and, before amendments in 1930 and 1937, largely excluded from wage regulation. This left unskilled workers without any protection and because these workers were mainly black the Act reinforced the industrial colour bar, impeding the organisation of African workers. The legislation of 1924, following the defeat of the white workers in the 1922 general strike, was a move to eliminate or at least prevent strikes by means other than direct repression. It had been suggested in the Report of the Economic Commission of 1914 that Conciliation Boards be established, and that the statutory recognition of trade unions would 'create responsibility' (Davies, 1976, pp.10–11). The 1914 Report had also expressed the fear (repeated by the Judicial Commission inquiring into the 1922 strike) that Africans would rapidly learn the value of combination and strike action if industrial legislation was not introduced (ibid., p.9).

The racism expressed by white workers parroted that of the ruling class but was more virulent. In one respect it was part of a struggle as old as trade unionism itself. In Europe, as Michael Mann (1973) shows, similar issues had appeared, even if expressed differently:

> If workers possessed full class consciousness they would seek among their other goals workers' control of industry and society. . . . But few important working-class movements have pursued this all-embracing goal with any conviction. Instead, industrial action has generally split off from political action, and industrial action has itself split into two subordinate and separate spheres. By job control, I mean issues

arising out of the worker's attempts to maintain a measure of creativity and control within the given work process surrounding him. The type of trade union action which corresponds to this sphere is usually termed job regulation, for it seeks to exert control over the work area agreed with management to be 'his'. . . . [J]ob regulation is essentially conservative — it seeks to establish *de jure* what has already occurred *de facto*. . . . It is very rarely that a trade union action is orientated towards an increase in *actual* job control, and this distinguishes job regulation from instrumental demands (p.295).

Mann maintains that job control also destroyed shop floor unity and cut across collective action. What one group of workers gained was at another's expense, and in the South African context black workers could see little distinction between white workers and the bosses: both were addressed as '*baas*' (or boss).

The white working class seldom saw beyond the narrowest of industrial demands, whether for 'job control' or financial improvement. The one political party that claimed to represent its interests, the South African Labour Party (SALP), was segregationist. Shortly after the passage of the IC Act, the National Party, in alliance with the SALP, took office and tabled new legislation to protect the status of the white worker and maintain the ethnic separation of workers. There were differences in the perception of workers' rights inside the government: the Labour Party demanded that all Africans be sent back to the Reserves and that employment be reserved for whites, while the National Party, led by General Hertzog, appealed to Afrikaner workers on grounds of 'nationhood' and white supremacy. The change in political control led to the advancement of sectional interests through speculation, patronage or orthodox economic moves: the setting up of tariff barriers; the framing of the Apprenticeship Act (which effectively barred all but white youth); the setting of minimum wages; and the replacement of African (and other black) labour by whites in the civil service, on the railway and harbours, and in secondary industries.

In practice, the IC Act did not assist many workers. It was operable only where workers' and employers' associations existed and agreed to form Industrial Councils, and there were few trades in which workers were sufficiently well organised to meet this precondition in 1924/25. The craft unions that existed and represented workers on Councils were only interested in their own differential pay (Lucas, 1927, Part 1). In other industries there were no agreements and fears were expressed in Parliament that wages would be kept so low that blacks would oust white workers or, alternatively, if wages were set on a 'civilised scale' employers would replace white labour with black.

The Wage Act of 1925

To protect these vulnerable semi-skilled and unskilled white workers the Wage Act of 1925 was passed, establishing a Wage Board to investigate wages and conditions of work in any industry, trade or undertaking with the exception of farming, domestic service and parts of the state sector. The Board would meet at the request of the Minister of Labour, a registered trade union or an employers' association. If these did not exist, the request could be made by a representative number of employers or employees in the industry. The Board could only recommend that employees be paid wages that would allow them to enjoy 'civilised habits of life'; and had to ensure that employers could afford to pay such a wage, unless the Minister authorised otherwise.

There was an outcry from employers, and the Chamber of Mines in particular, but the legislation was approved by Parliament and most fears proved to be groundless. In the first decade of its existence, the Wage Board made no more than 54 wage determinations, 13 of which were declared invalid by the courts (Van der Horst, 1942, p.259), and the Board never subjected the mines to an investigation.

The Wage Act was designed to provide an alternative to social welfare legislation for unskilled white workers and, accordingly, the Board dealt mainly with 'white' wages. Even when the Act was amended in 1937, shedding the clause on civilised standards, and the Board was able to investigate wages paid to African workers more freely, their recommendations referred mostly to Coloured workers in Cape Town. The wages prescribed for them were so miserly that Revd S.W. Lavis, in a stinging rebuke, said that 'the assertion that the unskilled [Coloured] worker has been adequately protected by Wage Board determinations and Industrial Council awards is sheer nonsense' (c. 1943, p.7). Nevertheless, the Joint Council of Europeans and Natives, the Society of Friends of Africa, and organisers of African trade unions, all used the Wage Board to argue for higher African wages, and in the late 1930s this became the springboard for organising unions throughout the country.

The Amended Wage Act

The Johannesburg Joint Council presented claims for higher wages for Africans at all its appearances before the Wage Board from 1926,[3] when the Board was invited to set a minimum wage in Bloemfontein following the riots of the previous year (Lucas, 1927, Part 2). The Joint Councils gave evidence wherever the Board met, submitting budgets based on the calculated minimum cost of living for an African family of five persons (Jones, 1930a, p.177). The figures were pared down to the absolute minimum and excluded medicines, clothing, travelling (except to work), schoolbooks, newspapers, toys, writing materials and so on, providing only 18s to 20s per week for the family's food. The 'budget', which became the basis for all wage claims, was set at £6–£6 14s 8d per month in the cities, and £4 10s–£5 10s in the smaller towns. It implicitly accepted segregated townships, slum housing without amenities, third class transport, rudimentary diet, poor schooling and a lack of medical facilities. Few families could survive on these wages and yet, ironically, African trade unions had to use the Wage Board and present 'Native family budgets' in order to win improvements for the workers. They then had to ensure that all wage determinations (under the IC Act or the Wage Act) were honoured by the employers. In this they won the grudging cooperation of the Department of Labour, which claimed that it had no finances to pay labour inspectors.

The crucial change in the Wage Board's proceedings came with the amendment to the Act in 1937 and was prompted by the need to placate the semi-skilled and unskilled white workers, whose increasing militancy and radicalisation was of concern to the ruling class (Lewis, 1981). A wages bill setting 10s per day as the minimum wage was proposed, but rejected by employers. The South African Trades and Labour Council (SATALC), the federal body of registered unions, concurred because the new wage did not differentiate between white and black (Report, Society of Friends, 20 March 1935). At its 7th Annual Conference in 1936 the SATALC suggested that the minimum wage be set at 10s per day for white workers and 5s for blacks. The employers would not budge, however, and on the insistence of the Chamber of Mines the bill was withdrawn.[4]

J.H. Hofmeyr, Minister of Labour, addressing Parliament on the amendment to the Wage Act said that it incorporated the provisions of the ill-fated Minimum Wages Bill but allowed for greater flexibility and did not interfere with the principles of 'self-government and consultation' that had prevailed hitherto (Parliamentary Debates, 1937, Cols 4324–6). Because the 1937 Act made no reference to 'civilised habits of life', the Minister could direct the Wage Board to an investigation 'in respect of all employees, or of any one or more class of employees in any trade or section of trade in any area'. This clause, which had far-reaching consequences for trade unions, was not discussed in Parliament, nor was the instruction that 'the Board shall, in connection with every investigation, give to persons interested an opportunity of making representation to it'. The Board could have a member of a registered trade union present at its sittings but the wages recommended were to be colour free. The IC Act was also amended to give the Minister and the Industrial Councils the power to impose rates of pay and conditions of work without consulting African workers.

These bills made it even more difficult for workers to strike while, to tighten further the controls on black workers, the Native Laws Administration Act of 1937 was passed. It stopped the 'influx' of Africans into the towns and removed those deemed to be there illegally (Senate Debates, 1937, Cols 1186–8). Senator P.W. le R. van Niekerk explained:

> It was not really his [the Minister's] purpose to remove the native from the urban areas, but he did it in order to create better opportunities for the employment of Europeans in the cities.
> I understand from him that it is the intention to remove the redundant natives who do not belong there, and the young natives who should be on the farms, but are now in the locations. . . (ibid., Col. 1195).

From Wage Boards to union organisation

Liberal spokesmen used the terms of the new Wage Act to secure wage increases for African workers. As indicated by Frank MacGregor, successor to F.A.W. Lucas as chairman of the Board,

> The interests of Native workers are represented, often very ably, by such organisations as the Institute of Race Relations, and the Friends of Africa, frequently . . . with representatives of the unregistered but none the less active trade unions. These unions appear generally to be organised by interested Europeans who usually lead the case for their members. . . . [T]heir presentation of evidence and their grasp of the issues at stake and of the ebb and flow of argument is generally more effective than is the case when presentation is in the hands of the less experienced Natives. . . (Stein, 1977a, p.45).

Professor R.F.A. Hoernlé of the Joint Councils and the SAIRR said much the same, with the same paternalistic overtones:

> [In] interviews with white authorities . . . the white members of the [Joint] Councils 'know the ropes', as no Native can know them. Whites can best judge what procedure and what arguments are most likely to be effective. . . .
> The white members of these Councils act as a sort of bridge between the dominant and the dominated sections. They offer a unique channel for the practice of the spirit of trusteeship in the social field. . . (Hoernlé, 1941, p.97).

A new, more sinister light was thrown on Wage Board appearances by W.G. Ballinger, former adviser to the Industrial and Commercial Workers Union (ICU), in a letter to the Secretary of the Department of Social Welfare on 12 September 1942:

> it has been the policy of this office to encourage trade union activity among Africans and other Non-Europeans, but specially to direct [the word 'divert' is scratched out!] that activity into the legitimate channels of agitation, and it has given practical assistance towards this direction by initiating requests for investigations of industrial conditions by the Wage Board, by preparing statements for presentation to the Board where investigations have been authorised by the Minister of Labour, and by providing spokesmen for the workers on the occasion of public enquiries by the Wage Board.

The letter was written at the height of a strike wave and that could account for the strong stress on 'legitimate channels'. In addition, the letter was written in order to solicit funds for the work of his organisation — according to Ballinger, there was 'a specially urgent reason for our request for assistance':

> [There] is a rapid awakening of the African's consciousness of his desires, and what he regards as his rights, which is likely to make him, and is in fact making him, impatient of the pace of evolutionary change in a democratic society (*sic*), particularly in one where he is himself largely inarticulate. In such circumstances, it is of vital importance that there should be available to the African at this time experienced, sane and balanced advice and assistance which will both encourage him to hope for and to work for improvement in his conditions, but will also hold him stable against influence which would stampede him into impatient extravagant and possibly disastrous action. . . (Copy in *Ballinger Papers*, Cape Town)

For Ballinger the process was clear. The workers' confidence could be won through appearances at the Wage Board and the trade unions could be 'directed' (or 'diverted'?) into legitimate channels. What might have started as acts of 'practical assistance' were transformed into moves to insulate workers from socially unsettling 'channels of agitation'.

Notes

1. Quoted by Ivan L. Walker, Secretary of Labour, in a letter to the Johannesburg Joint Council, 20 September 1934, answering queries about directives recently issued in Natal. *Rheinallt Jones Papers*.
2. This is, of course, only part of the story. Men had moved on to the labour market to secure money, and also arms and ammunition, long before measures were taken to force them off the land. See Chapter 1.
3. Report of J.D. Rheinallt Jones, Appendix A, Second Annual Report of the SAIRR, 1931.
4. SATALC, National Executive Committee, 'Memorandum on the principle of a national minimum wage, 1935', *Ballinger Papers*, Cape Town; Minutes of the 7th National Conference, SATALC; Parliamentary Debates, 1937, Col. 5093.

4. Rebuilding the African Unions, 1932–40

Trade unions in the colonies

Just before his death Leon Trotsky (1940) wrote an essay on the nature of trade unions in 'the epoch of imperialist decay' in which he called once again for concerted working class action to check the spread of fascism and the corporate state, about which he had warned throughout the 1930s.[1] He feared that corporatism would grow and inevitably dominate society unless the working class rose to overthrow the bourgeoisie. He condemned labour leaders who allowed the subversion of the working class and called for the 'complete and unconditional independence of the trade unions in relation to the capitalist state', trade union democracy, and revolutionary socialist leadership of the unions. Trade unionists had to abandon the policy of 'political neutrality' and confront 'a centralised capitalist adversary . . . bound up with state power'. The unions would either 'police' the workers on behalf of monopoly capital or 'become the instruments of the revolutionary movement of the proletariat'.

By 1939 European trade unions were in a parlous state. Trotsky referred to the workers of Italy, Germany and eastern Europe, who had suffered a series of disastrous defeats, and to the Spanish syndicalist movement that had been destroyed. The workers of France had not recovered from the collapse of their 'sit-ins' in the mid-1930s; the labour movement in Latin America had also been savaged. Trotsky called for the revival of independent working class action to prevent imminent disaster: though his direst predictions were not borne out, it seemed at the time that fascism might triumph in Europe. In that event, the working class movement would face a long and bitter period of oppression — which made it all the more urgent to reorganise the socialist movement.

Europe did not fully emerge from the depression before war broke out, and the workers never recovered sufficiently from the demoralisation of large-scale unemployment to build a fresh revolutionary movement. Consequently, they did not intervene as a class to alter the course of events in western Europe. When war came they joined the armies and kept the industries functioning. Class identities were forgotten by men who fought and died for king, for *führer*, for *duce* or for the general-secretary; for the greater glory of Reich, Empire or Mother Russia.

Trotsky also wrote of the colonies under imperial control, monopoly capital, and traditional backwardness. Native capitalism would be weak, he said, and the working class would build trade unions controlled by a labour aristrocracy and bureaucracy which would come to depend on the protection of native governments. The holders of local capital would resist the pressures exerted on them by expatriate capital, and would be 'compelled to a greater or lesser degree to lean on the proletariat'. If, however, the governments of those backward countries found it more profitable to ally themselves with foreign capital, they would destroy the labour movement and institute a more or less totalitarian regime.

Trotsky's global analysis did not provide an 'instant analysis' for every country, and his remarks could be applied more readily in South Africa to the white unions than to African organisations. The Afrikaner bourgeoisie had taken a section of the white working class under its 'protection', and many Afrikaner workers joined the National Party, which promised them protection from the degrading conditions that applied to black workers.

The Nationalists also extended their patronage to the all-white Labour Party in 1924, sharing their detestation of the Chamber of Mines and determination to protect white workers against black worker encroachment. But there could be no alliance between the white bourgeoisie and the black workers, and the extension of trade union rights to Africans (as envisaged by Sidney Webb, Secretary of State for Colonies in the short-lived British Labour government of 1929—31) was not found acceptable in South Africa.

Webb recommended in his dispatch of 17 September 1930 that (black) trade unions be encouraged in the colonies as a 'natural and legitimate development' and that the Trade Union Act of 1871 be used (Bowen, 1954). This Act had legalised British trade unions but had been accompanied by a second bill imposing a ban on picketing and, according to Webb, had been considered a defeat for trade unions in Britain at the time (Webb and Webb, 1907, p.266). Now as Minister for Colonies he suggested his own accompanying restrictions:

> I recognise that there is a danger that, without sympathetic supervision and guidance, organisations of labourers without experience of combination for any social or economic purpose may fall under the domination of disaffected persons, by whom their activities may be diverted to improper and mischievous ends (quoted in Bowen, 1954).

Webb's proposals lay in abeyance, even though trade unions were declared to be neither criminal nor unlawful for civil purposes. Disturbances in the West Indies in 1937 revived the issue, and when the Colonial Development and Welfare Act was passed in 1940, provision was made for the existence of unions and advisers sent to assist them.

Webb's dispatch of 1930 had no effect on official thinking in South Africa, but there seems to have been some response to the events in the West Indies in 1937 and, in October 1938, Harry Lawrence, the Minister of Labour, announced plans for placing African trade unions under government control, 'not along orthodox trade unionism, but along lines as defined by the Native Affairs Department in consultation with the Department of Labour'.[2] Here indeed was the cooptation of trade unions as foreseen by Trotsky.

Trotsky's writings on trade unionism are taken as a point of departure partly because they capture the mood and focus on some of the perceived needs of the working class movements of the time, and partly because his writings influenced socialists in Johannesburg who tried to apply his ideas in their work in African trade unions.

Organising the work force

> Trade unions, even the most powerful, embraced no more than 20 to 25 per cent of the working class, and at that predominantly the more skilled and better paid layers. The more oppressed majority of the working class is drawn only episodically into the struggle, during a period of exceptional upsurge in the labour movement (Trotsky, 1938).

The African trade union movement on the Witwatersrand claimed a membership of some 80,000 in 1945. A further 15,000 were said to be members of unions in Pretoria, and about 60,000 in the rest of the country.[3] If the 20,000 mine workers are excluded, the total nominal membership of some 50 unions averaged just over 1,000 each.

The problems facing the unions were immense. They had no legal standing, although they were not illegal. After 1937 the new Wage Board Act allowed them to present evidence for minimum wage awards, but strike action was always forbidden. The most elementary matters presented new problems: Africans had no right to occupy premises in the town and subterfuge was needed to rent offices, without which they could not survive. Financing the union was even more daunting. Wages were so low that subscriptions were not always forthcoming and the unions were starved of funds; only in exceptional cases was the paid-up membership as high as 10 per cent of membership lists.

Despite these difficulties the unions survived and some made notable progress: membership grew and the unions secured improvements for the workers. Furthermore, those who did join came to meetings, demonstrated, and defied the law by striking. And with them came hundreds and thousands of other workers who never formally joined the union, but participated in many of the most militant industrial confrontations.

Information about workers' attitudes to the unions is still rudimentary but it seems that membership was erratic and enthusiasm somewhat uncertain. When action was required a remarkable number supported the complainants and the union, but thereafter many drifted away. Thus, according to an un-named speaker:

> In 1934, that was the year that marked my disrespect for the white man. I worked at a laundry. I used to earn one pound ten shillings a month and I used to sleep in a house full of bugs and my food was bad. Then in 1938 somebody came along by the name of Wilfred, he had an assistant called Freddie. They organised us to join the trade union. Our employer protested extremely. The people used to start at six in the morning, they used to knock off at 5.30 in the afternoon. Since then what we discovered was that the long period we worked was cut.
> Then again in 1939 came in the Wage Board, then there was a slight increase in

wages, then little by little they gave us some increments. In 1939 it [the union] was left to drop, because according to the custom of Africans, once they see some betterment then they leave struggle, as a result the union became weaker and weaker and the employer started oppressing us once more. Then we said, but surely the trade union was helping us. Again we combined. It was true. Once more we saw some new and good development.[4]

There were just over 1,600,000 African males employed or employable in South Africa in 1937. Of these over 550,000 were migrant labourers on the mines (a figure adjusted for the average contract of 9–10 months) (*Native Farm Labour Commission*, 1939, p.8) and a further half million were employed on the farms or as domestic servants, as shown in Table 4.1.

Mining, domestic and rural workers — two thirds of the total work force — were the most difficult to organise because barriers were placed in the way of organisation, or because they were scattered, or isolated inside the household, and there was little that could be done to improve their conditions. Furthermore, they were excluded from the provisions of wage legislation and that prevented trade unionists gaining meaningful improvements for them.

Table 4.1
Number of Africans employed (000)*

Occupation	1930	1932	1936	1939	1945/46
Mines					
Gold	213	229	324	348	318
Coal	30	21.5	28.5	32	
Diamonds (not alluvial)	16	2	3	4.4	
Private industry	81	55.3	120	140	230
Government					
Govt/local govt and railway workshops		15	10		
Railways	33	26	38.5	47	63
Stevedores			16		
Provincial roads				40	
Clerical and distributive			25		34
Teachers					
Male			4.8		7.5
Female			3.4		6.5
Servants					
Male			114		152
Female			242		404
Rural			320		343

Sources: Van der Horst (1971); *Union Statistics for Fifty Years: 1910–1960* (1960); *Report of the Native Farm Labour Commission, 1937–38* (1939).
* All figures are rounded and many are averaged.

This did not stop would-be organisers. There were campaigns to organise farm labourers in the late 1920s and several attempts at organising domestic servants, while the organisation of mineworkers was perhaps the most important project attempted in the 1930s and 1940s.

If these three groups of workers are seen as representing special cases, the number of African workers who could be organised was relatively small. There were the 120,000 working in industry or construction; 25,000 in distribution; and over 65,000 employed by government, provincial or municipal authorities. There were also some categories that are not listed in Table 4.1 — workers in power stations, wattle plantations, plant nurseries, car, van and bus driving, nursing, or newspaper vending. In the rash of wartime unionisation unusual groups of workers formed unions and took strike action — for example, golf caddies, plant nursery workers, shoe repairers and power workers. Although most have been overlooked (partly for lack of information) they were important at the time, both for the workers who created them and also for the spirit they breathed into the working-class movement.

Unfortunately worker organisation was cut down in extent and consequently in influence by the failure to build national unions. Trade unions in major towns (Cape Town, Port Elizabeth, East London, Durban and Pretoria) concentrated almost exclusively on the workers within their municipal boundaries or regions. Even Johannesburg unions, which were the biggest and most important, only occasionally ventured outside the town.

There were reasons for this parochialism. Conditions differed in the main urban centres with respect to industrial foci, ethnic composition and wage structures. Coloured and Indian workers were not excluded by law from joining registered trade unions and they had little inducement to join an exclusively black trade union movement. Unskilled African labour was covered by wage determinations based on local living conditions, making national organisation a less obvious priority. Further, the main centres of industry were hundreds of miles apart and transport was beyond the means of the unions. In any case few union officials had 'exemption' passes, without which travelling was always difficult.

Even if these obstacles had been removed, the concentration of most industry on the Rand meant that there was little purpose, for workers in most occupations, in trying to link up with scattered factories in far distant towns. The Rand had an urban African population of nearly 600,000 in 1936, three times larger than the combined total for the eight largest towns outside the Rand: 60 per cent of African male workers were employed in this region. Johannesburg was therefore the centre of the trade union movement and witnessed an extensive strike wave in 1942—43. It was here, at the centre of the gold belt, that the workers' movement rose and fell. It emerged in the aftermath of the country's economic recovery and its collapse marked the end of an era in the working class movement.

The state of the unions, 1930—35

The trade unions organised on the Witwatersrand in the late 1930s did not always start from scratch. There were threads, tenuous and often broken, that started with the ICU, continued through the first black industrial unions on the Rand (organised by Communists expelled from the ICU), and were then rescued from oblivion by men expelled from, or disagreeing with the policies of, the CPSA.

We know little about the workers who joined the new unions and can only guess at probable continuities with previous organisation. The ICU maintained a shadowy existence in some centres and was reported to be split into eight separate and independent ICUs, each with its own headquarters and all claiming several branches.[5] The East London section was involved in strike action in 1930 in support of the railwaymen's demand for wage increases:[6] thereafter, like most other sections, it was largely dormant. In other areas, such as Pretoria, a few leaders were involved in political agitation but this slackened when they tired of politicking (Mokgatle, 1971, pp.179, 215). Workers in shops or factories were therefore likely to look elsewhere if they wanted to press their demands.

In 1928 the Communist-led unions combined in the Non-European Federation of Trade Unions and affiliated to the Red International of Labour Unions (or Profintern). The Federation claimed a membership of 10,000 and demanded equal pay for equal work, with an end to all discriminatory laws (*Umteteli wa Bantu*, 7 September 1929). But these were revolutionary unions, rejecting all reformism in line with Profintern directives, and they paid little heed to the workers' immediate needs. They called time and again for strikes, and when these inevitably failed the workers just drifted away.

The unions had little success and were weakened by internal strife in the CPSA. When most of the leading trade union organisers were expelled from the Party, the Federation went out of existence and only a few unions survived. T.W. Thibedi, the veteran Communist and one of those expelled, formed the Communist League of Africa (Opposition), and claimed in a letter to the *Militant* (6 August 1932) that he had taken with him (or reconstituted) laundry and baking workers' unions, together with the nuclei of both mine and municipal workers' unions. Gana Makabeni, another veteran Communist and trade unionist, and also one of the expelled, kept a much diminished African Clothing Workers Union alive, aided financially by the Garment Workers Union (Report, Society of Friends of Africa, December 1936).

From 1933 to 1940 the CPSA in the Transvaal was in disarray and had little influence in the African trade union movement. Small groups of party adherents initiated organisations through which they could operate in a period of minimal party activity. Some entered the Labour League of Youth, others were active in the Labour Party and, although these activities were uncoordinated, they were all directed at recruiting sympathisers.

In his 1933 report, Ballinger listed only three extant African unions in the country: the Clothing Workers and Laundry Workers unions, and a union of dock workers in Cape Town. He also mentioned two 'white' unions (in the leather and the textile industries) which admitted African workers.

Nonetheless, Ballinger warned that no union was financially solvent, and that weakness came from inefficient leadership, maladministration, growing poverty following the long drought, and repressive legislation.

New beginnings

The story of African trade unions in the 1930s is also that of the Trotskyist groups whose members had been expelled from the CPSA. First there was Thibedi. Then, when he seems to have dropped out of politics, leadership of the African Laundry Workers Union was assumed by Murray Gow Purdy and his successor Ralph Lee, both members of the Workers Party of South Africa.

Purdy's stay was short and turbulent. He presented the laundry workers' claims to the employers and, although modest, they were rejected by all but three of the firms. The workers asked for weekly instead of monthly payment (hoping thereby to secure two to three days' extra pay every month); wages in lieu of board and lodging (which absorbed up to a quarter of their monthly wage packet); and an end to the victimisation of their shop stewards.

A lock-out at one of the firms led to a 'wild-cat' strike by 180 workers, without preparation and without funds. Purdy affiliated the union to the South African Trades and Labour Council (SATLC) on the day of the strike and was later accused by the Council (SATLC Annual Conference, 1935, minutes) of having done so in order to secure legal expenses and food for the workers. A court judgement went against the employers but many of the workers were laid off. Purdy withdrew and went to India, where he joined a small revolutionary organisation and was arrested after a raid on a post office van. Lee took over. The Laundry Workers Union grew to just over 300 members, but when the employers made no concessions its strength declined.[7] Lee also formed a union of steel ceiling workers, but a 'wild-cat' strike in which 'scabs' were violently handled convinced many in the Johannesburg branch of the Workers Party that there was little they could do in South Africa. They sailed for Britain in 1935 and helped found the Workers International League (Interviews with Heaton Lee and Millie Kahn/Lee/Haston). During the war Lee returned to Johannesburg, formed the local Workers International League, and participated in the Progressive Trade Union Group (PTU) (see Chapter 8).

Max Gordon and the liberals

Max Gordon, a member of the Workers Party, left Cape Town in 1935 at the age of 22 and came to Johannesburg, where he assumed the leadership of the Laundry Workers Union. He came from a poor family and, although supported by a relative at university, was unable to complete a pre-medical course. He used his knowledge of chemistry to secure employment in a shoe firm, but an industrial accident left him with a permanent disability.[8] Several factors were to shape Gordon's strategy. His primary aim was to organise mineworkers: to do that he needed a framework through which to recruit them.[9] From the outset he aimed to win higher wages and to convince workers of the value of trade unions. He was wary of strikes, particularly after a 'wild-cat' strike in December 1936 almost destroyed the union. In the court case that followed the thirteen accused 'strike leaders' were discharged on a technical point, after which Gordon exercised considerable restraint on his members.

Strike action in the 1930s seldom succeeded: restraint was needed while the unions built their strength. Gaur Radebe, secretary of the African Cement, Stone, and Building Workers Union, learned this lesson in September 1937 when six of his workers were dismissed from a constructional steel firm after an appeal for higher wages had been rejected. Over 100 men immediately came out on strike. Radebe appealed to Ballinger and Gordon for assistance, but officials of the Native Commissioner's Office prevented them addressing the workers. The strikers were arrested, then released and paid off. Two days later pickets were confronted by police, white workers and some of the bosses. *Sjamboks* were wielded, stones thrown and shots fired. One bullet, apparently fired by the managing director, shattered the jaw of a worker — but it was the workers who were arrested and charged with public violence. Sixteen received six-week prison sentences and two youths got fourteen strokes.[10].

If strikes failed, other means were needed to improve the position of workers. Gordon transformed his union's offices into a meeting place for the unemployed, and employers contacted the union when extra staff were required. He also arranged legal assistance for those who fell foul of the law; medical attention for the ill; and even assistance for workers in arrears with their rent. In the evenings the offices became a school for workers, with lessons in literacy, arithmetic, bookkeeping, procedure at meetings, and history. This school was eventually closed under police orders because, they said, the history course (taught by Fanny Klenerman) had a distinct political flavour (*Saffery Papers*).

But these ancillary activities could not sustain a trade union movement, nor raise the money to pay organisers, the rent and other incidental expenses. The workers had to be convinced that joining the union and paying subscriptions could get them higher wages and better work conditions before they would part with their hard-earned coins.

A project started by the SAIRR in late 1936 was to alter the course of Gordon's work. Initially the Institute commissioned Ballinger (who was given a fee of £300 for one year) to report on wages paid to Africans, their relation to the cost of living over the past 50 years, and the effect of wage determinations and agreements on black wage levels.[11] He was also to use the information to make representations to the Department of Labour and the Wage Board. Three reports were submitted at quarterly intervals in 1937 and Ballinger made representation on behalf of some workers. But an economist to whom the reports were referred stated that the work provided 'no information which any knowledgeable person could not have ferreted out for himself within a relatively short time'.

This led to acrimonious correspondence and a breach between Ballinger and leading members of the SAIRR which was never altogether healed. The paths of Ballinger (for the Friends of Africa) and the SAIRR, particularly on African trade unionism, henceforth tended to diverge. In the third of his reports to the SAIRR Ballinger wrote that he had been assisting his wife in her campaign for the seat as Native Representative of Parliament in the eastern Cape. While he was away, he stated:

> I made arrangements with Mr Max Gordon, Secretary, African Laundry Workers Union, for the carrying on of the more urgent aspects both of my own work for the Friends of Africa and some of that implicit in my agreement with the Institute, such as preparations for Wage Board Enquiries and matters affecting the relations of Native workers and their employers.
>
> Mr Max Gordon, whose activities are being subsidised from the grant given to me by the Institute of Race Relations, reports that he attended to about 150 complaints of Native workers against employers of labour during the period May to August 1937 covering claims for wrongful dismissal, wages in lieu of notice, underpayment of wages according to agreement and payment for overtime. [Sums of] £1 to £50 were obtained totalling approximately £260 (Third Report, 30 August 1937, in *Ballinger Papers*).

Ballinger gave details of Gordon's submissions to the Wage Board on conditions in bakeries, and of representations made to the Industrial Council of the Newspaper and Printing Industry on behalf of the workers in the Printing Workers Union, requesting a rise of wages from 15s—20s per week to a minimum of 24s—27s 6d. The payment to Gordon was criticised as not fitting into a 'wage and cost of living enquiry', but nonetheless the SAIRR arranged through the Bantu Welfare Trust (which they administered) to provide £10 per month for Gordon to work full time in the unions. Gordon was also to receive 'considerable secretarial and other assistance in the preparation of evidence for sittings of the Wage Board'.

The SAIRR extended its assistance to African unions after receiving, in August 1937, a memorandum signed by organisers of twelve African trade unions all urgently needing help against employers who underpaid workers or broke agreements (including those supplementing Wage Determinations). Assistance was also needed for workers who fell foul of various Native Acts. In January 1938 it was decided that the restricted funds of the Bantu Welfare Trust be spent on two projects: trade union work and legal aid.

This brought Gordon closer to Lynn Saffery, secretary of the SAIRR, who made trade unions his special interest, and Ruth Heyman (later Mrs Saffery), the first full-time organiser of the Legal Aid Bureau. This cooperation allowed Gordon to concentrate on building the unions, while Saffery provided resources from the SAIRR. Together with Julian Rollnick, librarian at the SAIRR, Rheinallt Jones and others, Gordon and Saffery appeared before Wage Boards up and down the country.[12]

The Wage Board provided Gordon (and others) with the instrument through which African unions could be built and sustained, and it was central to their burgeoning in the late 1930s. The use of a government body to secure wage increases introduced a factor with obvious dangers, however. Organisers were to learn that unions could obtain wage increases only when the government permitted, and when wage awards were curtailed, and wages pegged, workers drifted away and unions crumbled.

It was 'Catch 22'. Without the Wage Board, the unions would probably have foundered; but, by working through the Board and not preparing alternative strategies, the unions were placed at the mercy of the government. Gordon was aware of the precariousness of the position, and he meant to build a movement which would survive in the event of a confrontation, but it is doubtful whether many of those who followed him took steps to prevent the collapse which followed. The basis of Gordon's optimism can be found in a conversation in 1938 which was later recounted by Peter Abrahams (1954, p.260). It indicates Gordon's awareness of the limits to which the Wage Board could be used and of the need for a strong independent movement able to withstand a government attack. In the encounter Gordon is reported as saying:

> One day, a vigorous and strong Native trade union movement will grow up. None of the government's prohibitions and restrictions and arrests will count for anything then. And that movement is going to play a key part in the political emancipation of all non-whites. So, for the present, I ask for a threepenny rise [which laundry workers obtained], for a recognised and proper lunch hour, and for decent and safe conditions of work. It's a small beginning, but it's a beginning. That's what was wrong with earlier efforts. They didn't know how to start.

Gordon knew how to start: he set up six unions in the years before the war, and a General Workers Union in which to enrol workers who would form the nuclei of further unions. Included amongst these were the mine workers whom Gordon had contacted. Gordon also formed a Joint Committee of African Trade Unions with himself as secretary and a combined membership estimated at 15,700 by 1939 (Saffery, 1941a).

The other African unions in Johannesburg were those established by Gana Makabeni, who started as an organiser in the ICU and then the CPSA. During the late 1930s he would not work with Gordon: it is not certain whether this was because of the latter's self-proclaimed Trotskyism or Makabeni's belief that there was no place for whites as officials of African trade unions. Ten unions were grouped together under Makabeni but there is little information about their activities. He was general secretary of the Co-ordinating Committee of African Trade Unions to which they all belonged. By 1939 the total membership was estimated as under 4,000 (Saffery, 1941a; Ballinger report to Friends of Africa, 1936, *Ballinger Papers*).

The two trade union committees continued along separate paths and their differences persisted through the years. Appearing inside the trade union movement time and time again, these divisions were later to plague the Council of Non-European Trade Unions (CNETU) (see Chapter 8). The factors dividing the organisation are not easily delineated, clouded as they are by differences of personality, political philosophy and trade union tactics. The antagonisms that split the left into warring factions were transferred to the trade union movement. In the Transvaal the situation was made even more fissiparous by the nationalism of Makabeni and others. It was a matter of black versus white, Trotskyists versus Stalinists, reformism versus militancy — and these ingredients appeared in endless permutation.

Yet the Trotskyist Gordon seems to have worked without help from members of the Workers Party — although Jack Godwin, also reputedly in the WP and the organiser of one of the three Steel Workers Unions, worked along parallel lines. Furthermore, few of Gordon's union organisers ever joined the Trotskyists, except for Daniel Koza, and there is little indication that organisers discussed political issues with workers in their contacts over union matters.

Interviews with Guy Routh and Rolene Szur indicate that Gordon obtained assistance from young socialists who were attracted to the work he was doing, and it is conceivable that in the 1930s, when there was considerable disquiet over the Moscow trials, his anti-Stalinism stood him in good stead with members of the liberal South African Institute of Race Relations. But the cooperation he found there was also connected with his style of union leadership, and it has not been possible to disentangle the strands that made up his relationship with Institute officials.

Gordon's victories and ultimate downfall

In June 1938 the Wage Board strategy brought the first substantial victory: unskilled workers at bakeries had their wages increased from 16s 6d to 29s 3d per week — a considerable sum for the time. This was followed by an agreement covering laundry workers in May 1939. The Joint Committee's major triumph, the agreement in the commercial and. distributive trade covering everyone from counter-hands to labourers and night watchmen, came on 22 December 1939. Unskilled workers in Johannesburg received 27s 8d per week, with provisions for annual paid leave, overtime pay, and special rates for work on public holidays. Payment elsewhere on the Reef was slightly lower but still proportionately high compared to other unskilled workers (Hellmann, 1953, p.12).

The new determination received wide publicity. Ballinger reported to the Friends of Africa in 1939 that workers in commerce 'subsequently gathered in Johannesburg in an open air meeting in numbers that have not been equalised since the days when Clements Kadalie . . . held mass meetings'. He saw this as providing a new impetus to the whole African trade union movement. Naboth Mokgatle, at that time an unskilled worker, also attended the meeting and after discussions with Gordon agreed to form a branch of the Commercial and Distributive Workers Union in Pretoria (see Chapter 9).

Max Gordon.

Gana Makabeni.

J.B. Marks.

Lynn Saffery.

Organising workers through the barbed wire fence.

Wage determinations usually took 18—24 months to complete from the first sitting of the Board to the final report, ministerial agreement and gazetting. Gordon did not sit passively waiting for the outcome. With the cooperation of the Department of Labour he took up every complaint brought by aggrieved workers. In 1938 he recovered £3,200 for members of the Commercial and Distributive Workers Union, over £5,000 for members of the General Workers Union, and £3,000 for the 900 members of the Bakers Union (Saffery, 1941a, p.29). Other unions recovered smaller amounts for their members and this became a vital part of all union activity.

Where the unions were unable to secure improvements, they lost members. This was not unique to South Africa but that was small consolation to Gordon, who wrote in a memorandum to the Bantu Welfare Trust that the African Printing Workers Union

> has suffered a severe set-back and many of its members have become disillusioned. . . .
> The membership of the Union has fallen but its activities are still kept [up] by a few enthusiastic members. If the [Industrial] Council fixes a decent minimum wage [30s per week was requested], there is a good possibility of a strong union . . . being built up. Many of its members have become disillusioned by the repeated promises of the Secretary of the Typographical Union, and the Industrial Council (*Saffery Papers*, No.1).

Gordon ensured that the legal rates were paid, and that wages were paid in lieu of notice, but only a 'few enthusiastic members' maintained the union.

Members of the SAIRR took a certain pride in the achievements of the trade unions. By providing legal aid, technical assistance, finance, expertise on wage agreements and so on, the Institute made itself indispensable. This might have raised questions about the possible effects of such relations with a body which had such close contacts with members of the establishment: nevertheless, the unions grew ever closer to the SAIRR.

By 1938—39 the officials of the SAIRR seemed united in their evaluation of work in the trade unions, although tensions were to appear when Saffery wanted the Institute to take a more active part in their organisation. In late 1938 Saffery arranged a six-month tour of Britain to meet organisers of agricultural labourers and unskilled workers, with the assistance of the Trade Union Congress.[13]

The role of the SAIRR was acknowledged in January 1939 when the Minister of Labour, H.G. Lawrence, told its annual conference that African unions could not be recognised under existing legislation, but that their right to exist had been protected. Since the government could not supervise their activities, there were fears that they would be exploited by agitators. The question of non-statutory recognition was being considered and 'it would be useful if bodies such as the Institute of Race Relations would consider the subject and submit their suggestions' (*Sun*, 13—27 January 1939).

The SAIRR seemed set to extend its hold on the trade unions even further, with government backing. If there were signs of difficulties, inside the SAIRR or among the unions, these were obscured by the euphoria which accompanied the wage determinations. The first hiccup came unexpectedly in the aftermath of riots at Nkana in Northern Rhodesia. On 3 April 1940 troops shot workers who were demanding higher wages, leaving 17 dead and 65 wounded. Dan Koza drafted a leaflet calling a mass meeting for the Bantu Sports Ground and this was issued under the names of Makabeni (for the Co-ordinating Committee) and A. Thipe (of the Joint Committee). The translations were more colourful than the original English but the latter was considered sufficient to have the meeting banned in terms of the wartime Emergency Powers Act. It read:

> Come to protest against the action of the Rhodesian Government, which has killed African workers who were fighting for their rights. If European workers had their wages increased, why should wages of African workers be increased by guns? Come in great numbers. Support the children and widows of the comrades who have been shot without sin.

The police accused Gordon of advising the executives of the trade union movements to convene the meeting and, despite his denials, he was instructed to cancel the meeting or face arrest. When he was interned later that year, one of the government's accusations was that he had called the meeting (see *Saffery Papers*, No. 1). Officials of the SAIRR formed a United Committee of African Trade Unions to consider matters arising from Nkana, and planned to send an investigator to the Copperbelt, offer names of candidates for a Commission of Enquiry, and obtain legal assistance for Africans involved in the riots. Renamed the South African Committee on Industrial Relations, and including members of the SATALC, African trade unions and the ANC, it became the vehicle through which the SAIRR hoped to direct the work of the unions, campaign for recognition, provide training for officials, and assist unions in their day-to-day work.

In June 1940 Gordon was interned and the direct link between the SAIRR and the Joint Committee was broken. Jones, Saffery, Fanny Klenerman and others expressed fears that the unions might fall apart, money be misappropriated and, above all, that the Communists would use the opportunity to take over the Joint Committee, the unions, and the workers. It was the belief of officials of the SAIRR, and of Rheinallt Jones in particular, that whites were essential for the efficient running of the black unions, and also that Africans were easy prey for Communists unless protected. Jones saw the Director of Native Labour on 4 June and urged that Saffery be allowed to visit Gordon to get information on union matters that were pending when the arrest took place, and to arrange with Gordon that Saffery take his place on the Joint Committee. He put his views in writing:

> Mr M. Gordon who has for some time been engaged in organising Native trade unions, has been interned. As a result these unions have been thrown into considerable confusion and it is most important that they should at this moment be offered competent guidance and direction, more particularly in regard to the control of funds and the maintainance (*sic*) of contacts with employees. I have reason to believe that unless this is done efforts will be made by undesirable persons to secure control of the organisations. In fact, such efforts have already been made. After very

careful consideration, the President of the South African Institute of Race Relations (Professor Hoernlé) and myself, after consultation with the treasurer (Mr J.L. Hardy), feel that the Institute should offer the organisations the voluntary help of its secretary Mr A.L. Saffery. . . . Mr Saffery would bring to the Executive Officers of the Institute any development of an untoward nature with a view to the attention of the authorities being directed to this.

Unless some such action is taken there is great danger that the funds of the organisations (of which there are eight, with a membership of nearly 20,000) directly under Mr Gordon's direction, will be dissipated and the Native workers will suffer.

As chief executive officer of the Institute I can give you the assurance that Mr Saffery will confine his activities entirely to the financial and industrial activities of the organisations.[14]

The letter continued on these lines, and added that the suggestion was subject to the willingness of the unions to accept this help.

Saffery visited Gordon at the internment camp at Ganspan and brought back proposals for maintaining the union's activities. On 18 June 1940 Saffery and Jones met members of the Joint Committee and called for a petition to secure Gordon's release, but, according to Saffery, Jones 'made [the] mistake of suggesting that the reason be that the unions could not manage without Gordon'.[15] Koza was furious and his opposition to Saffery's appointment split the Joint Committee. After much personal abuse and recrimination Jones walked out of the meeting, vowing that he would have no more to do with the unions or with Gordon's release. The meeting was a watershed for the unions, and for SAIRR involvement in their affairs.

Koza proved to be correct. The unions managed without Gordon and Saffery, and without the assistance provided by the SAIRR. The real struggles of the workers were just starting: Koza was soon to show the way by securing the biggest wage rises for his union. The dispute had opened up the issues of white paternalism and liberal stewardship, attitudes which lay at the heart of SAIRR policy. The trade unionists who supported Koza had broken with a tradition into which Gordon, largely unwittingly, had led the movement.

Gordon was interned for approximately one year. Although he was allowed to return to trade union work, he did not find a new niche in Johannesburg. He worked with Saffery and the South African Committee on Industrial Relations, and through them was invited by white trade unionists and socialists to visit Port Elizabeth in 1940. In ten weeks he set up seven trade unions and established contacts with workers in three further trades, before handing the unions to local organisers. Continued police harassment then persuaded him to leave the field and retire to private life in Cape Town (Hirson, 1977, pp.191—2).

Lynn Saffery's position in the SAIRR was undermined when Rheinallt Jones, on losing his seat in the Senate to Hyman Basner in 1942, wished to take over the directorship of the Institute. Jones never regained his position, but an acrimonious interview with Saffery hastened the latter's resignation. Then came the announcement in *Race Relations News*:

The Institute does not concern itself with the actual organisation of trade unions. The organisation and administration is left to the unions themselves, and officially, the Institute's only connection with the unions is to give them the assistance and guidance which it gives to any other bodies and individuals who ask for help (Vol. 4, No. 3, March 1942).

It was the end of the road for Saffery. Three months later he and his wife left for the Northern Rhodesian Copperbelt, at the request of the Colonial Office, to report on social conditions there. His report, which was printed, was not published until Zambia gained its independence, when the work he had done gained belated recognition.

Notes

1. There were elements of 'corporatism' or state control of institutions in systems as different as fascist Italy, Nazi Germany, Hiroshita's Japan, Franco's Spain, and Roosevelt's 'New Deal' United States.
2. *Forum*, 7 October 1938, and *Guardian*, 14 October 1938, report Lawrence's address to the Convention of Federated Chamber of Industries, in which this was made known.
3. Minute attached to letter from the Council of Non-European Trade Unions to SAIRR, dated 4 June 1945, *Rheinallt Jones Papers*.
4. The speech (translated into English) is recorded in the Conference of Local Committees of SACTU, probably 1956, Hemson microfilm.
5. W.G. Ballinger, 'Report on the Industrial and Commercial Workers Union of South Africa', typescript, 1933. My thanks to Charles van Onselen for drawing my attention to documents at the ILO.
6. Henri Danielle Tyamzashe, *Summarised History of the Industrial and Commercial Workers Union*, typescript, n.d., pp.30–5, gives an insider's account.
7. See R. Lee, 'The Native Question in South Africa', *New International* (New York), May 1935, pp.110–11, for an impressionistic account of the laundry strike.
8. I owe details on Gordon to Paul Kosten (one-time co-editor of *Spark*), Charles van Gelderen (one-time editor of *Workers Voice*), and D.S. Linney, who met Gordon in Johannesburg after his release from internment in 1941. A taped memoir by Fanny Klenerman also provided data.
9. Conversation with D.S. Linney. N. Sneh (Skikne), formerly of Johannesburg, now at Beersheba, mentioned this independently in an interview.
10. 'The Strike at Sayle and Rossack', a statement by W.G. Ballinger, *Rheinallt Jones Papers*. Also, W.G. Ballinger, 'Interim Report to Society of Friends of Africa', 28 October 1937, *Ballinger Papers*, Johannesburg.
11. The correspondence on the project is contained in the *Rheinallt Jones Papers*.
12. This information is to be found in the Second Annual Report of the South African Bantu Welfare Trust, 1937–38, Minutes of the Trust (quoted by Stein, 1977a, p.43). Further background information was obtained in discussions in London with Ruth Heyman Lazar.

13. Correspondence with Transport House, London, 1938. My thanks to the TUC for copies of the letters.
14. *Saffery Papers*, No. 2. These papers are not generally open to the public, and were made available to me by Lynn Saffery. In answer to my questions, Saffery wrote shortly before his final illness that he had no clear recollection of what had transpired so long ago. It was an event which would have to be seen in the context of the war situation. Furthermore, he wrote, he would never have done anything contrary to the interests of the workers.
15. Notes made by Saffery on the emergency meeting, dated 18 June 1940. This comment is inserted by Saffery in parenthesis. *Saffery Papers*, No. 1.

5. Organising Domestic Servants

Cheeky servants must go!

In 1938 mimeographed letters were addressed by the African Domestic Servants League to 'All Employers of Domestic Servants' asking them to send their employees to discuss the organisation of the League. Employers were assured that the objective was 'to improve relations between employers and servants'.[1] It was not clear from its 'programme' whether this was an employer's or a servant's organisation. Point 4 concerned '[h]ow best to protect the interests of Domestic servants, to advise in the proper method of dealing [with] irritable housewives'; Point 5 proposed to 'ensure security of service through sick and benefit funds . . . proper training in domestic service, and . . . respectable testimonials' to be issued by the League. These were at best ambivalent, and did not offer much to the worker. The first three aims, however, were straight out of the housewives' charter. Point 1 offered lectures, cookery demonstrations, 'moral exercises' . . . to inspire servants 'to take a keen interest in their work'; Point 2 aimed to 'put an end to all saucy and impertinent servants'; and Point 3 sought to end 'thieving and other vices prevalent among domestic servants'.

Four months later posters appeared on walls and lamp posts, directed to householders and advertising a Grand Cookery Demonstration for servants (see p.52). The fee per quarter was 2s 6d for servants, and 5s for employers who became 'honorary members'. The League seemed to have become primarily an employment bureau. 'Honorary members' would get 'dependable servants', and 'cheeky servants' would be weeded out. The protection of servants from 'irritable' housewives had been dropped.

In this decade of emerging trade unionism it is not surprising that attempts were made to organise domestic servants. This was the largest group of workers in the country, a body of men and women who were paid miserable wages and subjected to excessively long hours of work. The mimeographed letter and the poster raise further questions, however, about the motives of the organisers and the nature of the League they were forming. Was this really a serious venture and did the founders seriously believe that servants would be attracted, or that employers would wish to join as honorary members?

The 'patrons' (if indeed they had agreed to serve) were not particularly concerned with trade unions, or with 'cheeky servants', although they might have been concerned about the 'morality' of women servants in the town. The officials of the union and their associates are of more concern. D.R. Twala, of the Bantu Sports Club and the Bantu Men's Social Centre, was

African Domestic Servants League

P.O. Box 6975.   151, MARSHALL STREET, JOHANNESBURG.

Under the Patronage of:

Revs. J. BRUCE GARDNER, R. RAYNES, Miss D. MAUD, Mrs. E. HELLMANN.

GRAND COOKERY DEMONSTRATION

FOR EVERY DOMESTIC SERVANT

ALL ROADS LEAD TO THE

BANTU SPORTS CLUB
On SATURDAY, MARCH, 5th 1939

at 3 p.m.

SEND YOUR SERVANTS TO COME AND LEARN TO BE OF GREATER SERVICE.

SOLVE THE SERVANTS PROBLEM.

Improve the services of your houseboys and girls.

GET RELIABLE, TRUSTWORTHY AND WILLING SERVANTS.

HELP TO WEED OUT UNDESIRABLES.

CHEEKY SERVANTS MUST GO!

To ensure good Servants insist that every employee become a member of the League.

Let us help one another to better the behavior of Domestic Servants.

HOUSE-HOLDERS BECOME HONORARY MEMBERS OF THE ABOVE LEAGUE IN ORDER TO GET DEPENDABLE SERVANTS.

HONORARY MEMBERS pay 5/- a quarter.
MEMBERS -   -   - pay 2/6 a quarter.

Cookery Demonstrations every Fortnight until further notice.

By Order, Executive Committee,

D. R. TWALA, Chairman.

interested primarily in football: he might have been providing a postal address, but otherwise his presence is unexplained. J.G. Coka had been an organiser in the ICU, then a member of the CPSA until expelled in 1935 for 'petty bourgeois' (that is, business) activities. Subsequently editor of his own journal, he also organised trade unions in close collaboration with W.G. Ballinger. Others who joined the League's committee included Self Mampuru, later adviser on trade unions and cooperatives to the Friends of Africa (and Ballinger's assistant after Coka's departure); Dan Tloome, trade unionist, later Vice-President of the Council of Non-European Trade Unions, paid treasurer of the ANC (and adviser to Dr Xuma) and member of the CPSA; Nkagaleng Nkadimeng, trade unionist and assistant secretary of the Transvaal ANC; and Albert Segwai, later secretary of the League and associated unions, and secretary of the 'militant' Progressive Trade Union Group.[2]

'House-boys' and 'house-girls'

> The domestic labourer has a semi-feudal relationship with her employer, where she is paid partly in kind; and is tied to the employer by a series of obligations, by economic needs, and sometimes by law. (Belinda Bozzoli, 1983.)

> But even in Johannesburg a native is sometimes fed and housed with extreme crudeness. There are people who build their boy's room with shelves of concrete for beds, and they give their cook-boy only his mealie-meal, and perhaps — not necessarily — a daily ration of meat. In practically all households, if the boys have bread, it is special Kaffir bread; if they have sugar or tea or syrup, it is specially inferior sugar or tea or syrup. . . . (Sarah Gertrude Millin, 1934, pp.274–5).

One had to be a very poor white not to have employed a servant in the 1930s. It was the prerogative of every white man, woman, and child to have one or more servants, male or female, Coloured or African (or, in exceptional cases, white). As nannies, chars, cooks or gardeners, the servants tended their mistresses and masters, providing the leisure time enjoyed by the privileged minority.[3]

The colour of the servants was partly a matter of geography. Most Coloured and Indian servants were in the Cape and Natal respectively — but African servants were available everywhere, in the towns and in the countryside. The number of Africans in domestic service is not certain. One government commission in 1937–39 ignored census returns, and estimated that there were 275,000 men and women in service: that is, one African for each white family in the Transvaal and Natal (*Report of the Native Farm Labour Commission, 1937–38*, 1939, p.8). In the available statistics rural and urban domestic servants are grouped together: the overall figures tend to conceal such features as the predominance, at least until the mid-1930s, of male servants on the Witwatersrand and in the main towns of Natal.

The distribution profile for domestic servants depended in part on the sex ratio in the towns: a predominance of males in the early days of urban

Table 5.1
African domestic servants (urban and rural)

	1921	1936	1946
Men	88,953	114,502	151,803
Women	162,905	242,405	403,706
Total	251,858	356,905	555,509

Source: *Union Statistics for Fifty Years, 1910–1960*, 1960, A–33.

Table 5.2
Distribution of African servants by province

	Male		Female	
	1911	1921	1911	1921
Cape*	11,624	25,352	31,768	76,599
Natal	19,417	17,845	6,335	13,882
Transvaal	40,466	38,328	16,371	33,371
Orange Free State	17,925	7,428	22,804	39,053
Total	89,432	88,953	77, 278	162,905

Source: Census figures quoted by Gaitskell et al., 1984, p.96. Figures for Coloureds in service (including hotel employees), *Union Statistics for Fifty Years, 1910–1960*, 1960, A–31.
* In 1921 the number of Coloureds in 'service' in South Africa (which included domestic service) were: men, 8,988; and women, 50,167. Most of these were in the Cape.

Table 5.3
Urban African domestic servants, 1936

	Male	Female
Cape Town	1,554	1,086
Port Elizabeth	955	4,007
East London	1,042	6,036
Durban	13,708	5,377
Pretoria	6,941	5,302
Johannesburg	22,297	22,391
Witwatersrand	31,897	38,297

Source: Census figures quoted by Gaitskell et al., 1984, p.96.

settlement — a consequence of the determination of African patriarchal authorities to retain control over female labour — led to their employment as servants in preference to women. But historic and geographic factors also determined which of the sexes would be employed as servants. The proximity of Reserves or the Protectorates tended to increase the number of women available for domestic labour in nearby towns, unless specific regulations (in Natal or the western Cape) prevented their entry. By contrast, the scarcity of Reserve Lands in the Orange Free State led to a dispersion of Africans across the province, and to a more even distribution of the sexes in the towns (except where there were diamond mines), which led to a predominance of female domestic servants.

Table 5.4
Number of Africans in Johannesburg

Year	Males	Females
1896	12,961	1,234
1904	55,765	3,840
1911	97,614	4,357
1921	102,960	12,160
1936	168,130	60,992

Source: Gaitskell, 1981, p.359.

The increasing number of women in the towns and cities (as shown for Johannesburg in Table 5.4) was a reflection of the growing impoverishment of the rural areas and an increasing demand for male labour elsewhere. The movement of women from the countryside, despite the limitations on the work available, was also a necessary corrective to the abnormally distributed sex ratio. The ratio of African men to women in towns throughout South Africa changed from 3:1 in 1921 to 2.2:1 in 1936 and 1.8:1 in 1946 (Van der Horst, 1971). The situation was obviously less 'normal' in Johannesburg and the overall balance throughout the country was still severely skewed in 1946. The disparity was lessening, although family life was still disrupted by the requirement that servants 'live in'.

The flow of women into the towns was not without its problems. Unmarried women were not given permits to live in the locations and had no independent access to housing. Many claimed 'marriage' to secure shelter and, possibly, companionship, sexual satisfaction, or a base from which to brew beer (Simons, 1936, pp.357–8). Alternatively, where women secured jobs as domestic servants and occupied rooms in the back yards, men claimed 'wives' and shared the accommodation, albeit illegally.

Table 5.5
African women in urban employment, 1936

Teachers	3,441
Nurses	669
Medical aids	151
Welfare workers	16
Managers/officials	16
Clerks, typists	209
Shop assistants/saleswomen	7
Hawkers	371
Factory operatives	*

Source: *Union Statistics for Fifty Years, 1910–1960*, 1960, and H.J. Simons, *African Women: Their Legal Status*, as quoted by Cynthia Kros, 1980, p.73.
*   The number employed in manufacture is not certain. *Union Statistics* gave 3,372 (of which 2,609 were general labourers — cleaners?) while the commonly quoted figure for 1939 is under 1,000.

Women in the towns did not have many alternatives in employment or self-employment. In the early 1920s a few women with primary school education could train as teachers or nurses, but even in the mid-1930s the total employed in these fields was small (Table 5.5). Another small group employed in manufacture (as ironers in laundries or pressers in the big bazaars), numbered 144 in 1935 and 422 in 1939 in Johannesburg (Wells, 1982, p.270; Hellmann, 1939, p.184). Others who were listed as 'working in industry' were mainly employed as chars: there were few other positions available, as shown in Table 5.5.

The facilities for legal self-employment were limited, although in many cases the wife's contribution was an 'imperative necessity. . . . During a wife's confinement, when expenses were abnormally heavy, the poverty is often appalling' (Hellmann, 1939, p.46). Women hawked mealies, sugar cane, buns and lemonade, offal or fruit and vegetables; approximately 40 were licensed to push carts, known popularly as 'Cafes-de-Move-on', hawking mugs of tea, cakes, ice-cream, fruit, etc. in the city centre. Another outlet, for which there are no figures, was home washing. In the days before the washing machine women collected bundles of clothes from white families and spent up to five days per week fetching, washing, ironing and then delivering the bundles. Estimates of the amounts they received, after expenses, varied from 1s per week to 3s or 4s (Gaitskell, 1981, p.139).

An unknown number of women were involved in illicit beer brewing and prostitution. Women in the slum yards, townships and locations brewed beer or more potent concoctions, known in Johannesburg as *Shimiyana*, *Skokiaan*, 'Kill-me-quick' and *Qed'iviki* ('Finish the week'), guaranteed to provide rapid oblivion. This led to a cycle of police raids, arrests, fines or imprisonment, and to location anger, scuffles and ultimately riots.

The only alternative for most women was domestic service: of those legally employed in the towns, over 80 per cent were so occupied. Yet because the pay was low the demand was insatiable: as Sheila van der Horst once said, 'if the cost of labour is zero, the demand would be infinite; as the cost was almost nothing the demand was almost infinite'. Simons (pp.359—60) put the pay as low as 10s to 20s per month, but it did reach £3 to £4 — varying from town to town, suburb to suburb. There were some women in the early 1930s who received nothing but their rooms and some food in exchange for specified house duties; some used the rooms as a base for beer brewing or prostitution and there was little secrecy about the situation.

Table 5.6
Urban African women servants as percentage of gainfully employed women in 1936

Town	Women over 10 years old	Gainfully occupied No.	%	As servants No.	%
East London	10,426	6,805	65.3	6,036	90.6
Durban	12,507	6,539	52.3	5,377	84.2
Pretoria	12,888	5,922	46.0	5,302	90.9
Johannesburg	49,313	24,781	50.3	22,391	91.6
Other Rand towns	35,752	17,952	50.2	31,897	89.3
Cape Town	3,285	1,343	40.9	1,086	84.6
Port Elizabeth	10,608	4,434	41.8	4,007	91.3

Source: Gaitskell et al., 1984, Tables V, VI.

The 'immorality' of servants (by whom, the warning ran, VD would be transmitted to innocent children) was a constant topic in the newspapers. The lurid picture did not come from the media alone: missionaries, appalled by slum yards, the breakdown of the family, and the twin evils of liquor and sex, urged that the situation be controlled (see e.g., Mrs F. Bridgman, 1928, p.63). These Jezebels had to be removed from the towns because they had not only been 'exposed to the temptations of town life' but had also brought their 'unmentionable' customs with them. They were 'driven to sin', 'became dissolute, and . . . in turn demoralised decent boys' (Hertslet, 1920). By regulation or legislation, local authorities aimed to remove 'surplus' women (those unemployed, or without male support) and return them to their 'natural' place in the rural areas. Passes for women were introduced in Free State towns in 1913 and again after the war, and night passes were tried in 1925, but these measures failed because of locally organised resistance. The government intervened, amending the Urban Areas Act in 1930 to further restrict the entry of women into the towns.

The preparation of women for domestic service, first as servants then as housewives, appeared in the programmes of the first colleges for Africans in South Africa. Some schools later phased out such programmes for the more academically minded girls, but the training continued. One of the more significant initiatives came from the Helping Hand Club which started a small training school for girls going into service in 1931. The Club, founded by the American Board of Commissioners for Foreign Missions in the 1920s, planned to build hostels which would also provide leisure facilities and schooling for black women in the towns. Local ratepayers prevented them from being built. In the few existing hostels the schooling was rudimentary, but the Club placed over a thousand servants between 1928 and 1931 (Gaitskell, 1981, pp.244ff.).

Another programme to train girls for service was devised by the Wayfarers, a black guide movement. The organisation aimed at 'the deepening and strengthening of character, and inculcating of loyalty to authority, emphasising the necessity for self control and teaching the joy of unselfish (*sic*) service' (Mrs Bridgman, 1928, p.66). The Home Ways tests were designed to fit this aim — with badges for housework, cookery and laundry. For the first badge the girls:

> had to polish silver, clean the kitchen and the stove, and light the fire; dust furniture, books and ornaments, clean windows, get rid of vermin, and turn out a sitting room: do the daily work necessary in a bedroom, answer the door and where possible the telephone, take messages and wait at table (Gaitskell, 1981, p.287).

Wayfarer leaders prided themselves on providing 'the only simple domestic training possible for those whose parents cannot afford to send them away to institutions'.[4] Yet the schools and clubs reached few women with their programme of training for 'domestic service', and it was this gap that the organisers of the African Domestic Servants League intended filling.

Unions for domestic servants

The organisation of domestic servants has always been difficult. In disputes with employers, the confrontation has always been too individual and too isolated to afford the worker much possibility of success, and it has been difficult to establish a corporate identity cutting across separate households. In South Africa, the colour barrier which kept servants in the back yard made it even more difficult for them to succeed in their struggles. The social networks which existed in every suburb, comprising church groups, hometown groups, beer brewing circles and informal leisure activities, afforded servants little opportunity of directly affecting working relations (see S. Gordon, 1985, pp.6–7). Even when it was possible to intervene by introducing friends to fill a vacancy in a neighbouring house, conditions of employment always rested with the employer.

Many organisations, from the ICU in 1925 to the National Liberation League in 1937, resolved to form unions for servants, but it is not certain that they ever succeeded. Other attempts, like that of Lucy Twala to form a Bantu Girls Domestic Servants Association in the late 1930s to protect the interests of ex-boarding school servants who had been trained for service, also failed (Gaitskell, 1981, p.128).

In 1938, when African trade unions were still small, [?] Mvula started a Domestic Servants League — but it collapsed when he died. The League was resuscitated by J.G. Coka, who appointed a committee and offered membership to persons whose names were sent to his journal, the *African Liberator*. Funds were to come from social functions, the first to be held jointly with an 'institution for the politically victimised Jews': this was probably an exercise in attracting Jewish patronage (A. Segwai, Minutes of the Domestic Servants League, 3 November 1939). The strategy failed, after which Coka dispensed with the first committee and reorganised the League. Members were now required to pay 1s per month and a new committee was appointed which included Self Mampuru and others associated with Gana Makabeni.[5]

Coka circulated handbills to householders about the League. He also wrote a sixteen page pamphlet (*c.* 1939) with subtitles: Where Will Anti-Semitism End? Where Are We Going? Does 1939 Open a Promise or a Menace? Save the Health of the Community? The pamphlet does not address itself to the four questions, but states that it has not been easy to build the League, the policies of which are given:

> In the best interest of Blacks, Africans must support this League because among other things, it will put an end to the cheeky, *skokiaan* brewing, insolent, impertinent and thieving servants, who cast a slur on the name of the Bantu people by their irresponsible conduct. To relieve the peace of mind of many White Ladies who are rightly irritated by the conduct of many servants it is essential for them to give the League every assistance. We must get reliable, trustworthy and efficient servants even if it means fetching them direct from school.

This programme has little or nothing in common with trade unionism, and yet the League (from which Coka was expelled in 1939 for expropriating funds) included on its committee men who were all active through the war years in the trade union movement; and both Coka and Mampuru worked with Ballinger, who kept a close watch on trade union developments. What precisely was the function of the League? Did committee members believe they could improve conditions of work or pay? Or were they battening on men and women in a helpless position, promising improvements that could not be achieved?

Answers to these questions are neither easy nor simple. Coka had always been a keen protagonist of workers' organisation but this did not stop him taking money from the League. Segwai did likewise and he became secretary of three associated unions: The Hotel, Boarding House and Flat Workers Union; the African Catering Workers Union; and the Domestic Servants League (or Union). Workers in the first union were covered by a wage determination in 1941 and the union assisted workers who were underpaid. Little could be done for other service workers. The Servants Union was incorporated into the Hotel Workers Union, their membership fees going into the kitty as a bonanza.

A case of corruption?

It was already obvious in the late 1930s that there were men who, with few outlets for their entrepreneurial proclivities, sought their livelihoods through the unions. In some cases they undoubtedly helped their members secure improved conditions, but in instances such as the League little could be done, because servants were specifically excluded from the Wages Act. The organisers were aware of what they were doing — and a survey of Segwai's other activities throws light on his work in the unions. He appears to have been connected with a white associate, on a purely business basis, in an employment agency, and on Sunday he conducted services at his own church in the township. He said that he received no pay but that members of his congregation brought him gifts of food.[6] Despite all this, Segwai became the (unpaid) secretary of the ostensibly militant Progressive Trade Union Group in 1944–45.

The extent to which money was misappropriated and the workers made to pay for the misdemeanours of trade union officials will never be known. Periodic exposure in the newspapers or before the courts was only the visible tip of what was happening. Inevitably this spread a certain amount of disillusionment, although many workers preferred to overlook these deficiencies if they believed that the secretaries and organisers were ultimately assisting them. They might also have reasoned that the amounts taken were in fact minute, or at least not excessive.

Nobody was as hard on men who milked the unions as W.G. Ballinger. He never tired of reporting cases of expulsion for misappropriating money or failing to keep proper books — as in his report to the Society of Friends of

Africa for January–July 1944, when he noted that

> the tendency for certain Secretaries of African Unions [to] regard [them] . . . as
> their own personal enterprise shows signs of increasing. Some of [them] . ·. have
> gone to the extreme lengths of changing the constitutions of their organisations so as
> to confer all control, particularly financial, upon themselves. . . .

Ballinger did not refer to the League, although he must have known of conditions in the organisation. In December 1936 he said in his report that it was gratifying to record that Coka was organising industrial groups of workers in Benoni and Germiston. Thereafter Ballinger and Coka rented joint premises in a Johannesburg building.

At some point Coka left the office and Mampuru, a man of diverse interests, moved in. Besides working with (or for?) Ballinger, he was aspiring president of the Transvaal African Congress in 1943; adviser on cooperatives and trade unions, and secretary of an African businessman's association. He was also a founding member of the African Democratic Party and an active participant in the bus boycotts and the shantytown movement during the war years. Ballinger referred to Mampuru in several reports as founder of the Domestic Servants League (October 1940–January 1941; June 1943), but he was in fact the League's adviser. When Segwai was away, Mampuru took his place. Perhaps, under Mampuru, the union funds were safe, but neither he nor Ballinger could have had any illusions about Segwai, or the destiny of the money. Ironically, Ballinger's attack on secretaries who 'regard their Unions as their own personal enterprise' was a quotation from a report by Mampuru.

There appear to be no reports on the actual activities of the League, on membership figures or finances. Nonetheless during the war years Segwai visited residential suburbs and enrolled members. What happened to these members can only be conjectured. There is some evidence that there were domestic servants who were less than happy about the union and its leadership.

The union of 100

Despite the difficulties involved in organising a servants' union, Lawrence Mlambo of Parktown North, Johannesburg, wrote to the SAIRR in August 1943 saying that he had enrolled servants in a union and required assistance. Rheinallt Jones replied, pointing out that it was extremely difficult to organise domestic or farm servants, and advising Mlambo to contact the Council of Non-European Trade Unions. Gosani, secretary of the CNETU, informed Mlambo that there was a Domestic Servants League, and he wrote again to the SAIRR in November:

> . . . I sent back that I know very well the African Domestic League is already exists
> but the matter is this if is not satisfied is not much help to meet the Domestic servant
> Requirements. I say to theme I ask theme give permits of to form the Domestic
> Union under the name [African servant trade union]. . . .

Mlambo heard no further from Gosani, and determined to form his union he wrote to Dr Xuma in December, addressing him as 'My Dearest Honest Leader of All Africa':

> Sir, we are writing to ask your kind advice as your children are all the Employees of the Domestic Servants of the private houses having now formed our own union and named it the name of African Domestic servants Trade union we are now nearly 100 — members being joined under the now named name are now desire to open our own office therefore we are asking your advice how can we open it does any thing to be demanded from the official or not from any authority or not
>
> your faithfully servant
> Lawrence mlambo

There is no indication whether Xuma replied, or whether the initiative shown by Mlambo was appreciated, yet it was this eagerness for organisation that was tapped, and dissipated, when the posters and handbills were printed and distributed in 1938−39.[7].

The story of the domestic workers' union is one of failure. That must raise the question why it should be included in a history of the working class, and why it should appear at the beginning of our account. The fact that it failed, and had little effect on the trade union movement, does seem to indicate that it was of little consequence and should be relegated to the curiosities of the period. But that would only help to create a wrong impression of these first attempts at organising African trade unions. Many unions were launched during this period, appealing to workers in production or distribution. Some were ineffectual, others were ephemeral and many seem to have left no records. All recruited workers, yet their failure spread disillusion amongst many who believed initially that here was a new instrument for obtaining their rights.

There are also positive reasons for including the story of this union. This was the one source of employment for women: permission to stay in the towns depended on their securing work as domestic servants. Furthermore, after mining this was the largest source of employment for men and it seemed to the leaders to be an easier field for organisation. The union was amongst the very first to be launched, and remained independent of the two main bodies of the time. What is perhaps surprising and worth recording is the group of men (there were few women involved!) who turn out to have been associated with this union: Coka, the one-time ICU organiser; Tloome, the future Vice-President of the CNETU; Ballinger of the Friends of Africa; Mampuru, his future assistant; and Segwai, future Secretary of the PTU group. This mixed assembly of characters, all hoping for an entry into black trade unionism, chose an 'easy touch' by going to the servants. It was an ill-conceived move, and reflects on their political sagacity and possibly on their integrity.

Notes

1. Undated letter signed by Miss E.T. Daba, J.G. Coka, S.K. Tutu; enquiries to D.R. Twala, Bantu Sports Club. The meeting was called for 20 October 1938. *Rheinallt Jones Papers.*
2. Names included in Minutes of the African Domestic Servants League, 3 November 1939. Segwai's diverse interests are discussed below, the Progressive Trade Unions in Chapters 8 and 9.
3. Domestic servants were part of the working class and theoretically class has no ethnic boundaries. White workers, however, shared this class privilege with the petty bourgeoisie — and this included Coloured, Indian and even affluent African families, who all employed servants.
4. Report by Edith Rheinallt Jones to Fifth National European–Bantu Conference, July 1933, typescript, *Rheinallt Jones Papers.*
5. See *Bantu World,* 20 November 1937, for a report by Makabeni of plans to extend the African Clothing Workers Union with the assistance of D. Tloome, A. Segoai (*sic*) and others.
6. See letter from Dr Xuma to Segwai, 28 August 1945, about a 'white sub-tenant'. *Xuma Papers,* ABX 450828b. Other information from conversations with Segwai, Johannesburg, 1945. He only smiled when asked about hopes for improvements for domestic workers.
7. Mlambo's original letter is not available. The reply from Jones is dated 23 August 1943. The November letter is undated, but was received on the 10th. I have retained the original grammar and spelling. All these letters are to be found in the *Rheinallt Jones Papers.* The December letter is in the *Xuma Papers,* ABX 431201a.

6. Vereeniging: 'To Hell with the Pick-up!'

A 'lack of organisation'?

There were riots in the Old Location, Vereeniging, on the weekend 18–19 September 1937. On Saturday, a crowd at the public square turned on a raiding party of police and drove them away with stones. The police returned with reinforcements on Sunday and once again there was violence; three policemen (two white and one black) were killed and three injured. The police fired several volleys before retreating, hitting an unknown number of residents. The following day some 450 men and women were arrested and held in custody.

White communities, with press and government backing, called for revenge. The 'weakness' of the law and the 'liberalism' of government and administration were condemned. Resolutions at meetings asserted the 'right of every European to shoot down any black savage who has the temerity to raise his hand against a white person', called for the use of tear-gas and recommended a demonstration by Air Force planes over locations. Reds were thought to be hatching plots and the press reported calls for the outlawing of Communist propaganda (*Cape Times*, 28 September).

Politicians invoked the memory of the *voortrekkers*, whose centenary dominated the rhetoric at the time. Prime Minister Hertzog led the way for the government when he spoke in Pretoria on 28 September. Whites, he declared, were determined as 'in the days of the *Voortrekkers* to rule the country in terms of European civilisation'. He threatened more draconian laws and even 'stricter supervision of the Native's freedom of movement' if thought expedient. Hertzog also spoke of a Communist plot and a 'deep-rooted and far-reaching, perhaps organised hostility on the part of the Native towards the white man'.

The CPSA issued a pamphlet (1937) on the riot denying any involvement. This was confirmed by the Commission of Inquiry appointed by the government. In 1927 defecting members of the ICU had formed a branch of the CPSA in the location (Johns, 1965, p.378), but in the long and bitter strife of the early 1930s the party was almost destroyed and nothing further was heard of this branch. *Spark*, the organ of the Workers' Party, blamed the authorities for creating riot-prone conditions, declaring in November that:

> The question at issue is not whether we deplore or whether we do not deplore the Vereeniging incident. Such a question would be simply stupid. It is superfluous to emphasise that, whether we like it or not, such incidents do occur and undoubtedly will occur, as being the natural outburst of people under intolerable conditions. To attribute such outbursts to revolutionary propaganda is merely ridiculous. They

prove exactly the opposite; they point to the *lack* of revolutionary influence, to the *lack* of revolutionary propaganda and agitation. They always prove lack of organisation.[2]

It was this crucial question of organisation that had to be addressed in both the major urban centres and the smaller towns in the 1930s. With growing industrialisation, men and women crowded into the townships or were housed in compounds. There they found companionship based on such factors as clan, occupation, leisure activities or the church.

There were no revolutionary organisations in Old Location in 1937, nor any of the known national movements, but undocumented associations undoubtedly did exist, such as a vigilance association or a stand holders' group formed to contest advisory board elections. There were church bodies and hometown groups — some of the latter associated with dance groups that practised and performed on the public square, and were present during the riots, together with their supporters. These were not 'revolutionary' bodies, but they acted as pressure groups and provided networks for communication and mobilisation. At the enquiry it was said that women who supported the dance groups urged the men to attack the police, and, although this could have been spontaneous (and no evidence was brought to show otherwise), there was a consensus that suggests a common cause in the riot.

The eclipse of all national movements in the 1930s threw communities, particularly in the smaller towns, back on their own resources. It was only the formation during the war of the trade union branches in Vereeniging that linked sections of the working class with wider provincial organisation. But in 1937 the trade union movement had not yet extended beyond Johannesburg. When the inhabitants of smaller towns were faced with crises, they looked inward to known groups for a chain of command. Without further evidence, the historian can only guess at likely sources of leadership but what is clear is that heightened frustration in Old Location, and the failure of formal channels of protest, led to crowd reaction against provocation from the police. They met force with force and committed the 'sin of sins' — killing two *white* policemen.

From 'Old Location' to Sharpeville

The use of the word 'Old' by white burghers to describe the location in Vereeniging meant only one thing: they wanted a 'New' location, well away from the present site which blocked their expansion in the centre of the town. The location in which some 8,000 people lived in 1936 was not old, though nobody could have described it as modern or contemporary. The Medical Officer of Health, writing in 1942, had little doubt that conditions were deplorable:

> The quality of the houses in the location [is] as inferior as anywhere in the world. Scraps of tin, bundles of filthy rags, mud and stone formed the basis of their construction. These were the huts, houses, and hovels for the accommodation of black people.

The streets were sand tracks, and the two- or three-roomed houses, each accommodating ten or more residents, had no running water, internal latrines or electricity.[3]

There were only 5,000 residents in the location in 1934, but poverty in the countryside and increased urban employment brought immigrants to Vereeniging. They crowded into the location, welcomed by the administration because lodging permits cost one shilling for every man, woman and child. The location superintendent said this yielded over £200 per month and 'was to the advantage to the Municipality', but denied that the fee was collected as part of a policy to swell local revenue. Wherever the money went, new houses were not built.[4]

In April 1936 John Lillie Sharpe, the mayor, addressed a petition to the Administrator of the Transvaal requesting that the 'Old Location' be appropriated and its inhabitants moved well away from the existing site to a location that would be named Sharpe's Village, or Sharpeville. The petition showed no concern for living conditions in the existing location, but was blunt and to the point:

> owing to local development and expansion it will in the near future be necessary to extend Vereeniging township, and the only satisfactory direction in which to extend, in view of local conditions, is the North, on the land at present used for purposes of the Native location (Dixon, c. 1946, Part II, pp.2–3).

The mayor spoke of grave discontent among the whites of the town that could be traced back to the agreement of 23 December 1889, in which the South African Republic gave the South African and Orange Free State Coal and Mineral Mining Association the sole right to establish Vereeniging on the existing farms, together with control of the mineral, agricultural and other rights over an area of 1,000 morgen within the town (1 morgen = approx. 2 acres). The company had sited the location near the centre of town, providing a conveniently placed labour supply. 'Despite entreaties by the Town Council to place it elsewhere', the principals refused, agreeing only in 1936 to the removal of the location, while retaining some of its original rights to the land.

The company (which operated in the gold fields under the names of its principals, Lewis and Marks) also owned Springfield colliery; the farm lands known as the Vereeniging Estates; and Union Steel Corporation, the biggest and oldest steel producer in the country, which had resmelted scrap iron since 1912. Bricks for the steel furnace were manufactured by the company-owned Vereeniging Brick and Tile Works (Richards, 1940; Leigh, 1968, pp.122–31). In 1930 Iscor bought the controlling interest in Union Steel for £100,000, but this did not affect the work force appreciably: black labour was not replaced by whites in this plant, as was the policy at Iscor. In 1928 Union Steel employed 378 whites and 1,067 blacks. This dropped to a total of 1,401 employees in 1933, before rising to 1,942 in 1937. Of these more than 1,000 were black (Richards, 1940, pp.270,293).

A commission heard evidence on the location on 9 November 1936, and the mayor presented the case for its gradual removal to Sharpeville to 'rectify the original mistake of Mr Marks'. Neither company nor council offered compensation to stand holders: only an offer to transport stones used in the existing structures to the new location. The proposed move undoubtedly led to deep disaffection in Old Location. Removal would result in higher transport costs and new uncertainty about housing and lodgings. Stand holders stood to lose from the demolition of their shanties if compensation was not paid, as is evident from the copy of one available letter from A.I. Motsuenyane, Secretary of the Advisory Board in 1939 (Dixon, *c.* 1946, Part III, p.1).

Law and disorder in the location

More than 8,000 people lived in Old Location, a further 7,000 (including colliery workers) in nearby compounds, and an estimated 23,000 in the adjacent rural area.[5] Many of those living nearby would visit the location at some time, meeting friends or seeking alcohol. Others might be at the public square watching the *marabarara* (nine-man-morris) players or the teams of dancers. The square, which achieved notoriety as the scene of the riot in September, was known for its orderliness, as was the location. Crime was low by urban standards, and in the twelve months October 1936–37 (which included the days of the riot) the police were notified of one murder, 102 assaults, 10 housebreakings and 90 'less serious' crimes. Arrests were mainly for defaulting on lodger permits, pass offences, poll tax evasion and beer brewing. Of the 4,723 cases brought to court that year in the region, 3,621 were for such 'statutory offences' (*Star*, 15 October 1937).

Until mid-1937 weekly raids were conducted by resident African police. On Monday mornings most of those who had been charged were fined, some imprisoned and others ordered out of the district. Police raids couldn't stop the beer brewing, however, or ensure that men carried all their documents. At a later date, Lewis Nkosi (1965, p.40) was to write about the 'inevitability' of arrest:

> Africans have accepted the status of being outlaws from society and have an elaborate system of escaping, hoodwinking and baffling the law. They know every time a policeman encounters a black man in the street he assumes a crime has been committed. . . .

Those stopped by the police were usually arrested; those who protested were assaulted. Under such conditions, wrote Nkosi, 'why bother to live a legal life'.

The position was more complex: many tried to 'live a legal life', but laws were broken, and although there were 'elaborate systems of . . . baffling the law', everyone knew the penalty if caught. Those arrested went quietly, provided no excessive force was employed, and it was this that led an Advisory Board member to say: 'The location superintendent [H.U. Davidson] often raids the location but there is no trouble because he treats the people well.'[6] In fact Davidson took no part in beer raids because of the hostility encountered by his predecessor for so doing, but in other respects the comments were apposite: the people obeyed him because he treated them 'well'.

In June 1937 the mood altered, a change universally ascribed to the appearance of 'pick-up vans' in Vereeniging. Arrests increased by 150 per cent and there were allegations of police violence in the vans (*Star*, 15 October). Residents complained that the police used sticks and *sjamboks*, a matter afterwards raised at Advisory Board meetings and by witnesses at the inquiry conducted in October 1937. There was no explanation for the new policy in Vereeniging. Police denied the allegations, although the issue was by no means new in South Africa.

'To hell with the pick-up!'

> . . . bands of armed hooligans are terrorising the people in the locations. In the ordinary course one would appeal to the police for protection, but in this case we cannot do that for the police are themselves the hooligans (Statement in court, E. Roux, 1933).

> Look at the Police Station
> There are policemen there
> That is the greatest disease
> In this place
> (Location children's song, Shore, 1975).

In 1933 the pick-up vans were described as follows:

> At any time of the day or night, but mostly during the week-end, when people . . . are visiting their friends . . . the police come out in a motor van. They proceed to any populous locality . . . and arrest anyone they can lay their hands on. The arrested persons (all Natives, of course) are bundled into the van, often seriously assaulted . . . taken to the lock up, and brought before the magistrate the next morning . . . charged with contravening the pass law, poll tax ordinance, liquor laws, urban areas act, location regulations, etc., etc. If the police are at a loss, they can always charge them with being drunk or noisy.
> The magistrate sentences them in batches of ten or twenty at a time. (A magistrate is considered efficient if he can finish off a couple of hundred cases in an hour or two!). . . (Roux, 1949, pp.285–6).

The CPSA called for look-outs in every location to warn of impending police raids, and defence groups against brutal attacks by the police (ibid., pp.285–7). They also started a campaign against the van and Roux spoke at a mass meeting on Dingane's Day, 16 December 1933 under the slogan 'To Hell with the Pick-Up!'. He was arrested and charged with incitement to violence because of his condemnation of police brutality and received a six-month sentence. A call by the CPSA for an independent commission of inquiry collapsed for lack of support.

Violence was a standard part of police practice. Gilbert Coka told of being accosted by police when returning home from a temperance meeting with friends. 'Suddenly, without warning, [police] surrounded my friend, shook him, and then like a bale of wood threw him into the van.' The whole party was arrested and kept overnight in police cells. Coka was discharged by the magistrate next morning but was arrested on three occasions between 22 July and 14 August 1933; eventually, in the last case, he was fined 5s for contempt of court.[7]

Ray Phillips of the American Board of Missions described third degree methods used to extort confessions, and assaults by drunken police over several months in Johannesburg during 1933. He said he was informed by a police sergeant that:

> there is pressure brought to bear on us by our superior officers to keep a regular supply of Native prisoners coming forward. If we do not deliver a certain supply of Natives charged with various offences we are given to understand that we are regarded as not being sufficiently active (*Rheinallt Jones Papers*, Box B, Statement No. 4, Para. 3).

In another statement, Phillips recounted an event in October 1933 that became the 'subject of enquiry by the District Commandant':

> On Sunday afternoon, while sports was going forward at the Bantu Sports Club ground, a Police van approached the ground and off-loaded a half dozen constables armed with stones. They advanced upon a number of Native spectators who were watching the sports from outside the fence and attacked them by discharging their missiles. Some of the Natives took refuge in trees nearby and these were in turn attacked by the police, who threw stones at them (*Rheinallt Jones Papers*, Box B, Statement No. 10).

Eventually the manager of the club, A.W. Cloete Smith, 'expostulated with these constables' and persuaded them to leave, after he had '[q]uieted the Natives who were preparing to make a [counter] attack. . . .'

In September 1936, Justice Lansdown chaired a commission on the police force to investigate the high turnover of young men.[8] This problem was so urgent that an interim report was published within two months of the commission's sitting. The commission also reported on recruiting and training, promotion, the implementation of laws on liquor and illicit diamond and gold buying, and police conduct in the carrying out of their duties. According to the final report, recruits were usually of limited education and pay was low. Whites received four to six months' training; Africans attended a few drill sessions at the police station. White policemen received £150 p.a. rising to £282 after eighteen years' service (unless promoted). They objected to low pay and 'unjustified' complaints against the way they carried out their duties. African policemen got £48 p.a. in the first two years of service, rising to £66 after seven years. Even sergeants (the highest grade) received only £95 rising to £105 after five years. They complained of low pay and a range of grievances: allowances, uniforms, promotion, length of leave, medical attention for families and absence of married quarters. New wage scales were recommended, giving whites £150 p.a. rising to a maximum of £330 after twelve years, and Africans £60, rising to a maximum of £84 after nine years. The other issues were dismissed as being too costly to rectify.

Evidence was heard from several sources, including the ANC and the Joint Councils, about the relationship between the police and the black population; some was heard *in camera* (with no reason given); other accounts in open session gave details of police misconduct or brutality. Evidence was given of African hostility to police 'methods of handling',[9] and there were many references to 'unpopular' laws couched in terms that called for reform rather than radical change. Thus the Joint Council was reported as saying that three statutory offences (pass laws, tax receipts and service contracts) 'were typical of a system which made happy relations between the natives and police impossible' (*Star*, 14 December 1936).

The commission produced a report which upheld existing discriminatory practices while urging restraint on the police, and in a much quoted passage declared that:

> We are of the opinion, after a careful survey of the evidence, that the relations between natives and police are marked by a suppressed hostility which excludes whole-hearted cooperation and which does harm both to the Force and to the natives themselves. This is due partly to the odium incurred by the police in enforcing unpopular legislation, but is contributed to by the manner in which such enforcement is carried out and the general attitude of some individual policemen to the native population. It is, therefore, of first importance . . . that every possible step should be taken to ensure that restrictive laws, such as the pass laws, native taxation act, and the liquor law are enforced with the maximum amount of consideration and regard for the ordinary rights and liberty of the citizen [*sic*], and that no effort should be spared to prevent their enforcement becoming, as it so easily can, an opportunity for practising harshness and oppression (Interim and Final Reports of the Commission of Inquiry, UG 50, 1937, p.74).

Finally, and ironically in view of what occurred in Vereeniging three weeks after publication of the report, the commission recommended that domestic brewing of beer, in reasonable quantities for home consumption, be allowed in urban areas. It also commended the use of the patrol van, but noted its misuse in the past to arrest 'passless natives'.

The first riot [10]

All accounts of the period leading up to the riots of 18–19 September refer to the appearance of the pick-up van in the location and mention the complaints at Advisory Board meetings. There were also accusations of police (white and black) finding excuses to body search women.

On Saturday afternoon, 18 September, a police van and two cars entered the location and enrolled several municipal police (or 'police boys', as they were called in court statements). Together they sought and found illicit stills, arresting several women. The cars then cruised around the location and converged on the public square where 'a large crowd of women' were watching the dancers. It was these women who seem to have been crucial in what followed. Witnesses said that five policemen jumped from their cars, confronted two men walking towards the square, and demanded their papers. The dancing stopped as, in full public view, the police tore up the papers of one of the men. He was brutally assaulted and thrown into the van. When an angry crowd shouted that they 'could not arrest a man when his pass was torn', the police opened fire and the crowd replied with stones. One policeman was hit and the van, its windows broken, raced out of the location.

The second riot

On Sunday afternoon when the location was filled with visitors the police returned with twelve additional men from nearby towns (carrying batons or revolvers) and six local municipal police (carrying sticks). Some went straight to the public square, others went in groups from house to house, demanding passes or lodgers' permits; they said they were looking for beer, although they did not have the usual probing irons. Men, women and children — at home, on their way to church, or even playing tennis — were ordered to go to the square. Some witnesses claimed that it was a revenge raid and had been prearranged. Revd Mashack Mahlaba reported police as saying 'Go to the square and do what you did yesterday', and Mrs Lily August told the SAIRR that the police had said that 'everybody who was there on Saturday must be there'. Those who hesitated were hit and kicked.

The people, whether forced to enter the square, or already there, were both afraid and angry. Precisely what started the riot, and who provided the leadership, is not clear. It may have been the dancers or their followers, or it may have been the brewers who were said to be mainly Sotho. The anger boiled over, stones were thrown, and ululating women urged the men on. According to Detective Snyman, 'A shrill cry by hundreds of Basuto women was the signal for the attack on the police.' They fired into the crowd, aiming to kill. When their twelve rounds were exhausted, eight men returned to the police station for more rifles and ammunition. Three of those who remained were killed and three injured (one of the dead and two of the injured being black). There was no mention of fatalities among those on the square, although the police 'aimed to kill'. Reports only mentioned the shooting of a number of men and women in the stomach and thigh. The following morning a large contingent of police arrested over 450 people in the location, mostly for statutory offences. The arrests were arbitrary and the police 'kicked, hit and thrashed the Natives, whether they had their papers or not, and arrested them wholesale'.

White town — black location

The location was separated from the town (by fence and by regulation) and this separation marked the difference between master and helot. At the same time there was a 'unity' based on the need of capital and householders for labour. The tensions this induced were always just below the surface.

Relations between white and black were not improved by the attempts to remove the Old Location, and in 1937 there were two further issues which brought the town to flashpoint. The first was the canonisation of the *voortrekkers* in the centenary celebrations, which coincided with the growth of 'shirt' or fascist movements espousing an especially virulent racism. According to D.W. Kruger, an Afrikaner historian (1971, p.190):

Ever since 1936 the historical past had claimed the attention of Afrikanerdom . . . from the great cities to the tiniest hamlet, Afrikaners were preparing to commemorate the Great Trek. It was considered the one event that had not only saved white civilisation in South Africa but had also laid the foundation of republicanism. . . .

Afrikaans newspapers and periodicals published . . . articles devoted to the history of the Great Trek and . . . speakers referred in glowing terms to the mighty deeds of the Voortrekkers. . . .

The celebrations were not as innocent as the passage implies. Hertzog (the Prime Minister), Dr Malan (the leader of the opposition), Oswald Pirow (the Minister of Defence) and others courted the support of the rightward-moving sections of the Afrikaner people. Pirow was in Berlin during the Nazi take-over and had enrolled unemployed youths in the paramilitary Special Service and Pioneer battalions since April 1934; by 1937 he had 'processed' over 6,000 recruits, and during the war he would organise the New Order fascist group. For Pirow, as for others, the centenary was a pageant aimed at the hearts, minds and votes of the Afrikaner worker and middle class.

The CPSA intervened opportunistically with a statement in *South African Worker*, 15 May 1937 that the *trekkers*

loved independence — they must turn in their graves to see their descendants tethered to industry by the Industrial Conciliation Act, the youth militarised in the Special Services Battalion and Defence Force to serve British Imperialism. . . .

This absurdity could not wish away the convergence, particularly in the Transvaal, of Afrikaner nationalism, racism and fascism, as was made evident at the time of the riots when the different tendencies vied with each other in the vociferousness with which they called for revenge. In the aftermath of the riots there were attacks on Africans in the town, resulting in serious injuries, and there were reports (*Star*, 22 September; *Bantu World*, 25 September) that Africans were afraid to leave the location. A white who dared protest on the Monday over the way police mishandled Africans they had rounded up, was assaulted and, after being escorted to the police station for his 'own protection', charged with obstructing the police (*Star*, 20 September).

A meeting called at the Market Square by the Greyshirts, the major fascist group in the Transvaal, was attended by a crowd of 1,500. Jews and Communists were blamed for fomenting the riot and it was resolved by acclaim to boycott any local attorney who defended blacks involved in the riot; other resolutions called for the lines of demarcation between white and black to be strengthened before they disappeared; and for the resignations of Smuts (Minister of Justice), J.H. Hofmeyr, and the Commissioner of Police.

The atmosphere of the time was encapsulated in the words of Revd P.J. Viljoen who officiated at the funeral of the two white policemen:

> It was heathendom that killed Retief and his men at Dingaan's kraal . . . and it was heathendom that killed Constables van Staden and Greyling. Unfortunately, today, white heathens are busy instigating black heathendom in our country, not only in Vereeniging, but throughout the land. . . (*Star*, 22 September).

There was no news of the burial of the black policeman.

The aftermath

After the arrest of the 450 residents on the Monday morning, 'thousands of others left the location, fearing that their turn would come next', and many industries reported that they were 'practically paralysed'. This led to instructions from Smuts that all those arrested, but not associated with the riot, be released immediately, and over 300 were freed (Roux, 1949, p.291). Whether the exodus was unwitting, or involved an element of protest, cannot be determined, but Roux's conclusion that direct community action had secured the release of the prisoners is undoubtedly correct.

Douglas Smit (Secretary of Native Affairs and an associate of Rheinallt Jones) together with S. Maynard Page (Chief Magistrate of Johannesburg), headed a commission of inquiry which took evidence on relations between police and Africans; on the pick-up van and its critics; on conditions in the location; and on the illicit brewing of beer. It could find 'no excuse whatever for the attack made by the Natives on the police . . . or for the brutal murder of the unfortunate constables', and recommended the speedy removal of the location site (*Star*, 16 October 1937). It also supported the greater availability of beer, but through regulated sources (*Bantu World*, 20 November 1937). The commission believed that 'the patrol van should not be used in such a way as to give ground for the belief that it is used as an instrument of oppression' and called for the *sjambok* to be banned (ibid.). Some six weeks later all police stations were instructed by the Police Commissioner to use less violence, and warned against mishandling Africans in the 'pick-up'.

Finally, the superintendent of the Vereeniging location was instructed 'to exercise very close control over the unattached Native women who came to the location possibly to brew beer and for purposes of prostitution. . . ' (*Star*, 11 October). The old bogey about too many women in the towns had resurfaced (see Chapter 5), and once again it was urged that they be sent back to the rural areas — in particular, Basutoland — whence they had come.

Of the 71 who had been held, seventeen were released. Local lawyers appeared for the defendants despite the threats they had received. No one was found guilty of having murdered the policemen but eleven were convicted on lesser charges: two were imprisoned for seven years, one for four years, and eight for three years (Roux, 1949, p.292).

There were some concessions for the residents of Old Location. By 1939 every house was allowed four gallons of home-brewed beer and members of the police force were not allowed to enter the location without a permit. The riot probably advanced the date of the removal to Sharpeville, however, and it almost certainly led to the eviction of 400 'surplus' women from the town.

Working-class action

Two years after the riot there were new indications of disaffection in Vereeniging, but this time the protests were industrial and inevitably affected the Lewis and Marks empire. On 30 October 1939, one week after a fatal assault by a white overseer on a coal miner at Springfield Colliery, 1,000 men refused to go on shift. Some 600 started on a thirty-mile march to Johannesburg to complain to the Curator of Portuguese Natives. The line straggled back over five miles and the marchers in front had got half way when they were stopped by over 100 policemen, fully armed with bayonets fixed. Ten men were injured in a baton charge and the rest retreated to the veld. They returned only after the Native Commissioner promised a full inquiry into their grievances.[11]

The miners' spokesman, Mahlupukani Jomo, supported by other workers, complained of an enforced 14-hour working day without overtime pay; of assaults by whites while underground; of idle days without pay when fuel was not required (usually on alternate Saturdays), in contravention of their contracts; of inadequate food, particularly over weekends or on days when they were laid off or came up late from work; and of being given castor oil (to stop them 'malingering') when they reported minor injuries at the hospital. Thereafter conditions at the colliery improved in line with recommendations which owed much to the leadership of Jomo. During the next three years branches of African trade unions were established in Vereeniging: the Brick and Tile Workers Union and the Iron and Steel Workers Union came in 1942–43, and then (among others) the Milling Workers, the Gas and Power Workers (VFP), and the Timber Workers unions.

In this period of industrial ferment it was often possible to set up branches, but their success depended on the ability to win improvements, which rested partly on the willingness of the union to take strike action during the war (see Chapter 7). Although many factors were involved, it was not accidental that the steel workers (who were restrained by their leader's refusal to strike) won few concessions. On the other hand, the Brick and Tile Union, under A. Morokane, did threaten strike action and obtained rises from 2s 3d per day in 1939, first to 3s 2d after a strike in 1942 in Johannesburg, and then to 7s per day in the Wage Determination of 1945, when few increases were being given.[12]

Organisation of the Vereeniging branches of many unions was hampered by the inaccessibility of workers in compounds. According to a report on the Brick and Tile Company (*Rheinallt Jones Papers*, Box B, File 3.1, p.10), married men (223 out of a work force of 1,066) were housed in the location and they provided the nucleus around which the branch was built. Organisers also found it difficult to meet workers in the steel works, the power station and the timber yards, but branches were formed and in 1945–46 there were hopes of wider organisation in Vereeniging.[13]

The optimism was short lived. The timber workers suffered a major defeat in January 1946 after a six-week strike. Workers were beaten up by police and replaced by scabs supplied by the Department of Demobilisation (*Socialist Action*, January 1946). The VFP Union also collapsed, and this was followed by a strike in Vereeniging, long demanded by men at Union Steel, in July 1946. Some 2,500 men stopped. work and were dismissed, leaving the union branch (and with it the rest of the union) in ruins.

It was not only the unionised workers who suffered defeat. In January 1945 Springfield colliery workers again came out after a fatal underground assault. This time the workers faced a hostile regime and the strike collapsed. This phase of working-class resistance, whether organised in unions, or generated 'spontaneously', was coming to an end. The difficulties were not specific to this one town but were part of a larger problem which affected the entire working class: nevertheless, Vereeniging demonstrated the speed with which workers were able to mobilise themselves, or respond to trade union organisation. This was the story in all industrial centres, and these local efforts could be neither more nor less successful than those in Johannesburg, where the unions were centred.

Notes

1. *Cape Times*, 30 September 1937, gives the names of the killed and injured. Henceforth the press referred only to the death of *two* (white) policemen.
2. *Spark*, November 1937, summarised the course of events as reported in the press.
3. Quoted by F.H.C. Dixon (*c.* 1946), Part II, p.1. He said there were 722 houses, accommodating 8,000 persons. See *Survey of Reef Locations*, pp.41–2, on external latrines and 26 stand pipes for domestic water in the location. (Thanks to Helen Bradford for copies of these documents.)
4. H.U. Davidson, evidence at Commission of Inquiry into the riot, quoted in *Star*, 15 October 1937.
5. According to the 1936 census there were 14,864 Africans in Vereeniging, 8,654 being in the location. The number of rural dwellers was given as 23,403. The *Survey of Reef Locations* stated that by 1938 the urban population had increased by 25 per cent to 16,694 (*sic*).
6. Minutes of meeting of Advisory Board, 22 September 1937, with the Native Commissioner (H.U. Davidson), Rheinallt Jones, R. Britten (one-time Chief Magistrate of Johannesburg) and Saffery (for the SAIRR). *Rheinallt Jones Papers*.
7. Taken from Statement No. 2, found among ten statements in the *Rheinallt Jones Papers*, Box B.

8. Interim and Final Reports of Commission of Inquiry, to Inquire into Certain Matters Concerning the South African Police and the South African Railways and Harbour Police, UG 50, 1937. (Copy kindly sent by Helen Bradford.)
9. See, e.g., evidence of E.W. Lowe, Chief Native Commissioner for the northern OFS, Transvaal and Bechuanaland, in *Bantu World*, 5 December 1936. My thanks to Clare Ghazi-Harsiny who searched through the South African press for information on the commission.
10. The account of both riots is compiled from: statements at an Advisory Board meeting and the above-quoted meeting with members of the SAIRR; evidence collected for the SAIRR by Rev. Tlaletsi (all found in *Rheinallt Jones Papers*); and press reports on the preparatory examination into the deaths of the policemen.
11. *Star*, 30 October 1939. Thanks to Dunbar Moodie for lending me his typescript with accounts of events at Springfield.
12. See Stein, 'The Non-European Iron and Steel Workers Union', for attitudes to the war. Also Interim Report, 'Vereeniging Brick and Tile Company', mimeograph, *Rheinallt Jones Papers*, Box B, File 3.1.
13. *Socialist Action*, October 1945. The report does not reflect the optimism felt at the time that the unions had established a base in Vereeniging.

7. The Politics of War and the Black Working Class

Indifference

There can be few events, outside natural disasters, that affect societies more than war. Governments assume new powers, armed forces are mobilised, restrictions are imposed on social activities, labour is recruited for new industry or to replace those joining the forces, imports are restricted and substitutes manufactured, and the volume of exports drops sharply. The prospect of war, and even more so once war is declared, generates a fierce propaganda campaign to rally the population and legitimate the governing party's action. The nation is 'in peril' and the enemy must be stopped, yell the headlines: critical voices are stilled as the nation is rallied behind the army in an all-out struggle for victory. That, at least, is the manner in which wars are envisioned by ruling classes — and, to a large degree, it is what has happened since civilian populations have been called upon to participate in the struggles between nation states. This was not the position in South Africa in 1939, however. The white population was divided in its sympathies, one section siding with the Allied and the other with the Axis powers. On the other hand, the Africans, called upon to act as non-combatants in the field, had small sympathy for whatever cause whites espoused and showed little enthusiasm for the war.

It was not the government alone that appealed to the population for support against the enemy. The two main black political groups, the African National Congress and the All African Convention, supported the war effort, and after the German invasion of the USSR the Communist Party did likewise. These groups, which had blown hot and cold in their opposition to fascism during the 1930s, now set aside much of their opposition to the Smuts government and called for the mobilisation of the African people. The government turned a deaf ear, ignoring all pleas for democratisation and calls for the arming of blacks.

During the first months of the war observers noted the truculence of the African urban population. There was little open talk among blacks about the war and an obvious indifference to what was happening outside the country. If the 'white men' wished to kill themselves, that was a matter that did not concern the black worker. There were many who hoped that the South African army would be severely trounced and even some who hoped for a Japanese victory as a first step towards securing liberation from white rule.

For over four years, socialists and trade unionists worked in this divided society under constant surveillance by the police. Those who were pro-war argued for internal reforms as a prelude to mobilising support for the armed forces — and to varying degrees appealed for industrial peace. The small anti-war (socialist) groups derided the claim that the war was being fought for democracy and, although this won them few converts, they were successful in organising trade unions and pressed wage claims without any consideration of 'industrial peace'. Through all this period, the African working class demanded better conditions. Where their trade union leaders, or community organisations, were prepared to lead them in struggle, they won concessions during the early war period. Where their leaders were associated with pro-war organisations, the workers were restrained and their conditions did not improve much. Only after the end of the war, when the government was no longer prepared to allow any further concessions and the trade union movement was in decline, were restraints dropped. By then, it was too late for much of the work force and they were led into a series of disastrous strikes that left the trade union movement in ruins. This story, covering the period 1939—46, is glossed over in most histories but needs to be recounted to understand the rise and fall of the first industrial working class movement in South Africa.

Recruits for the army

South Africa joined the Allied forces in war against Germany on 4 September 1939, sending a volunteer army of just over 300,000 to fight in North Africa and Europe. The National Party opposed the war and strong pro-German sentiment in the country precluded conscription. A substantial force was consequently kept in the country to contain enemy agents and (white) subversion, while all recruits who volunteered for service abroad wore a red tab on their epaulettes.

A quarter of those recruited were members of the Cape Coloured Corps, the Indian and Malay Corps, and the Native Military Corps (NMC). But despite the slogans under which the war was fought — 'Freedom and Democracy' for example — segregation was as much a way of life on the battlefront as in South Africa and African recruits remained under the Natives Affairs Department (Grundlingh, 1984).

Blacks were restricted to non-combatant roles and unmarried men were paid 1s 6d per day, 6d more than the allowance paid to internees. Clerical workers, transport drivers and some others received an extra 1s per day. None could rise to a rank higher than sergeant,[1] and all earned less than the 5s per day paid to white privates. There were consequently few inducements to blacks to join the army. Clement Makabuza, formerly acting sergeant instructor in the mechanical transport section of the NMC, wrote to Dr Xuma on 13 November 1941 (*Xuma Papers*, ABX 411113a):

> Trainees are beaten up and if retaliation is made the Native is threatened with detention or actually detained and fined for insubordination for which he was provoked to. We are addressed as bloody bastards, niggers [?], *dom* kaffirs. This has created a wave of indignation throughout the camps.

> We have officers and NCOs who have come to assert their authority in no uncertain terms. Parades called to tell us that Natives are *nothing* in the army. When they [the Africans] demand an explanation the answer is detention.

Makabuza complained, and was demoted without right of appeal. He now asked Dr Xuma to secure an investigation, and continued:

> Are you going to leave us in the lurch. Are we in concentration camps or in camps of a democratic country (*sic*). What have we got arms for against Nazism if terrorism is practised in our midst?

Against such a background, the recruitment of 80,000 blacks was no mean achievement. Grundlingh suggests that some men were motivated by loyalty to the Allied cause, if not directly to the government, and some joined to learn a trade, or gain status by being in uniform. Others volunteered to escape the tedium of daily life, and perhaps to ensure regular pay, clothes, and housing. Most, however, enlisted for other reasons. Some 80 per cent came from the rural areas, devastated by drought in 1941—43 in the north of the country, and by a disastrous mealie harvest due to crop disease and pest infestation (Grundlingh). Starvation in the Reserves, or dismissal by white farmers after crop failure, was a powerful factor in black recruitment. As Lt Col R. Fyfe King, former Chief Magistrate of the Transkei, said: 'The best recruiting districts both for the Army and the Mines are those which reap little.'[2] It would, perhaps, be more accurate to say that the mines gained most from the districts 'which reap little'; the rest had little option but to join the armed forces.

Division on the left

The declaration of war brought confusion to the ranks of the left, who had campaigned against fascism for some time but opposed the war. Some Trotskyists, fearing the triumph of fascism in South Africa, went underground or dissolved their groups; others opposed the war as an imperialist conflict, but declared their defence of the USSR as a 'degenerate workers' state'. Gordon declared at the SATALC (Tenth Annual Conference, 1940, p.81): 'I am anti-Nazi and anti-imperialist war'; he attacked the role of Britain in her colonies, and the part played by the Western powers and the USSR in the defeat of the workers in Spain. He denounced the CPSA and declared that their opposition to the war was opportunistic and would melt away if Russia was attacked.

There was also tension inside the CPSA, whose members had participated since the mid—1930s in anti-fascist organisations; others were confused by the Stalin-Hitler pact, the partition of Poland and the Russian invasion of Finland. Some left the party and a few joined the army immediately (Simons and Simons, p.532). The CPSA faltered and welcomed the emergency regulations of 13 September, which gave the government powers of detention, as an attack on 'pro-Nazi elements in the country, and their irresponsible followers'. The party paper (then called *'Nkululeko*) also stated in September 1939 that the war was not 'imperialist', because:

> There is a sharp division between fascist countries which have brought about the war by their policy of aggression, and democratic countries in which the people can hope for progress only if they resist aggression and fascism, both inside their countries and outside them.

Soon after, however, the CPSA reversed its call for war on fascism and, ever loyal to the USSR and the Comintern, described the war as imperialist.[3] Arguments by party analysts were tortured. 'Vigilator', the *Guardian* columnist, started uncertainly, saying on 22 September that the German-Soviet pact might still be renounced; or that Hitler might be overthrown and the non-aggression pact converted by Russia into one of mutual assistance. Two weeks later (6 October) he said that the Soviet-German pact was 'a symbol of Hitler's abandonment of the drive to the East', and that Hitler was no longer a menace to the USSR. The fact that von Ribbentrop dined in Moscow with two Jews present was 'a symbol of the smashing of the anti-Comintern pact' (*sic*).

Other socialists were also divided. One group, which was later to form the Socialist Party, condemned the Stalin-Hitler pact as one more betrayal of the Russian revolution, but also blamed the outbreak of war on the imperialist powers. They disagreed with the Trotskyists and supported the war effort (albeit critically) because, they said, of the need to smash the Nazi war machine. The division inside the South African left reflected the rift in the international socialist movement. For members of these groups the differences were all-important, but few workers were interested in the debates. Two factors did affect black views of the war: firstly, many young Indians, incensed by British policies in India, were attracted to the CPSA; secondly, the maintenance of the colour bar in the army, and the refusal to arm blacks, made the Allies' 'Four Freedoms' slogan farcical.

The presence of openly pro-Nazi groups was a source of embarrassment to those socialists who opposed the war. Shortly after the declaration of war this was apparent in a short CPSA statement ('What is the War About?') that spoke of Poland fighting to keep her freedom while the South African government retained 'the pass laws, poll tax, low wages and inhuman exploitation of the Non-European workers'. The CPSA called for all blacks to have a 'part in the government of the country', but

> At this moment they [the blacks] must see that the Hertzog-Malan-Pirow group does not take over the Government of the Union. They must demand that the Smuts Government suppress the Nazi supporters who are out to enslave the Non-Europeans still further.

The statement was criticised at the annual conference of the CPSA in March 1940 because it weakened 'the line of struggle against the war, since it meant a passive acceptance of the Smuts Government and therefore of its war policy'.[4] During the discussion, leading members of the party suggested that it would be possible to appeal to Afrikaner workers, because

> Potentially there exists a wide feeling against the war providing all the basis needed for a real anti-war movement. For the first time perhaps in the history of South

Africa there is the possibility of developing common action between hostile racial groups on a single issue. . . .
The Afrikaners are opposed to the war because it is an imperialist war, not because they are pro-Nazi. There is need among them for an anti-imperialist, anti-war movement. The party must supply one.

Such assertions are inexplicable. Sam Kahn, a leading party member, even thought that the pro-Nazis could be won over. He said:

Those Afrikaners whose sympathies seemed to be with Nazi Germany, must view more sympathetically the communists: if it is possible for Hitler to co-operate with Russia (*sic*), so it must affect the people here whose sympathies were with Hitler. We will be able to get more readily the ear of the Afrikaners to the line of the CP.[5]

These pronouncements had little effect. In 1940 the CPSA claimed a membership of 280, 150 of whom were in Johannesburg (A. Brooks, p.25). The party was isolated and unable to address the simplest tasks raised by the war situation, despite all previous agitation for peace, for democratic rights, and for socialism. Of the Trotskyists, only one group in Cape Town and a few individuals in Johannesburg were active. Nonetheless, these small groups played a significant part in the developing trade unions, and their appraisal of the war influenced their work.

African responses to the war

Africans were not consulted about the war, and their white 'representatives' in parliament had no mandate to vote on the issue. Smuts counted on their votes when war was debated in Parliament and was not disappointed. He also received expressions of loyalty from some chiefs and members of the Native Representative Council, and with these too he was satisfied. Yet there were warnings that Africans did not support the war. Govan Mbeki, one of the first to express dissent, argued in *Territorial Magazine* (November 1939) against 'hasty comment either in support of the war or of neutrality'. Africans had no political rights, he said, and urged the 'wisdom of silence . . . [because] our own problems are as fierce as those on the European Western Front'.

One month later a resolution passed at the annual conference of the ANC stated that 'unless the Government grants the Africans full democratic and citizenship rights, the ANC is not prepared to advise the Africans to participate in the present war, in any capacity' (Karis and Carter, 1972–77, Vol. 2, p.155). The ANC leaders rejected this resolution and supported the government, while calling for full citizenship rights, privileges and duties, and the removal of the colour bar in recruitment.[6] The All African Convention (AAC) also supported the war, and the executives of the two bodies met together in July 1940 to reaffirm their policies (Karis and Carter, 1972–77, Vol. 2, p.339). The call for equality in recruitment and citizenship rights was ignored, as was a resolution along the same lines at the next session of the Native Representative Council, according to M. Ballinger

(1969, p.161), because it could only embarrass the government and 'cause trouble'.

Moses Kotane, General Secretary of the CPSA, found African reactions to the war 'hard to describe' in the columns of *Freedom* (March, 1940), but said:

> there is one thing certain . . . there is no enthusiasm among them for the war. The reason . . . is that they are not convinced of the truth of the causes and aims of this war and that they as an oppressed people do not figure anywhere in its aims.

Kotane might have been discounted as biased, but others confirmed his impression. In late 1940 Margaret Ballinger, a Native Representative, wrote to General Smuts about her 'great surprise' at the responses of her audiences. 'No one spoke in support of the war', and few raised the subject — not even to complain of the low rate of pay or the withholding of arms. 'The people were absorbed in their local difficulties and grievances', and at one meeting a speaker said:

> Why should we fight for you? We fought for you in the Boer War and you betrayed us to the Dutch. We fought for you in the last war. We died in France, in East Africa and in West Africa, and when it was over, did anybody care about us? Why should we fight for you again? What have we to fight for?

This was the feeling of the great majority of the people, she wrote, adding that Donald Molteno, Native Representative for the Western Cape, had found that

> while the people apparently fully appreciate the necessity of defeating Nazism, they have no intention of doing anything about it themselves, unless there is some clear indication of a change in Government policy towards them.[7]

In October 1942, contributing to a series of articles on the war in *Common Sense*, Mrs Ballinger stated that: 'With significantly few exceptions the African people are simply not interested in the war.' When pressed they claimed there was no democracy to defend and, if they did fight, they said, 'Shall we get back the right to buy land? Shall we get back the franchise?'

Z.K. Matthews, a leading member of the ANC, had also explained to the readers of *Common Sense* (July 1942) why, while Africans would not sabotage the war effort, neither would they respond to recruiting nor to appeals for war funds:

> The African has experienced so little of the freedom and democracy for which we are fighting, that he is tempted to ask, 'In which cheek has the White man got his tongue when he makes such statements to us?'
>
> Africans are not impressed when told that a German victory will lead to a worsening of his position. . . . Neither the Native policy of the Union, nor British Colonial Policy, nor indeed . . . [that] of any other Power, represents a cause worth fighting for.

H. Sonnaband, a sociologist at the University of the Witwatersrand, reported that a poll showed 69 per cent of Africans opposed the war effort under existing conditions; 91 per cent wanted equal pay and pension rights for all soldiers; and 93 per cent wanted Africans to carry arms. If these demands were met, 80 per cent said they would support the war (*Common Sense*, September 1942). He found that 'educated' Africans tended to be more inclined to support the government. This was supported by a memorandum of the Transvaal African Teachers Association (TATA) to the Secretary for Native Affairs, requesting higher wages and stating that they were 'live agents of the government in spreading propaganda among the children and parents against Fascist and Nazi subversive activities. . . .' Two members of TATA, however, felt it necessary to add that

> so long as the status of the black man brands him as a social outcast, so long may he intelligently imagine that the difference between Nazi totalitarianism and South African lily white democracy is the difference between tweedledee and tweedledum.[8]

Subversion?

The South African state seemed to face threats from two sides during the war. Firstly, there were the Nazi sympathisers: these included members of the 'shirt' movements, who dressed and acted like Nazis, and were anti-black, anti-semitic, and anti-Communist; the New Order group, with strong Nazi inclinations and led by former defence minister, Oswald Pirow; and sections of the National Party who kept a discreet silence. Daily clashes in Cape Town and other centres between pro- and anti-war elements often erupted during the midday observance of a two-minute silence. Skirmishes between troops and laymen were common in towns and villages. Other developments included a wave of bombings and sabotage, the smuggling of local Nazis into the country after training in Germany, an aborted insurrection, and a plot led by members of the police force to overthrow the government (Lawrence, 1978, Ch. 14; Parliamentary Debates, 1942, Cols 17,663).

Several hundred people were interned after the plots came to light: a few were charged and convicted, and one received the death sentence (later commuted), but many remained free to propagate their brand of Nazism (Lawrence, 1978, p.136). In the internment camps they got away with swastikas, receiving and transmitting sets, pictures of Hitler on the walls, their own postal censorship and sanctions against anti-Nazis, many of whom were violently assaulted.[9] Their targets included communists and white trade unionists like Fellner, who reported on release that he had been attacked one night and mercilessly beaten.[10] Amongst the pro-fascists were a future Prime Minister and President, the future head of the Security Police, and other officials of the post-war state.

The second challenge to the state was more potential than real. Communists and Trotskyists opposed the war but there was no call for the defeat of the Allied forces, no sabotage and no 'subversion'. On 9 June 1940 Dr Dadoo, Secretary of the Transvaal Non-European United Front, member of the CPSA and leader of the (Indian) National Group, told the Indian

National Youth Organisation of the sacrifice of lives throughout the world by 'robber-imperialist powers . . . to fill the coffers of the finance-capitalists'. The language was radical, but the message was reformist:

> There is only one logical and righteous attitude that the Indians together with African and Coloured people could adopt to the question of war, and that is to render no support to the present war, but to unite amongst ourselves and bring about such a powerful front of Non-European peoples and it can intensify the preparation, organisation, and struggle for the achievement of complete economic emancipation and full rights of citizenship.

Though some of its members were gaoled, the Indian National Congress opposed the war until Russia was invaded in June 1941. Then D.A. Seedat (one of the leaders) refused to accept restrictions on his activities and stayed in gaol a further forty days in September 1942 (Roux, 1949, p.319).

Few socialists were detained, although police surveillance continued and individuals were warned to desist from some of their activities or face arrest. Several leftists were held in detention camps for periods of between nine and fifteen months, including Arnold Latti (of the CPSA in Port Elizabeth), Max and Louis Joffee (active members of the CPSA), Max Gordon, Fritz Fellner, J.E. Brown and E.J. Burford (who ascribed his detention to disputes inside the Labour Party). The reasons given for their internment were vague. Burford, who led a deputation to the Minister of the Interior and asked what was subversive about a person connected with African trade unions, was told that 'any organisational activities amongst natives was looked upon with suspicion'.[11] It was not suggested that the war was an issue: Latti, amongst others, was pro-war when interned (*Guardian*, 24 September 1942).

There were others who had anti-war attitudes of which little is known, and many might have agreed with Bloke Modisane and his Sophiatown circle who 'privately cheered the military advance of the armies of the Third Reich; it was not so much a question of admiring Hitler, but an emotional alliance with the enemy of South Africa' (1965, p.81). In just one reported instance were such sentiments translated into action. Stephen Sebe, Commander-in-Chief of the African Legion, gathered a group of unknown size which collected money 'to help the Japanese and Abyssinians free us from white slavery' (*Star*, 11 June 1943). Sebe, in imitation of Garvey, styled himself 'Prince Yusuf' or 'Prince of Abyssinia' and his commanders 'Knights of the Grand Cross'. But it was wartime and the tactics were different to those once used in Harlem. The secretary of the Legion recorded in the minutes that Africans would be rallied 'if our army should awaken our people by throwing a bomb in the centre of the town'. Reports on the trial of Sebe and his lieutenants are perfunctory: there is no news of the sentences, nor of the support he received. Yet it seems that many took him seriously and Kadalie, who sensed the mood of the time, announced that people who purchased the membership cards of his Independent ICU would be protected when the Japanese landed in South Africa.[12]

CPSA opposition to the war stopped abruptly when Russia was invaded on 22 June 1941. It was claimed later that the policy was consistent (Simons and Simons, p.536), but it can hardly be said that it was determined by local considerations, or was in the best interests of the workers in South Africa.[13] Before June every article in the party press, or the publications of its front organisations, condemned Britain and France as 'reactionary and pro-fascist' and called 'for the immediate cessation of hostilities and a complete restoration and extension of the democratic rights of the people'.[14] After the fall of France in mid-1940 the Johannesburg District Committee condemned the government for involvement in 'a terrible and disastrous imperialist war', and for destroying 'the few democratic rights we possess'. No one escaped their wrath: Smuts and the Nationalist leaders were condemned as 'a terrible menace to the people of this land', and Smuts lambasted because he was 'obedient only to the desires of a handful of finance capitalists abroad who are the real rulers and controllers of South Africa'.[15]

The arguments were now inverted. The government had to be supported in the great fight against fascism, which

> would be a great triumph for the progressive and democratic movement in all countries, including South Africa. It would enable the Soviet Union to throw her weight on the side of the workers and oppressed people throughout the world. It would create conditions that would be favourable for a successful struggle against race and national oppression.[16]

The author demanded the liberation of blacks 'so that they could play their full part in the war against Fascism'. This 'was progressive in itself', he wrote:

> The Non-European peoples will understand and agree with this policy if we explain to them what the Soviet Union means to the workers and oppressed people of all countries.

The 'Non-European peoples' did not understand, and the CPSA turned to the white population, attracting a large number of petty bourgeois supporters to the Friends of the Soviet Union (under the patronage of Colin Steyn, the Minister of Justice), Medical Aid for Russia, and the Left Clubs in Johannesburg and Cape Town. The anti-war phase of the CPSA was forgiven, and the Nazi-Soviet pact interpreted by members of the party as a master stroke by Stalin to gain time in building Russia's defences. The Atlantic Charter of August 1941 and the 'Four Freedoms' were now universally acclaimed, and it was widely believed that the troops abroad would come home as carriers of progress. The Springbok Legion, claiming 40,000 members in the armed forces, set out to 'secure a fair deal for soldiers, ex-servicemen and their dependants; preserve unity between the races; defend democracy and promote Liberty, Equality, Fraternity' (Simons and Simons, p.540).

It was believed in liberal circles, and in the CPSA particularly, that change could not long be delayed. Some 30 years later the Simons wrote (pp.540−1):

> The Battles of Britain, Stalingrad and Alamein turned the tide against the Axis. Enthusiasm for the Red Army mounted. . . . The Soviet Union, that 'Colossus of Europe' in Smuts's phrase, had confounded the critics and vindicated the faith of its

most ardent admirers. . . . The Army Education service opened the minds of front line troops to progressive ideas, while the Springbok Legion organised them for political action on a liberal programme. . . . Victories on the battle front and high profits at home engendered a mood of euphoria in the pro-war parties. . . . Optimists thought that the time was ripe for a reversal of apartheid policies.

The CPSA grew, and the pro-Soviet *Guardian* increased its circulation from 12,000 in 1940 to 33,000 in June 1942 and 42,400 a year later (ibid., pp.538–9). Party members or sympathisers who had worked in the SALP or the Labour League of Youth, and had been anti-war, now 'came out' as members of the CPSA. The party recruited leaders of the 'mixed' trade unions in the coastal towns and the African unions in the Transvaal. But the real growth was among the white petty bourgeoisie and few workers, black or white, were recruited. Party members contested parliamentary and municipal elections in predominantly middle class suburbs, and in August 1943 won three seats in Cape constituencies, to be followed by one victory in Johannesburg — the 'capture' of Hillbrow by Hilda Watts (Bernstein).

The dissolution of the Comintern was welcomed by a writer in *Inkululeko* (5 June 1943) as an advance to greater working class unity: now the CPSA's 'programme for liberty' would mobilise 'the people in order to win the war'. The ultimate move to the right by some party members followed reports that Earl Browder, Secretary of the Communist Party of the USA, had in July 1942 pledged his party to support the government in the war, and offered not to raise the issue of socialism lest national unity be disrupted (Findlay, 1944, p.2). In December 1943 he extended the call for class collaboration, and declared that the Teheran agreement, signed by Roosevelt, Churchill, and Stalin, laid the basis for the peaceful co-existence of capitalism and communism in the post-war world.[17]

On 10 January 1944, Browder 'called for a new "national unity" to bring full employment, peace and an end to periodic economic crises'. He would welcome monopolies and cartels in the rebuilding of Europe after the war, because this would ensure full employment in the USA, and he called on the banker J.P. Morgan to join the grand new coalition. The communists, he repeated, would 'not raise the issue of socialism in such a form and manner as to endanger or weaken the national unity' (Haywood, 1978, p.531). He said that America was not ready for socialism, dissolved the Communist Party of the USA, and launched a Communist Political Association to 'disseminate political education' (Findlay, 1944, p.1).

The publication of Browder's January speech divided the CPSA: the majority rejected the main conclusions, while stressing the need for national unity during the war; a large minority supported Browder fully. The Central and local District Committees were divided, and the party journal carried the debate on Browderism.[18]

The war and the unions

When Max Gordon was interned in May 1940, and detained for over a year, the unions were inevitably disrupted. In the first months subscriptions fell by two thirds and some unions collapsed. The Joint Committee ceased functioning and individual secretaries joined forces with the ANC (and with Gana Makabeni) or the CPSA, while the rump stayed with Dan Koza and the African Commercial and Distributive Workers Union (ACDWU).[19] The unions revived in time, but it was only in 1941–42 that they experienced their greatest expansion amidst an unprecedented strike wave. The development of the workers' movement was influenced by three interlocking factors: the increasing reliance of the rural population on money from the towns, following crop failures; the inflation caused by wartime shortages;[20] and the continued demand for labour (semi-skilled and unskilled) in shops and factories, to meet the needs of the armed forces and the home market. The ability of trade unions to take up workers' complaints and secure improvements led to their expansion, and amongst the many contributing factors was the action taken by the ACDWU in defending the gains secured in the wage determination of December 1939. The workers ignored the war and other political issues: they were ruthlessly exploited, and were determined to secure the increased wages to which they were entitled.

The strike wave of 1941–42

In 1940, when the CPSA opposed the war, the number of workers involved in strike action was 1,900, and of these only 700 were black. This was the smallest annual total of strikers since 1933, when the country was emerging from the depression. After the invasion of Russia, and despite the clamour for industrial peace, the number of workers on strike increased, as can be seen in Table 7.1 (which is taken from official sources and does not include all the strikes reported to the Department of Labour).

The strikes of 1941–42 were mainly over wages and more than half took place in Johannesburg and Durban. The strikers in Johannesburg were predominantly Africans and their actions (always illegal) were linked to the economic pressures felt by themselves and their families. In Durban the strikers were mainly Indian and their actions, permissible under the Industrial Conciliation (IC) Act, were a response to rising costs of living and the threat of replacement by lower-paid Africans — that age-old ethnic tangle, in which Indians feared redundancy and Africans believed they were being blocked at the workplace. This prevented joint action in industrial disputes when working-class unity might have advanced their claims.

The authorities tried to contain the situation, making concessions or (in one case) calling in labour leaders to form a union to get power workers back to work. But after 1943 police or troops were used to crush strikes or demonstrations. Municipal workers were shot down at Marabastad on 28 December 1942, and the Native Military Corps was drafted in to smash a strike of the power workers in January 1944 (discussed in later chapters). Legislative steps were also taken to curb working-class action: in December

Table 7.1
Strikes in South Africa, 1940–45

Year	No. of strikes	No. of strikers (000) Whites	No. of strikers (000) Blacks	Man-days lost (000)
1940	24	1.2	0.7	6.5
1941	35	0.7	4.8	23.2
1942	58	1.3	12.8	49.5
1943	52	1.8	7.4	47.7
1944	52	0.2	12.0	62.7
1945	63	1.5	14.7	91.1

Source: Clack, 1962, Appendix C.

1942, War Measure 145 outlawed all strikes by Africans and gave the Minister of Labour the right to submit all disputes to arbitration. Contravention of the new measure was punishable by a prison sentence of three years or a fine of £500. Finally, in August 1944, War Measure 1425 prohibited meetings of more than 20 persons on proclaimed ground (under the gold laws), and this effectively prevented the organisation of mineworkers. Other unions, less dependent on large gatherings, were hampered by the new regulation, and gatherings in the townships, particularly in Alexandra where residents were engaged in a struggle over bus fares, were halted.

The development of the trade unions will be discussed in later chapters. What concerns us here is the response of the political parties and their trade union associates to the strikes. On 29 December 1942, a day after the shooting at Marabastad, Dr Xuma wrote to General Smuts asking that he see a joint deputation from the Council of Non-European Trade Unions and the ANC: his declared object was to put before Smuts 'certain aspects of the situation', which would lead to 'the settlement of recent strikes and the prevention of further or impending strikes'. He continued:

> We are alarmed at the number of avoidable strikes that have taken place recently.
> It would seem to us that the methods used to deal with some of the participants in these strikes are not calculated to improve the situation.
> The use of soldiers and armoured cars against unarmed strikers in the recent Marabastad Municipal Compound strike (*sic*) has shocked the African community, and we fear, may be wrongly construed by the rank and file of our people, and this might tend to undermine the war effort and the patriotic attitude of the African people.
> We deplore the occurrence of any strike at the present time, as we realise that they tend to impede the national war effort as well as to strain race relations between white and black.
> We feel that the causes and factors involved in these strikes are so varied that only the Prime Minister need be approached for a solution.
> We are very anxious not to embarrass our Government during this trying period (*Xuma Papers*, ABX 421229).

Xuma and his friends were ardent supporters of the war effort, but the remarks of Z.K. Matthews et al. in *Common Sense* showed that there was no 'patriotic attitude of the African people'. Marabastad (where there was no strike) was not being 'wrongly construed' but was interpreted correctly as a sign of continued repression. To state further that strikes would 'strain race relations', was to undermine everything the workers had achieved. Most damning, however, was the omission from the letter of any mention of War Measure 145. The desire of Xuma and his confrères to limit and even prevent strikes was not merely a wartime stratagem, as they were to show in 1946 when they gave scant support to the mineworkers' strike. They had little sympathy with direct working-class action, in the factories or in community struggles, and they used the issue of wartime production to conceal their own petty bourgeois prejudices.

The CPSA also opposed strike action, but its position was ambivalent. A statement by the Central Committee on 22 October 1942 spoke of the justice of the workers' claims, and noted that workers did not lightly embark on strike action. The CPSA condemned War Measure 145, and opposed compulsory arbitration, but the logic of class collaboration during the war required that workers 'make every effort, by arousing public opinion and developing all forms of pressure available, to obtain a satisfactory settlement while avoiding any stoppage of work' (Brooks, 1967, p.47).

Strikes were a 'danger', to be avoided in the interest of the war effort. Where unavoidable, they were to be restricted to the struggle for higher wages. The party published a pamphlet entitled *More Money*, outlining the functions of trade unions. The mechanics of trade union organisation were explained: the union office, the constitution, the role of the secretary, treasurer and committee, the need for a financial statement. The authors described negotiations, arbitration, Wage Boards and Conciliation Boards; they demanded the recognition of trade unions under the IC Act. The right to strike had to be protected, but there was a war; victory was vital, and every effort should be made to settle disputes before calling a strike:

> These hold up supplies of weapons, of arms, of uniforms, to our army fighting for our freedom. Strikes today can help our fascist enemies destroy our own armies . . . and enslave us. Wherever workers can win demands without strikes which stop the flow of goods from our factories, they should do so.

The CPSA faced an insoluble contradiction: workers were striking and would continue struggling for better working conditions. Furthermore, there was disaffection in the large towns after massive police raids in April 1943, in which over 6,370 men were arrested, in Johannesburg alone, for contravening the pass laws.

Consequently, the authors of *More Money* coupled their exhortation for industrial peace with a call for continued struggle against repressive legislation and laws which made striking illegal. Workers had to unite and use every available weapon to obtain higher wages, but they were not to strike. The contradiction, however, could not be concealed. At the CPSA conference on 15–17 January 1944, alongside a call for the intensification of the war in Europe and the opening of a 'second front', Dadoo urged full support for the recently launched anti-pass campaign (see below). Only the removal of 'these laws and other restrictions', he said, would win the full support of the African people for the war. Yet, '[s]everal African speakers explained that the Nazi-like restrictions imposed on the African people [made] it difficult for them to support the war'.

Ray Alexander presented the report on trade unions, and stressed 'the need for the expansion of production and for the improvement of working and living conditions'. On the issue of strikes she maintained:

> Our Party's policy is directed towards a peaceful settlement of disputes and avoiding of any strikes or any other action that will hinder the war effort. *But we do not regard this contribution of the working class as a one-sided arrangement.* Workers who labour under a sense of grievance, who are not able to maintain a decent standard of living, are certainly not in a position to apply their full strength and ability to production. . . .
> In our opinion a great body of low-paid workers have every justification for embarking on a national campaign for wage increases (CPSA, 1944).

There was no national campaign for wage increases, and the effect of the CPSA policy was to act as a brake on some of the key unions where workers called for strike action. In opposing strikes, the CPSA was devious. It urged that unions be better organised. 'Unity and organisation, not wild, unorganised strikes — is the way to better wages and freedom', ran one of its pronouncements (*Forum*, 2 January 1943) and although that advice was unexceptional, it only served as a cover for an anti-strike policy.

The march against passes

The police raids of April 1943 heralded a new state offensive against contraventions of the pass laws. Well over 10,000 males were arrested for sleeping in so-called 'servants' quarters' illegally, or on charges of 'vagrancy', or because they were without their passes. The African trade unions protested against this 'indiscriminate and unwarranted arrest of thousands of Africans along the Rand', and so too did the Native Representatives in Parliament.[21] The need for political action seemed more urgent than ever, but the ANC took no initiative, and there the matter might have rested had the CPSA not called a conference on the pass laws in November.

An anti-pass campaign was first broached by C.S. Ramohanoe, President of the Transvaal ANC, in January 1942. In a letter to Dr Xuma he announced the inauguration of a 'great campaign against the pass system, the most outstanding example of the oppression of our people' (*Xuma Papers*, ABX 420108). Xuma did not approve and the campaign languished. Nor did Xuma respond to the April 1943 raids. The CPSA waited for the ANC to act, and then hosted a conference in Johannesburg on 21 November. Dr Dadoo took the chair and 112 organisations were said to be present.

Edwin Mofutsanyana gave the keynote address:

The time has come for us to fight the passes to the bitter end. We have called this conference to make a start on the greatest campaign in the history of this country . . . we must confront the leaders of our national movement with the demand that they conduct this campaign. We must use every channel that we have. We must petition the Government and tell them that we can no longer tolerate their pass laws. We must tell our representatives in Parliament that in the coming session they must move a Bill to abolish the pass laws. The [ANC] conference . . . must tackle this issue. . . .

J.B. Marks was somewhat more bombastic. He said:

This conference has passed sentence on the pass laws, the sentence of death. The pass laws are a national stigma, and can only be fought by all the black people standing and fighting together. We have been humiliated by these laws. To hell with passes!

The authorities acted to stop the campaign, threatening Dadoo with internment and *Inkululeko* with suppression. At the ANC conference in December there were calls for a national campaign, but Xuma only agreed in March 1944 to act as a trustee and preside at the forthcoming conference in May. Here there were calls for a petition, for pass-burning, for leaders to prepare for gaol to end the pass laws, and for a national stoppage of work if the government did not respond. This was too much for some CPSA members. The call for leaders to go to gaol, and for strike action, was contrary to the new Browderist philosophy, and was rejected by Umlweli (M. Harmel).[22]

The conference was held over the weekend of 20–21 May and the organisers reported that 504 'delegates' attended, representing 605,222 people.[23] The resolution adopted stated that:

the pass laws are in conflict with the high and progressive war aims for which our country, together with the other United Nations, is fighting. These laws hold the African people in conditions of abject poverty and subjection; they retard the economic and industrial development of South Africa; they hamper the growth of organisation of African workers and thus weaken the entire Labour movement; they are the cause of sharp racial friction between the peoples of South Africa; they uphold the cheap labour system which results in malnutrition, starvation and disease; they fill our gaols with innocent people and thus create widespread crime (Karis and Carter, Vol. 2, pp.396–8).

Then, on Sunday afternoon, between 15,000 and 20,000 people marched through the streets of central Johannesburg, parading behind 'Chief Marshal' Moses Kotane. A report in the *Guardian* noted that:

The demonstration was a magnificent and impressive sight as, headed by a great Congress float and bearing hundreds of banners demanding the repeal of the pass laws and accompanied by two brass bands and singing national songs, the marchers made their way through the streets of the city.

The centre of Johannesburg was non-residential and empty on Sunday: impressive as the march might have been, few were there to see the spectacle. The march was to be the precursor of a national campaign to obtain one million signatures by the end of August for presentation to the government on 'National Anti-Pass Demonstration Day'.

The campaign flopped. The working committee could not muster a quorum and, even after co-options, the majority were said to be 'apathetic and uninterested'.[24] Despite attempts to get the campaign off the ground, the petition contained far fewer than a million signatures. The acting Prime Minister, J.H. Hofmeyr, refused to see a deputation and when they demonstrated with 5,000 supporters outside Parliament in June 1945, the leaders were arrested and charged with leading an unlawful procession. Dadoo, Selope Thema, S. Moema and others were fined, and, although there were attempts in June 1946 to revive the campaign and commence a mass struggle, culminating in a national work stoppage and the burning of passes, nothing more was heard of this initiative (Roux, 1949, p.330).

Notes

1. Alfred Bitini Xuma, typed draft of Presidential address to ANC annual conference, 15 December 1941, Hemson film; see also version in CAMP, Reel 8A, 2:DA14:30/11.
2. From a letter dated 28 September 1942, quoted by Grundlingh, 1984.
3. The anti-war stand was presented by J. Morkel (H.J. Simons ?), reporter for the Politburo, Minutes of Conference of the CPSA, 23–24 March 1940, in CAMP, Reel 3A, 2:CCI:32.
4. Morkel, Minutes of Conference, CAMP, Reel 3A, 2CCI:32; also quoted in A. Brooks, 1967, p.24.
5. This is reprinted in the *Report of the Select Committee on the Suppression of Communism Enquiry*, SC 6–52, pp.370–1. Kahn, cross-examined on the passage, confirmed that this was his position in 1940.
6. *Guardian*, 26 January 1940; also quoted in Bunting, 1975, p.102. Karis and Carter do not mention this rebuttal and Walshe, 1970, does not refer to the resolutions on the war.
7. 'Report of a tour of the Eastern Province by Margaret Ballinger M.P., in October and November 1940, for the information of the Right Hon. J.C. Smuts', in CAMP, Reel 9A, 2:XB2:62.
8. The memorandum, and the reservation, both in Lekhethoa and Mbobo, 1944, pp.11, 16.
9. George Heard, 'Tyranny in internment camp: reign of terror under fanatical Nazis and OBs', *Sunday Times*, 8 December 1940. Found in Saura Woolf's album of press cuttings, with items on the internment camps.
10. Reported in *Forward*, 22 November 1940. Cutting included in Saura Woolf's album.
11. Report on a deputation from the Civil Liberties League to the 11th Conference of the SATALC, October 1941, p.106.
12. Lodge, 1983, p.50, has a brief note on the Legion. It is not clear whether the same persons were involved in the events he describes in 1946 and those that took place in 1943. The item on Kadalie came from Helen Bradford, 1984, in response to my initial paper on the war.
13. Roux, 1949, p.317, said the CPSA was 'subordinating the South African struggle to the needs of the world situation'. But the switch needs to be expressed in terms that do not obscure the slavish subservience of local Communists to Comintern demands.

14. E.S. Sachs, speaking on an anti-war resolution which was supported by the Communist trade unionists, 10th Annual Conference of the SATALC, April 1940. It was reprinted (approvingly) in the organ of the Non-European United Front, *The Call*, Vol. 1, No. 4, April 1940.
15. Johannesburg District Committee of the CPSA, 'For the defence and independence of South Africa', mimeographed, n.d., SAIRR collection.
16. H. Morkel, 'Why we must support the government in the war against fascism', *Freedom*, No. 9, April 1942. Note the transformation of J. Morkel, who opposed the war in 1940, into H. Morkel, who was pro-war!
17. Browder's views were published in *The Worker* (USA), 26 March 1944. An extract, available in South African bookshops, was in *Left* (London), No. 95, September 1944. See also Haywood, Chapter 20.
18. Findlay describes disagreements in the CPSA in his diary. See also L. (Rusty) Bernstein, 'We're not in a vaccuum: a reply to George Findlay' and R.K. Cope, 'Economic aspects of Earl Browder's policy', both in *Freedom*, Vol. 2, No. 8, June 1944. These were dismissed by Findlay in his entry of 11 July 1944 as 'feeble', and Bernstein's 'attack' made him 'laugh'. Despite the intensity of the debate on Browderism inside the CPSA, the topic received scant attention in post-war publications.
19. Documents on Gordon's internment, and its effects on the unions, are in the *Saffery Papers*.
20. See letter from Selby Ngcobo to W.A.G. Champion, 10 August 1941, *Champion Papers*, comparing the increased cost of living since the war began: for whites it was 8.3 per cent and for blacks 50 per cent because of the rise in prices of staple foods.
21. *Star*, 6—24 April 1943, carried reports of arrests. On 16 April it gave the figure as 9,795 for Johannesburg and the Reef, and on the 24th said that the figure exceeded 11,000. It was also announced that no further figures would be published.
22. *Inkululeko*, 10 June 1944. Umlweli's attack was oblique. He likened a work stoppage and the courting of arrest to the strike in the coal yards — where, he claimed, other means should have been tried first to remedy the wretched conditions of these workers.
23. The only report is in *Inkululeko*, 29 May 1944. The author and two friends attended and 'represented' three of the 375 organisations, which included: trade unions, mines, peasants, political parties, churches, students, Advisory Boards, factories, compounds, and anti-pass committees.
24. Report of National Anti-Pass Council, presented to Second National Anti-Pass Conference, Johannesburg, 23 June 1946, Hemson film.

8. Trade Unions in Struggle

The African distributive workers

In South Africa in the early 1930s most commercial deliveries were made by bicycle or horse cart. From 4 a.m., when the milkmen wheeled out their cycles, until 5 or 6 p.m., when newspaper deliveries were completed, men rode through the suburbs carrying bread, milk and meat, or goods from shops, department stores, building merchants and hardware departments, or even blocks of ice, sacks of coal, furniture and scrap iron.[1] Larger deliveries were made by push-cart, horse and cart, or motor van. Except for some drivers, distributive workers in the Transvaal were Africans. Householders expected back-door deliveries, daily or weekly. Working with the delivery men, and helping to load the cycles and carts, were the packers, shelvers and loaders, many doubling up as cleaners, errand runners and 'tea boys'.

There were some 26,000 African commercial distributive workers in South Africa in 1937, all but a thousand listed as 'unskilled' (Van der Horst, 1942, p.258) although many repaired or assembled goods, or fitted curtains, carpets and linoleum (Stein, 1977, p.54). None served as counter-hands or at cash tills in shops: these jobs were reserved for the 52,000 whites. Even for whites, pay was poor and a 60-hour week not uncommon. Few workers received holiday pay and many were required to work on public holidays. White women received about £5 per month, rising to £9 when they were deemed 'qualified'; men's wages rose from £6 to £18. Many were paid far less, however; shop girls in Worcester received only 7s 6d per week, and those in Cape Town £1 7s 6d, with no additions for the 'qualified' (Herd, 1974, pp.41–8). In 1936 the National Union of Distributive Workers (NUDW) was launched, absorbing a few local unions (some dating back to 1914, though most shop workers had never been organised). The NUDW requested a Wage Board enquiry and asked for a 44-hour week, a two-to-one ratio of qualified to unqualified workers, and better holiday leave.

African workers, deemed inferior to white 'shop girls', received an average of 17s 6d a week in Johannesburg (and less elsewhere), with few amenities (such as wash rooms) available to them. They were excluded from the NUDW — although it was led by CPSA members or sympathisers — and in mid-1937 Max Gordon formed the African Commercial and Distributive Workers Union (ACDWU).[2]

Daniel Koza joined Gordon in the ACDWU and together they enrolled dairy workers, coal hauliers, shop workers and others: then they requested a Wage Board enquiry. Some distributive workers (including dairy workers) eventually formed separate unions, while the ACDWU continued to organise those workers covered by the terms of the Wage Board report of 1939. New regulations governing African wages and working conditions in the distributive trade came into effect on 1 January 1940, the same day that white workers gained considerable improvements under the Shops and Offices Act of 1939.

The development of African trade unions in the formative period before the war owed as much to Koza as to Gordon — together, they made a remarkable team. Gordon provided the overall strategy and the contacts which generated technical and financial assistance; Koza provided much of the organising ability and a close understanding of African workers' reactions. During his 'apprenticeship' Koza also. mastered the many strategies he would need in running a trade union, directing organisers and negotiating with the bosses. Then in 1940 he was called upon to take control of the ACDWU when Gordon was interned. He succeeded admirably.

Daniel Koza — trade unionist

In the early 1940s the African Distributive Workers Union under the able leadership of its secretary, Mr D. Koza, was acknowledged to be the best organised African trade union (Ellen Hellmann, 1953, p.23).

Koza led the ACDWU after Gordon's internment and until his own resignation in 1948. He led a number of successful strikes, advocated greater militancy in the African trade union movement, and became the effective leader of the Progressive Trade Union Group (PTU). He was intensely nationalistic, but spoke as an internationalist, opposing the war on revolutionary grounds.[3] He also believed that trade unions had a political role: at the first conference of the Council of Non-European Trade Unions (CNETU), in February 1943, he proposed that the ANC be invited to become the political wing of the African labour movement.[4] His motion was defeated. Instead, the conference recommended that all trade unions affiliate to the SATALC and achieve closer cooperation with the white workers — an idle dream, since no more than half a dozen African unions ever affiliated with that body.

On 29 July 1943 Koza proposed in a letter that the ACDWU executive meet with Xuma to discuss the basis of affiliation to the ANC (Hemson film). On the eve of the meeting, however, the Alexandra bus boycott commenced and meetings after working hours were cancelled. Koza's experiences in the boycott turned him against the ANC and this led first to his participation in the launching of the African Democratic Party and then to membership of the All African Convention.

Born in 1912 of poor parents, Koza studied at the Diocesan Training College for teachers at Grace Dieu, near Pietersburg in the northern Transvaal. In his third and final year of study he wrote to Dr Xuma asking where he could get training for dentistry.[5] There were no African dentists, nor places in the dental schools, and education abroad was closed to Africans in the 1930s. Like other Africans at college, he belonged to the tiny minority of primary school graduates; but Koza had no desire to teach, and the salary (£5 10s a month for a certificated teacher) was unacceptable. The only other outlets were in government departments, as clerks in the Native Affairs Department or the courts; or in the private sector as clerks on the mines, in legal offices or in certain firms. In most cases, wages were low and avenues of advancement closed.

Koza's entry into the trade union movement seems to have been an obvious step. He was probably introduced to the Trotskyists by his friend Peter Abrahams,[6] and that would have led him to Gordon. Koza was undoubtedly angry and frustrated, and his work in the unions provided an outlet for his passion and his energy — as is illustrated by his leaflet on the Nkana riots in Chapter 4. He also had a flair for organising and had become a competent trade unionist by the time Gordon was interned. Yet his obvious abilities isolated him from fellow unionists, and because he did not suffer fools gladly he appeared imperious and aloof. There are no records to indicate how he conducted the internal affairs of the union, but like other leaders his style of dress and bureaucratic approach to administration set him apart from the workers he represented, and he never assumed the leading role which his talents seemed to promise. Furthermore, like all trade union organisers in this period, Koza's salary set him apart from the workers — in aspiration and in style of life. There is no evidence that he ever stooped to the corruption that spread in the African trade union movement, but his ability to detach himself from the ACDWU in 1948, and his departure to London (on a bursary) was a measure of the gulf that existed between Koza and the workers.[7]

Strike in the coal yards

The wage determination for commercial and distributive workers gazetted in December 1939 set minimum wages for everyone from counter-hands to labourers and night watchmen. Unskilled workers in Johannesburg were granted 27s 8d per week, the highest unskilled rate in the city. Payment in Reef towns was lower, but still proportionately higher than wages in other occupations. There was also provision for annual paid leave, and pay for overtime and work on public holidays. The provisions of the determination expressly excluded workers in dairies, timber yards and coal yards. Before the determination was gazetted, Gordon protested, and the position of the coal hauliers was reviewed by the Wage Board on the instruction of the Minister. They remained outside the determination and Gordon complained again before he was interned. In June 1940 Koza applied once again through the Wage Board for the inclusion of the coal yard workers in the determination, but without success.

Africans in the coal trade received £3 per month for a 78-hour week; were required to work on Sundays and public holidays at ordinary rates of pay; and were housed in sheds at the coal yards. When the union's claim on their behalf was rejected, the men walked out and were arrested. Deliveries of coal stopped and the employers, unable to find suitable replacements, dropped all charges against the men. They offered to increase wages to £4 per month, pending further talks.[8] Then, to avoid honouring their promise, the employers all declared that they had become 'contractors' and therefore fell outside the provisions of the commercial distributive trade. Wages were reduced, in some cases to 32s 6d per month, and the employers refused to enter into negotiations. On 8 May 1941 workers at five coal yards came out on strike. This time convict labour was employed to maintain deliveries and 366 workers were arrested and charged under the Masters and Servants Act (*Guardian*, 21 May 1941; Report of 12th Annual Conference of the SATALC, April 1942).

The workers were advised by the lawyers, in consultation with Koza, E.S. Sachs and W.G. Ballinger, to demand separate trials. Only 83 workers, who accepted the usual practice of a collective charge, were found guilty, and fined £1 each. The others demanded separate hearings, and the court had to prepare 283 new charge sheets. The trial threatened to extend over several weeks, and the employers, needing experienced labour, entered into negotiations with the ACDWU. Pending a Wage Board sitting, the employers agreed to a minimum monthly wage of £4 2s 6d for adults and £2 for juveniles. Workers already earning more than these amounts were to receive an extra 2s 6d. Sunday work was to be paid at 4s above the going rate. The Department of Justice was notified of the settlement and agreed to release the men with a caution if they pleaded guilty. The Wage Board sat again, and proposed a minimum wage of 25s per week for a 52-hour week; juveniles to receive 16s 8d. Shortly thereafter, the Secretary of Justice instructed police not to arrest or prosecute Africans on strike until the matter was reported to the Departments of Labour and of Native Affairs, and until workers' representatives had been given an opportunity to settle the dispute.

Though the ACDWU protested against the new determination, there was jubilation in the committees of African trade unions. Despite a criticism in *Forward* detecting 'poor organisation', and a 'bad settlement', the workers had won an increase after striking, and the instruction to the police gave unions greater scope for organising and bargaining. The Minister of Labour also barred the future use of convicts as scabs.[9] The government concessions came at a time when the Allied forces had suffered heavy losses in all spheres of the war, and when several pro-German groups were particularly active and required constant surveillance. The government needed industrial peace and had few police to spare. Only at the end of 1942, when the tide of war had turned, and the government regained its confidence, were measures taken to curb the unions: it was at this time that strikes were declared illegal under War Measure 145. The ACDWU capitalised on their victory, and recruited members throughout the Rand and the country districts of the southern Transvaal. Demands were made for a general increase in wages in all commercial firms and a campaign was conducted in the coal yards to gain further improvements.

In September 1942 white workers were in dispute with the O.K. Bazaar, one of Johannesburg's largest department stores, over the recognition of union committees. At the time the ACDWU had asked the NUDW to make representations on its behalf at the Industrial Council, and when a strike was called at the O.K. 400 Africans came out with the 600 white employees. There were scuffles with the police as leading unionists were arrested, but management capitulated after one day and agreed to a closed shop in the store.[10] Koza wrote enthusiastically that:

> real history was made when black and white workers of the O.K. stood side by side for a common cause and succeeded. It should be a lesson to other workers, proving that joint action between black and white workers is possible (*Guardian*, 1 October 1942).

The NUDW arranged for Koza to present the Africans' case to the Industrial Council: as a result, minimum wages were raised to 37*s* 6*d* per week in April 1943, with 42*s* 6*d* to 47*s* for packers and 'sample boys', in Johannesburg, Pretoria and the Reef. This success was described by the *Guardian* as 'a tribute to the consistent work of one of the largest established of African trade unions' (14 March 1943).

The Department of Labour, maintaining that Africans were not covered by the Industrial Conciliation Act, would not ratify the new agreement. The Minister also said he was not satisfied that the ACDWU was fully representative of the workers! But this was doubletalk. The truth was that the government had decided wage increases were inflationary and pegged wages at their 1943 level throughout the country. Koza was able to secure just one more wage determination, which raised wages to 35*s* per week in the trade. Only in 1952 was this again raised by 1*s*, still lower than the negotiated minimum of 1943.

The ACDWU still had a problem at the coal yards. The workers threatened strike action on several occasions: when 'ringleaders' were dismissed; and when Koza and his assistant A. Matau were arrested at the instigation of the employers. In October 1942, after another threat of action, the employers agreed to the closed shop and the setting up of disputes committees: but there was no concession on the issue of wages (*Guardian*, 22, 29 October). In June 1944 over a thousand workers on the Witwatersrand walked out to press a demand for higher wages, stopping all coal deliveries except those to hospitals and charitable institutions. When Koza and Matau were arrested, 733 workers, headed by some 80 women, marched to the Marshall Square police station where they were being held. There they demanded arrest, stating that they would not return to work, and would accept no bail, until their leaders were released. They also demanded the appointment of an arbitrator to ensure that drivers and farriers got their wage increase. This had been included in the wage determination of January 1944, but the employers formed subsidiary companies to evade payment.

After meeting the acting secretary of the SATALC, the employers agreed to re-employ all workers without victimisation, and to include the drivers and farriers in arbitration. The workers were released after a week in jail and went back to the coal yards. When the state proceeded with charges, a panel of thirty attorneys and advocates was briefed for the defence. On the first day 122 men were discharged, but were subpoenaed to return the next day for the defence. On the second day the prosecution, confronted by court officials who could not cope with the collection, sorting and feeding of over 600 accused, and by impatient employers who faced the collapse of their businesses, closed the case without presenting any evidence. The case against Koza and Matau was set down for a later date, then withdrawn (*Guardian*, 29 June, 6 July, 21 September 1944).

Wage increases, backdated to 1 July, were gazetted for the coal yards in August, giving adult labourers 32s 6d to 35s per week, and juveniles 26s. A 46-hour week was decreed, with an extra two hours during winter months for delivery men. Overtime pay was set at one and a third, except for night watchmen. The ACDWU had secured an almost uniform wage for all its workers and this, together with a 5s wartime cost of living allowance, made its members the highest paid unskilled men in the Transvaal. Yet, according to the Commission on Bus Services (1944, p.17) the estimated essential minimum expenditure for a family of five in 1944 was £12 18s 6d per month. In other words, even these workers had a monthly shortfall of at least £4, if they were to live at subsistence level.

The account of the coal workers' struggle, important in demonstrating Koza's willingness to fight — and the loyalty he could expect from the workers — has moved the story through to 1944. But there was considerable activity at a number of levels in the trade union movement. The internment of Gordon weakened the organisation of all the unions grouped together in the Joint Committee, and finances were in a parlous state. In order to place the unions on a sounder footing and to provide means for improved organisation, sympathisers of the nascent unions urged their unity and centralisation. Once again the Institute of Race Relations sought the assistance of Gordon, and it was through his efforts that some unification was achieved. But Gordon could not have managed without the acquiescence of Makabeni on the one side and Koza on the other. In the process all the unions were brought together and seemed to speak with one voice although, in effect, the 'unity' only helped conceal differences that were unbridgeable (particularly under war conditions): the Council that was formed was soon irretrievably split. Yet, with all its flaws, this Council played a critical role in the subsequent history of the unions. Its formation and development must be considered at this point.

The Council of Non-European Trade Unions

The trade unions organised by Purdy, Lee, and then Gordon sought support from the SAIRR and the Friends of Africa for financial assistance, legal aid, and in preparing evidence for Wage Board inquiries. Affiliation to the SATALC was prompted by the need to win support for the workers in strike action, but it also rested on the belief in working class unity across the colour line — a belief to which the left clung, even though ultimately the black working class needed its own trade unions and its own federation.

In 1938 members of the Joint and Co-ordinating Committees discussed unity, but talks broke down ostensibly over a resolution barring whites from office in the black trade union movement (Simons and Simons, 1969, p.511). Gana Makabeni, who is quoted as saying the following year that white leaders were not needed in black movements, was an embittered man following his expulsion from the CPSA in 1931, but it is not certain whether his statement was aimed at Gordon because he was white, or because of his Trotskyism, which was anathema even to those expelled from the CPSA. Ultimately the state removed Gordon, but that did not lead to new unity talks.

The Joint Committee continued under the leadership of Koza and Gosani, maintaining a militant stance. In October 1941, in evidence before a government commission, they stated that workers did not easily resort to strikes but were forced into such action to improve their working conditions. This was a tragedy, but South Africa must sooner or later experience

> industrial upheaval unprecedented in its history, unless a change in the laws governing labour in the country is immediately effected. The events of recent years show that even where the workers are not organised, spontaneous strikes are taking place. . . . The Government has always taken up the attitude that once workers broke their contract of service by going out on strike, they are immediately arrested and sent to gaol. But, let it be understood, that very soon there will be insufficient gaols and these restrictive laws will prove a failure.[11]

The memorandum recommended that African unions get the same recognition under the Industrial Conciliation Act as 'the unions of other workers', and also associated the Committee's standpoint with that of the ANC.

Gordon was released from internment in June 1941 and, after negotiations, was given permission to work inside the trade unions. Unable to work with Koza, he found a haven in the Dairy Workers Union, led by Jacob Thipe, who broke with the Joint Committee after the confrontation with Jones and Saffery. At the prompting of the SAIRR new attempts were made to unite the African unions. On 20 November 1941 Gordon and Thipe met with Makabeni and W.A.R. Mokoena of the Meat Workers Union.[12] They made four demands in the name of their 5,000 workers:

1. African agents to deal with complaints on Industrial Councils.
2. The speedier operation of Wage Boards, and rejection of the Boards' stress on the industry's payability in assessing wage levels.
3. Basic wages to be calculated on a national basis.
4. Equal pay for equal work, provided that wages 'were not raised to artificial standards' (skilled rates of pay were criticised as being 'uneconomically high', and it was urged that they 'be brought down').

The first three demands reaffirmed the policy of working through state machinery, but the fourth took no account of then current debates. It was not the task of trade unions to attack 'uneconomically high' wages, but to break the industrial colour bar: Kotane, at a conference of the CPSA in 1938–39, had condemned the demand for 'equal pay for equal work' as a misuse of socialist doctrine which hampered unity between black and white. He argued that 'the only way for [blacks] to acquire skills is to undercut the European workers' standards' (Bunting, 1975, p.92). This was rejected and conference called for equal bargaining rights for Africans, though at the CPSA conference in 1940 Sam Kahn said that:

> the slogan 'equal pay for equal work' is not enough without saying that there must be work for which Non-Europeans can get equal pay. We suffer from white chauvinism without realising it, and we can only combat this influence by developing our understanding of the national question (CAMP, Reel 3A, 2:CC1:32).

On 29 November 1941, just nine days after the Gordon–Makabeni meeting, the All-in Conference of All African and Coloured Trade Unions met. The growth of CPSA influence since the launching of the AMWU in August was marked by the presiding role of Kotane, secretary of the CPSA. The CNETU was established, with Makabeni as president and Gosani as secretary. The main resolutions, which indicated that no militant action was contemplated, included:

1. A strong request to the government to include Africans under the provisions of the Industrial Conciliation Act.
2. A request to the government that the wartime cost of living allowance be given to all workers, including mine, agricultural and domestic workers.
3. A request for legislation for a minimum wage of £2 per week for all unskilled workers.[13]

The pre-existing federal bodies were dissolved and a commission, including E.S. Sachs and Dr Xuma, set up to eliminate duplicate unions. Beyond this, however, there is little indication of any activity by the CNETU.[14]

In February 1942 the Wage Board delivered its report on conditions in 34 industries in Johannesburg and Pretoria and recommended a minimum wage of 25s per week, an improvement for some workers, but well below the estimated poverty datum line of 37s 6d per week. The CNETU seemed to do nothing, and it was another six months before the CPSA responded.

> As you are aware, the Wage Board has . . . recommended . . . the scandalously low wage of 25s per week. There are reactionary forces, such as unscrupulous employers and the Johannesburg City Council, which have actually objected to even this mean and grudging recommendation as being 'too much'.
> In view of the extreme urgency . . . a representative Emergency Committee, consisting of members of all sections of the Labour and Progressive movement has been set up in Johannesburg [to raise] . . . mass pressure for the improvement of the wages of unskilled workers. It is proposed to launch upon an immediate whirlwind campaign to educate and bring home to the public the urgent necessity of securing a decent minimum wage, to arouse morale on the home front (*sic*) as a major contribution to victory in the great struggle in which we are engaged.[15]

The 'whirlwind campaign' to 'educate the public' was ill conceived, and collapsed. The white 'public' showed little interest, and black workers needed no rousing on 'the urgent necessity of securing a decent minimum wage'. Since 1941 they had been striking to secure that 'decent minimum wage', and needed no 'educating' on the issue — unless, that is, strikes were contrary to the arousal of 'morale on the home front'!

Throughout 1941–42 the number of black workers involved in strike action gathered pace: some 5,000 in 35 strikes in 1941, 12,800 in 58 strikes in 1942 — and to this must be added those disputes in which the employers conceded their workers' demands, and strikes averted by Department of Labour intervention. The main issue was wages, but there were also complaints over working conditions, overtime pay, reinstatement of victimised workers and the recognition of trade unions. There were also protests over the February wage determination — but at two different levels. For workers who would benefit, the delay in raising wages led to strikes, and a clash in Marabastad with troops; protests by others against the miserly rate of 25s increased the volume of strike action considerably in December 1942.

The first annual conference of the CNETU met on 20–21 February 1943. In the light of the strikes, War Measure 145, and the recent shooting in Marabastad, the agenda seems largely irrelevant:

The ACDWU called for recognition under the IC Act; for collaboration with the ANC; and for the full franchise.

The Mine Workers Union wanted a trades hall built for black workers, with offices for the unions.

The General Workers Union wanted a minimum wage of £2 per week; a new Wage Board, with an African member; a national Non-European trade union movement; and 'disciplinary action against . . . Trade Unions that continue to have European advisers'.[16]

The Iron and Steel and Metal Workers Union wanted all unions affiliated to the SATALC, to achieve closer cooperation with the white unions.

The Tin Workers Union called on the government to press the Allied War Council to open the second front in Europe.

Other resolutions called for the treatment of African soldiers on the same basis as whites; for free schooling for all African youth; and for an end to discriminatory industrial legislation.[17]

The right to strike

There were several gatherings at the end of 1943 at which problems of the trade union movement were discussed. On Sunday 10 October members of the SAIRR, Friends of Africa, the CNETU and a parallel Pretoria Council attended a conference on the recognition of African trade unions. There were few new ideas until E.S. Sachs rose to condemn any campaign for recognition of the unions under the IC Act. He claimed that success might be a political victory, but the Act had 'killed' the white unions. The correct tactic was to 'fight for the right of collective bargaining', otherwise black workers might find the Department of Labour even worse than that of Native Affairs. This view was rejected, and only Koza declared that he would rather maintain the status quo than have African trade unions become sections of the white trade unions.[18]

The next CNETU conference, meeting on 27–28 November, did not offer any new perspectives. Shortly afterwards, in December, the newly revived All African Convention held a meeting. It was on this platform that Koza, appearing as a delegate of the Fourth International of South Africa (FIOSA), presented his new appraisal of trade union tasks. Africans had to organise their own unions, he said, because unskilled workers had no other means of making claims, but 'Africans were not asking for recognition as a racial unit, because that would be suicidal'. Requests for 'special laws' for African workers could only be divisive and play into the hands of the employers. He also reformulated his policy on trade union recognition: this was adopted by the Progressive Trade Union Group (PTU) in the coming years, and was to become its hallmark:

> We do not want recognition under the NAD [Native Affairs Department] because in any case we are committed to a policy of full recognition with a legal right to strike with no restrictions whatsoever (such as the Industrial Conciliation Act contains even for the white workers) (*Inkundla ya Bantu*, 30 December 1943).

Koza asserted the right of Africans to strike during the war years and rejected the IC Act because of the further restrictions it added to wartime regulations. He led his own union on strikes when necessary, and was soon confronted by the need to intervene in the strike called by the milling workers when their wage agreement expired in May 1944.

Unskilled workers in the milling industry received 13s to 15s in the smaller towns, and 27s 8d for a 50- to 60-hour week in the larger towns. In line with CNETU policy, the African Milling Workers Union asked for £2 per week. The Department of Labour intervened and instructed the union to appear before the Industrial Conciliation Board. After several postponements, the union was informed in August that it could not be heard because it was not recognised under the IC Act. There was no reply to an application for an arbitrator.

Thus, after a mass meeting at the Bantu Sports Ground addressed by Makabeni and S. Molefi (the union's secretary), 2,000 workers decided to stop work on 11 September. They stayed out for ten days.[19] To circumvent the ban on strikes, the Milling Workers Union left the direction of the action to an ad hoc group of union officials, referred to as the 'General Staff'. Employers met representatives of the union and the CNETU on the first day of the stoppage, and promised to reply to the workers' demands, but there was no further meeting. Instead, scab labour was drafted into the mills. Picketing led to the arrest of some 600 workers under the provisions of Proclamation 201 of 1939, which prohibited gatherings of more than 20 persons. The secretary of the Non-European Railways and Harbours Union, L. Molapo, and E. Mokwena of the Office Workers Union were arrested under the Riotous Assemblies Act for inciting workers to picket.[20] Eventually 17 workers and the two union officials were charged with public violence. All were fined (*Guardian,* 21 September 1944). The intervention by the Labour Department, before the strike, was condemned by the advocate C.V. Berrange in court as 'deliberately delaying tactics for the purpose of provoking a strike' (ibid., 2 November 1944). Some trade unionists recognised in these tactics the hardening of government attitudes against further wage increases,[21] and members of the 'General Staff' claimed that only a general strike could stop the government's offensive.

In the closing days of the milling workers' strike Molefi sought the assistance of the Workers International League (WIL), of which he was nominally a member, and obtained a pledge of support for the enlargement of the strike action. Although this was fanciful, because there were neither the resources nor the support for such action, the suggestion sent a ripple of alarm through the SATALC and the CNETU. The 'General Staff' was vilified as a 'Trotskyist organisation' and attacked by Makabeni. Ronnie Fleet, a member of the CPSA and secretary of the Johannesburg Local Committee of the SATALC, maintained that the Trotskyists

> had even a so-called general staff meeting in the offices of the non-European Trade Union Council at which, if it had not been for the intervention of the local committee, the possibility existed of a general strike of the African unions taking place (SATALC, Minutes of Committee, 21 September 1944).

As the position of the milling workers became increasingly difficult, a delegation of the union, with advisers from the WIL and the CNETU, met the employers (*Socialist Action,* May 1945). An agreement provided for 70 per cent of the workers to return immediately, the rest to be reabsorbed within three weeks as the work normalised. The employers agreed to stop any further action against the pickets and to consider an increase of wages based on the arbitrator's award for the rest of the Reef.[22] Small interim increases of 2*s* per week were made and a new category of semi-skilled work, affecting mainly Coloured and Indian workers, was recognised.

The workers were saved from victimisation but the union had suffered a defeat. The 'General Staff' maintained that the strike showed the trade union movement was in disarray. 'The salvation of the workers lies in a strong, powerful council', said the 'General Staff' and, transforming itself into the Progressive Group of Trade Unions (PTU), it called for the removal of the leaders of the CNETU.[23] The PTU invited African organisations to an 'All Embracing Emergency Conference' on 23 September to discuss the strike, the use of scab labour, and the effects of Proclamation 201. The working class of South Africa, declared the PTU, was dissatisfied: this was shown by the number of strikes in industry and struggles in the townships.[24]

The conference never took place. The CNETU warned that attendance would be a 'breach of Council policy' and would lead to expulsion. At this stage a number of trade union officials left the PTU. Those remaining constituted themselves as a caucus within the CNETU, with Albert Segwai as secretary. Koza, who had not been involved in the 'General Staff', now moved closer to the PTU and became its effective leader until its demise in 1946. The WIL continued its association with the body, and its members were involved in organising some of the PTU's constituent unions.

In its leaflet the PTU complained about the influence wielded by Makabeni and his allies in the CNETU, claiming that they were used by 'semi-government bodies' to discipline the working class and citing the CNETU's role in breaking the strike of the VFP workers (see Chapter 13). Nonetheless, many of the 'progressive' union leaders were little different from those they criticised. Corruption had spread throughout the ranks of union officials, and Segwai's activities in the Domestic Workers Union hardly qualified him as a leader of democratic or radical trade unionism.

The policies of the PTU diverged increasingly from those of the CNETU. Initially the PTU (and the WIL) called for the recognition of trade unions under the IC Act, but following Koza's lead they demanded unconditional recognition. They also called for a £3 a week minimum wage, stating that no family could subsist on less. This proved to be contentious, although it was a realistic campaigning demand, particularly as some workers earned more than the £2 which the CNETU demanded. The WIL maintained that no trade union official should be paid more than the union was demanding: this would help eliminate corruption and enhance union democracy. The PTU argued for a campaign to back these demands and called on the CNETU to launch a mass recruitment to build the unions. The PTU was dismissed as a 'Trotskyist' front, however, and accused of being 'wreckers', 'fifth columnists' and so on: the demand for £3 was adventuristic, as was the demand for unconditional recognition. A report in the *Guardian* (2 November 1941) reflects the position at the time: a delegation of fifteen was elected at an ANC meeting to see the Minister of Justice to request the lifting of the ban on public meetings; at the meeting, said the writer, 'The Trotskyist, Koza, offered to lead "thousands tomorrow in passive action" but was howled down by the meeting.'

The delegation achieved nothing and the ban remained. The CNETU passed resolutions; the ANC sent a delegation; but the call for a determined campaign was howled down, and the *Guardian* approved. Before the year was out the residents of Alexandra asked the CNETU to call a stay-at-home until bus fares were reduced. The Council asked for a deferment until the new year, but the threat of a strike secured a fare reduction and in January 1945 the residents of Alexandra rode at the old fare. Once again the CNETU avoided taking action, thus failing to link the struggles in the townships with those of the workplace (see Chapter 11).

Notes

1. See, e.g., Dikobe, 1973, pp.47–9 for a description of milk deliveries; Mokgatle, Chs 22–3 for deliveries of meat and other parcels, and general duties involving errands, cleaning and tea making; Modisane, pp.82–6 for

shelving and deliveries in a book shop.
2. Report by W. Ballinger to the SAIRR in his letter of 20 April 1937. This issue is not raised in Herd and the reason for this exclusion remains unexplained, but it can be assumed that there was a mix of legal considerations and race prejudice.
3. See, e.g., ACDWU resolution to the SATALC Conference on the Second Front, opposing such action because it could only lead to the suppression of the workers' revolution. Quoted in *Inkululeko*, 11 April 1943.
4. Resolution of ACDWU at first National Conference of the CNETU, Carter and Karis, *South African Political Materials*, CAMP, Reel 13b, 2:LC1:30.
5. Letter to Dr Xuma, 16 February 1936, *Xuma Papers*, ABX 360216. The College is described by Peter Abrahams, 1954, pp.163–70. See also M.C. Williams (n.d.).
6. Abrahams does not discuss his association with the Johannesburg group in his autobiography, but writes of his intimacy with some of its members. His membership was mentioned in an interview with Nathan Adler, London, 1978.
7. Koza anticipated the collapse of the trade union movement, and studied part-time at the University of the Witwatersrand. He then proceeded to London but was unhappy and returned home. He was an ill man and did not return to political life.
8. Coal was used in the white suburbs for cooking and heating: supplies were delivered at the door. In the townships most cooking was done on braziers (leading to the early morning smog). The coal was obtained through the local stores. Reports on the strike differ in details, but the central features are agreed. This account is compiled from *Guardian*, 21 May 1941; *Forward*, 23 May 1941; *Race Relations News*, Vol. 3, No. 7, July 1941; Report of Friends of Africa, October 1940–June 1941; and the report of Koza to 12th Annual Conference, SATALC, 6–10 April 1941.
9. *Forward*, 23 May 1941; *Guardian*, 5 June 1941. Strikers were arrested again after December 1942; Rheinallt Jones wrote to the Minister of Justice on 7 December 1942, reminded him of the instruction of 1941, and complained about the recent arrests, *Rheinallt Jones Papers*.
10. Herd fails to mention the solidarity shown by the ACDWU in the strike. See *Guardian*, 17 September 1942.
11. Memorandum of Joint Committee of African Trade Unions to the Commission of Inquiry on the Economic, Social, Health, and Educational Conditions of Natives, October 1941. Signed by D. Gosani, Secretary, and D. Koza, Chairman. Hemson film. See also *Xuma Papers*, ABX 411031b.
12. There is little information on Thipe. At some stage he was accused of taking money from the Dairy Workers Union and forced to resign. He went to Pretoria and appears to have worked in the unions there. He died in the early 1940s. Mokoena, also accused of taking money from his union, was forced to resign shortly after this meeting.
13. Copy of resolutions sent by Gosani to Rheinallt Jones, December 1941, *Rheinallt Jones Papers*, Johannesburg. Roux, 1949, p.340, and Simons and Simons, 1969, p.556, mistakenly give the date as November 1942. The Simonses then state that Madeley (who opened the 1941 conference) betrayed confidences by promulgating War Measure 145 in December 1942. Without wishing to exonerate Madeley, the events are separated by over a

year, during which time much had happened, and the error gives a wrong impression.

14. Letter from Gosani to Xuma, 26 January 1942; and letter from Sachs to Xuma, 17 June 1942, Hemson film. Other members of the commission were Julius Lewin, George Carr (a Coloured teacher, and member of the CPSA), and Miss Msomi.

15. Letter to Xuma, dated 11 September 1942, inviting him to join the committee, signed by Gosani and Harmel (*Xuma Papers*, ABX 420911a). A second circular letter of the same date excludes all reference to morale on the home front or the great struggle (ABX 420911b).

16. Although it is possible to understand black trade unionists who wanted to be free of constraints in their activities, the resolution calling for an end to white advisers was incomprehensible while trade unionists co-operated with the SAIRR, the Bantu Trust (for donations), and with officials of the Department of Native Affairs. (See Chapter 13 for collaboration with these officials, in persuading power workers to go back to work.)

17. For the agenda and resolutions, see Hemson film; for report on the conference, see *Guardian*, 4 March 1943.

18. A report of this conference is in the *Ballinger Papers*, University of Cape Town. Those present included trade union officials; R.V. Selope Theme; J. Lewin, Rheinallt Jones; E.S. Sachs and Mike Muller (the only white trade unionists); and W.G. Ballinger, Self Mampuru and Mrs E.M. Binyon of the Friends of Africa.

19. *Inkululeko*, 23 September 1944 (with a report on the negotiations by Makabeni and Gosani); *Guardian*, 14 and 21 September 1944. See also statement by S. Molefi in *Progressive Trade Union Bulletin*, Vol. 1, No. 1, February 1945. (I have corrected those figures that are obviously typing errors.)

20. *Inkululeko*, 23 September 1944. See my account of the 'General Staff', *Internal Bulletin*, Workers International League, Vol. 1, No. 7, February 1946, CAMP, Reel 7b, 2:DW2:85/1.

21. *Inkululeko*, 23 September 1944, wrote of 'The gravest alarm . . . at what appears to be a concerted Government offensive against the trade union movement, and against African trade unions in particular.' The writer said it was 'not the policy of the CNETU to embarrass the Government's war policy . . . and officials have endeavoured to avoid strike action'.

22. *Guardian*, 18 January 1945, reported that milling workers were given increases to 30s–35s per week everywhere except where they were on strike.

23. 'The progressive group speaks', copy appended to 'Report on the split in the African trade union movement [1947]'. Thanks to Mark Stein for this document.

24. CAMP, Reel 13b, 2:LC1/1:47. The invitation was signed by A. Segwai, N. Calvert and J.C. Maoba, none of whom belonged to the WIL.

9. Organising Under War Conditions

Yours for the union

There were moments in the histories of the war-time unions that illustrated graphically their rise, struggles and demise. In selecting such moments as illustrative I have exercised a certain arbitrariness but they do nonetheless reveal the enthusiasm, courage and weakness of the workers; they show how their struggles provoked a counter-offensive from the employers and the state in which lives were lost. Indeed, the events at Marabastad in Pretoria became a symbol of worker oppression in South Africa, eclipsed at a later date by the shooting at Sharpeville. In developing this chapter I have drawn on the letters of William Bosiame, a phrase in one of which provides the heading of this section and the title of this book.

'How to get higher wages'

Before Lynn Saffery resigned his post in the Institute of Race Relations in June 1942 he addressed its Council and called for greater participation in the African unions:

> There are . . . supporters of the Institute who feel that the time has come . . . to give even more direct help, not only to the existing unions, but to organisations and individuals who are attempting to found and build new ones. It is generally recognised that the question of higher wages for unskilled workers is one of the major problems to be faced today. Inadequate housing, problems of delinquency, malnutrition, and disease amongst the Non-European people, are all directly traceable to low wages. . . . (*Race Relations News*, July 1941).

Saffery argued that there was 'no difference in principle between initiating clinics . . . and forming trade unions which will be instrumental in raising wages and thereby preventing people from getting sick'. Consequently, the Institute should become more involved in trade union work than hitherto. The Council rejected this call, but subsequently established a Southern African Committee on Industrial Relations with plans for training African organisers (Memo, RR 62/42, 17 April 1942). The SAIRR also published a practical manual on trade unions, written by Saffery (1941), entitled (perhaps misleadingly) *How to Get Higher Wages*. Not to be outdone, the CPSA published its manual, *More Money*, and the CNETU issued a leaflet, *Road to Higher Wages — Better Conditions*. All these publications explained the working of trade unions, provided instructions on how a union was organised, and discussed the procedures employed by unions in securing higher wages through negotiations with the employers.[1] Saffery's booklet was published first, and seems to have been the most successful. Besides discussing the structure of the union, Saffery explained how representations were made to employers and how evidence was given to Wage Boards. He also stated that ultimately workers could use the strike weapon, despite its illegality, in order to achieve their aims. Saffery provided a list of unions, explained why subscriptions were necessary (citing the failure of the ICU), gave figures of back pay secured by unions for workers, and listed other functions performed by trade union officials.[2]

Letters arrived at the Institute from villages and towns throughout South Africa (for examples, see *Rheinallt Jones Papers*). Some asked for information about the Wage Boards, others asked about trade unions. All were concerned about wages, and all hoped to find the solution at the SAIRR.

Phillip L. Mokhatla wrote from Mafeteng on 3 February 1944:

> Will you please do me a favour and give me address of Wage's Board. I think it is Native Wages Board. A Board which helps the Native people who are discharged from their services or jobs so cruelly without even given monthly notice, a Board or Council which helps natives from being paid small salaries, a Board or Council which compels his Employer to pay his native employee, his arrears after investigation realises that such a native has been treated unfairly by his Employer.

Jacks E. Ngwenya, a teacher at Oranjeville, wrote on 15 June 1943 that labourers at the nearby airfield had given him the pamphlet, and asked to have it explained to them because they wished to join the workers' union:

> I am writing to you, Sir, for an advice for when I get to explain the pamphlet to them I must get them together & might be to the eyes of the employers that will not be appreciated or perhaps having them together I will be contravening some law. I personally would like to be a member if only I could get the fullest details of the organisation. . . .
>
> Your pamphlet spoke the truth to my understanding and I only wish your organisation does not fade away like the ICU as it has done, you have said something about it in the pamphlet. . . .

Other letters were written in similar vein. J. Alfred Ncaca (organiser) at Cradock said (17 August 1943) he had started a union without consultation, and intended 'to take up Legal Aid'. He asked for assistance; and A.S. Mobita from Witbank wrote enthusiastically in April 1942 about Saffery's booklet, wanting information on fees and the union's address. He said he and several others had once joined 'at a certain man in the location here', and paid 1s.6d joining fees, but could get no information from him and were angry.

The 31 workers of Oliphantshoek

In June 1944 Willie Bosiame wrote to the SAIRR from the Irrigation Department, Oliphantshoek, Kuruman, requesting copies of Julius Lewin's *Africans and the Police* and Saffery's booklet. A postal order was enclosed and the note ended with the question: 'My dear sir can a trade union work in Kuruman district?'

Oliphantshoek was a village adjoining a new irrigation scheme in the northern Cape, possessing at most a few shops. Quintin Whyte, replying for the Director, assumed that the letter was about agricultural labourers, and warned that it was difficult to organise and almost impossible to sustain such a union. He nevertheless asked for more information about the workers, their occupations and their (registration) numbers.

Bosiame replied on 30 July:

> First I drop great apologies for delaying with your reply, Sir. I have received your letter [?] 16/6/44 had give me a pleasure to hear all the news. But I am really sorry. We are not large numbers we are small numbers. My dear sir I send you the names of all the men that want to form the Trade Union and their occupation, they have no number at work. We are 31 workers in that paper I send you. . . .

Appended was a list of 31 workers, their occupations and their pass numbers. The writer worked at the irrigation supply store; his brother Moses was the inspector of boring. Seven worked the government boring machines. One was a 'car boy' who drove for the doctor; three 'shop boys'; two municipal 'shop boys'; eight general workers; three 'yard boys'; one garage 'boy', and three boarding house labourers.

Once again Whyte wrote a discouraging letter, saying that the diversity of occupations made a trade union impossible. Instead, he asked, had they 'ever thought of forming a co-operative society for buying food and vegetables cheaply, on the local market if there is one?' Bosiame was evidently a patient man. He wrote back on 22 August, explaining as carefully as he could:

> Thanks for your dated 11/8/44, of which we gladly appreciated. So we again ask whether you cannot make us a union under one kind of work, As we all consider that this union will be of great help to us. It will be glad if you can try so.
>
> Your suggestion of forming a co-operative society is quite clear.
>
> But our minds are not in it because we haven't got a Local market and our Town is very small. We more or less look upon how to get higher wages we see great help in it. Awaiting on your favourable reply
>
> Yours faithfully
Willie Bosiame
for the Union

Whyte had erred in not stating that the SAIRR did not form unions, contrary to the impression given in the booklet, which Saffery had written when he still hoped to nudge the SAIRR towards such a policy. On 6 September, Whyte wrote that the correspondence was being handed over to Gosani, secretary of the CNETU, but on 3 October Bosiame complained that they had not yet heard from the Council.

On 7 October Gosani finally wrote, saying that the CNETU was discussing the feasibility of forming a General Unskilled Workers Union. Another letter was promised, but the matter probably ended there. The executive of the CNETU was dormant, and Gosani tendered his resignation a few months later after being accused of inactivity (*Socialist Action*, July 1945). There was no new General Workers Union and no drive to organise workers in the smaller towns.

After three years of ever widening workers' interest in trade unionism, the CNETU (which claimed a membership of 150,000, two thirds in Johannesburg) was beginning to disintegrate, its leaders now engaged in internecine struggle for control of the executive. The hopes of Willie Bosiame and his thirty workers would never be realised: and even if he had got his union, the time of general wage increases was over. It was this, predominantly, that led to the collapse of unions, since expansion had been so dependent on securing wage increases through government bodies. But even before wages were frozen, strikes were outlawed under War Measure 145 and, even more ominously, workers faced trigger-happy soldiers who shot to kill.[3]

Marabastad: the troops move in

Pretoria in the 1930s was a small provincial town, significant only because it was the administrative capital of the Union of South Africa. In January 1940 its total population was estimated as 77,800 whites and 42,700 blacks (mostly Africans). The largest single employer in the town was the state, followed by the provincial and municipal authorities. Whites monopolised the jobs in the civil service, the railways, and the state-owned ISCOR. Pretoria provided a market for the surrounding rural areas, a one-street commercial centre, and service workshops for local construction firms. There were few other industries of significance, and after Premier (diamond) Mines, one is left with a list of firms decreasing in size and significance: brickmaking, cement, glass, mineral waters and matches.

Although the African population of Pretoria was small, a number of its members had occupied leading positions in the ANC and the ICU. This was probably related to the presence of well-educated translators and clerks, who raised the level of discussion and debate among their confrères. H.L. Bud M'Belle, an interpreter of long standing in the Native Affairs Department, kept 'open house' in his centrally situated residence, and his frequent appearance before government commissions was undoubtedly a stimulus to discussions amongst his friends. Thomas Mbeki, also of Pretoria, was the first Transvaal secretary (and member of the National Executive) of the ICU, and this gave the union an early presence in the town. Like other branches, it had all but collapsed by the early 1930s, but seems to have maintained a presence through Ismael Moroe, who ran a branch of the ICU and spoke at meetings in Marabastad (Mokgatle, 1971, pp.221−2).

According to Max Gordon (Memo to Bantu Welfare Trust, 20 December 1938, *Saffery Papers*) the first branch of the Johannesburg unions was formed in early 1938 when some 200 workers joined the Laundry Workers Union and found an enthusiastic chairperson. Two years later, Naboth Mokgatle attended a meeting in Johannesburg to hear Gordon and his organisers announce the terms of the wage determination for commercial and distributive workers. After meeting Gordon, Mokgatle became part-time secretary of the ACDWU in Pretoria, working on a voluntary basis from his home in Marabastad.

Gordon was interned soon afterwards and Mokgatle states that in the ensuing turmoil the Johannesburg office did not answer his letters (pp.228–30). The workers became suspicious:

> A man who has paid his money always wants to know his fate. Doubts began to set in. Some suspected that I did not send on their complaints. To free myself from suspicion I had to write letters in their presence and let them post them . . . there was confusion. Complaints increased and stories began to circulate that my union was only interested in collecting money, not in the settlement of members grievances. I carried on. . . .

He was unable to carry on, however, even though Malesela Modibe, sent by the Joint Comittee to organise garage workers, assisted him in organising his branch.

Starting in August 1942 two competing trade union movements were built in Pretoria. The first was led by Mike Muller,[4] a young Afrikaner who had been influenced by Leo Marquard[5] in Bloemfontein and moved to the left. He went to Pretoria to study accountancy but left after a year to become a political organiser for the CPSA. Muller was pro-war and in 1944 became a fervent supporter of Browder, opposing strike action while hostilities continued.[6]

Ethel Binyon, who organised unions in opposition to the CPSA, had a different background. She had worked with her husband, warden of St Matthew's College in the eastern Cape, supervising the women students. Revd Calata was to say of the Binyons that they had been 'mother and father' to himself and his wife when he was a student (1914) and then a teacher (1915–20) at the college (CAMP, Reel 15a 2:XC3:94 and 91/1). After her husband's death (*c.* 1924) Mrs Binyon moved to Pretoria, served as secretary of the Pretoria District Non-European Health Service Association, and was a member of the Society of Women Missionaries, which issued a report on 'Initiation ceremonies for Native girls'. In 1936 she drove Calata through the northern Transvaal, a tour during which he sought to revive the ANC (ibid.). Listed on the Cape ANC letterhead as a patron, Mrs Binyon was a member of the Friends of Africa and, even more remarkably, was organising African trade unions by September 1943. These unions combined to form a Federated Association of African Trade Unions (FAATU) and Mrs Binyon hoped they would 'eliminate' the communists, whom she accused of fomenting strikes, and also remove Mike Muller, whom she referred to as her *bête noire*.[7]

Precisely what went on in the Pretoria trade unions remains to be unravelled. The Muller-Mokgatle (CPSA) group had 12–15 unions with 17,000 members by February 1943, and were united in a Pretoria Council with Muller as secretary. They joined with the Johannesburg unions to launch the Transvaal CNETU. In April 1943 the Pretoria unions organised a march of some 800 workers through the streets in a local 'campaign' for the recognition of African unions, but there are few indications of local union activity, and no news of strikes.

In September 1942 Muller started organising the Pretoria municipal workers. There were 17,000 municipal workers in the tramways, transport, cleansing, traffic and licensing departments on the Witwatersrand, and a further 4,000 in Pretoria. Their wages were 16s–18s per week, and the wage determination of February 1942 recommended that this be raised to a minimum of 25s. The Council of Reef Municipalities opposed the rise because 'this would impose a heavy burden on the finances of local authorities, already heavily burdened by wartime obligations'. They appealed to the Minister, and the increases were suspended until the next financial year. In November it was announced that the new minimum wage would be introduced from the 30th, but when the rise was not included in the first December pay packet, a one day strike was called in Johannesburg for 8 December. Some 2,000 workers came out, and the new wage was agreed. There were 400 members in the Pretoria Municipal Workers Union by November, and when their wage increase was not paid a meeting was called for 16 December. It was stopped by municipal police. On 21 December Muller, who obviously expected no trouble, went on vacation.

On 28 December the authorities called a meeting in the Marabastad municipal compound: for reasons never satisfactorily explained, troops were summoned and the compound sealed off. A soldier fired and killed one of his fellows, after which the troops shot wildly. Workers were crushed as they tried to escape. At the end of the day, sixteen men were dead and 111 were wounded.[8] An inquiry heard contradictory accounts of what happened, but witnesses agreed that the workers were addressed by two officials whose words were evasive and vague. Basner was told by the wounded in hospital that they were informed that the pay would be increased from November, but it was not made clear that this would be retrospective, and many understood the increase to be deferred. There was shouting and barracking, and then the troops appeared.

Marabastad became a symbol of government brutality. At the inquiry the CPSA was accused of being behind the unrest, although no evidence was produced to support this charge. Instead, observers either exonerated the Communist Party or claimed that the workers were 'so badly organised that no agitator . . . would have that influence on the Natives'.[9] Several spoke of dissatisfaction with the appalling conditions at Marabastad and Elias Gordin said that

> The location had been built in 1924 to accommodate 1,329 natives. Today the number had increased to 2,693. As far as I know there has been no attempt by the City Council to spend the £7,200 voted by it for improvements. . . .[10]

It was also stated that the accommodation in the compound was so cramped that 100 slept on the floor, and that 'the lack of air space was particularly marked'.

The inquiry was not given a satisfactory explanation for the calling of the meeting or the summoning of the troops. There was no explanation for the appearance of off-duty soldiers on the precincts; for the compound being sealed off; for shots fired at workers outside the compound; nor for the failure to give the workers their increased wages.[11] The commission blamed the Pretoria municipality for not implementing the wage determination. It found that tension had been exacerbated by living conditions in Marabastad and by the exclusion of Africans from any say in the management of affairs. Furthermore, 'the situation did not warrant the interference of a body of seventy-eight soldiers with firearms'. The report, in recommending that African trade unions be recognised, stated that 'misunderstanding' could have been avoided by communication through union structures.

Amongst those giving evidence at the Marabastad Inquiry was Jacob Modibe. He said he was secretary of FAATU to which 45 (*sic*) trade unions were affiliated, including a municipal workers' union with 200 members. His federation, he said, differed from 'another association' which only had fifteen affiliated unions.[12] This was the first public announcement of the existence of FAATU, and little was known then or subsequently about its activities.[13] Mrs Binyon opened an office and appointed 'agents' (*sic*) to organise the different trades. They were united under a Pretoria Council, and she looked forward to the establishment of a Johannesburg counterpart and 'a Transvaal Council overall'.

Accompanied by her 'protégés' (as she called them) Binyon visited employers and, she said, was accorded a good reception. In one letter to the Ballingers she reported that Labour Department officials would welcome the registration of African unions, because that would

> prevent such places as Boom Street [the CNETU offices] . . . which does not as it seems to me do anything but agitate the workers. We deal with Employers through constitutional methods — they do not!

This was a constant theme in Binyon's letters. She visited the Railway manager with Modibe, her main organiser, and asked for recognition of their union, which she thought would be granted. She also thought she knew why: 'The Communist Party try to get among the workers inciting them to demand higher wages — we go to the employer first. I explained this. . . .' She visited the Forestry Department, where officials told the men 'that Modibe spoke to them on the Department's behalf'; and then Iscor where, she reported, 'conditions . . . are good, with 6s per 8-hour shift, and very good food and quarters'. Binyon continued:

> Things are moving — largely thanks to the quiet steady work that you and William are doing — and the moment has come when we can usefully come out into the open, and *demand* I think. There is much to do. When we have done it, the Communists will point to it as *their* work! Their lack of straightforwardness does shock one. . . . They are a great help in strengthening the 'fascist' spirit in this country. . . .

On 1 March she wrote about the Marabastad inquiry, and of her work on the Riot Relief Fund Committee. Her tidings were that the unions had been accepted by the Railways, the Forestry Department and Iscor. In April,

Binyon again turned her scorn on the Communists:

> Too much is required of you both, but the 'Communists' ignore that you two are doing the work and make the illiterate [sic] Natives think *they* are! *Ugh!* Silly creatures, but the more intelligent (well behaved) Natives know better! Still I think more propaganda of William's work is needed among them.

W.G. Ballinger spent a weekend in Pretoria in May with the FAATU, advising 'on lines of negotiation to be pursued in respect of grievances among the workers'. The key to Ballinger's approach is contained in a letter written at the time. He wrote about 'complications'

> because of propaganda for recognition of trade unions rather than for recognition of Native workers as employees in terms of the [IC] Act. It is now getting complicated again by insistence on the right to strike when what we want is constitutional machinery to obviate the need for strikes.[14]

The Ballingers kept close contact with Pretoria: FAATU affiliated to the Pretoria branch of the Friends of Africa and Modibe was on the trade union subcommittee. Yet FAATU collapsed. In 1946 four unions in Pretoria (hotel and flat workers, milling workers, mineral water workers, and iron and steel workers) were listed as having premises in Vermeulen Street, and they seem to have been the remnants of the Federation.[15] If the authorities had toyed with the idea of recognising these unions, that time had passed, and organisers were no longer welcome at the railways, the forestry department and Iscor.

The irrepressible Mrs Binyon soon moved to new ground. She wrote to Mrs Ballinger on 12 July 1943 about 'native girls' who did not 'remain decent for long in town', and she hoped to establish hostels to stop servants living in back yard rooms. In that way the evil of venereal disease would be combated; but the solution, she thought, lay in the establishment of rural industries like weaving 'so that the parents could keep them at home under control'. The letter concluded: 'European policy has so messed up the Native people that one does not know how to tackle the huge problem that has been created.'

Splits and expulsions

At the end of 1943, the effects of state harassment were beginning to be felt. Some unions were still recruiting workers and even winning concessions for their members; but that was exceptional. Mokgatle, who became a full-time union official in August 1943, and was also secretary of the Pretoria branch of the Transvaal CNETU (TCNETU), records (p.245) that:

> It was hard for us all; some of us were lucky to get our wages regularly every month. The motto was sacrifice. Without it there would never have been African trade unions in existence. . . .

The difficulties faced by secretaries and organisers reflected the decline in membership and the resistance to recruitment. Workers would pay no subscriptions when the unions could secure no benefits; and the leaders had no alternative strategy to revive their organisation. Yet, if the letters of men like Willie Bosiame provide any indication, there was greater will and enthusiasm for organisation than the unions were ever able to tap.

The declining fortunes of the trade unions led to internal dissension and conflict over the best way to proceed. Both the CPSA and the ANC urged restraint over industrial action, although they differed amongst themselves over the ultimate role of the trade union movement. These fractions of the TCNETU nevertheless united to oppose the Workers International League, condemning it for being anti-war and for advocating strike action. Though the conflict between the CPSA and the ANC was papered over in the common front against the WIL, the strains became evident when Marks replaced Makabeni as president of the CNETU in April 1944. *Inkundla ya Bantu*, a pro-ANC paper, wrote in September of a 'vigorous tug-of-war between Dr Xuma and the communists for trade union support'. This was denied in *Inkululeko*, but the conflict became increasingly apparent and led ultimately to the split that destroyed the CNETU.[16]

When the African trade unions met in conference in April 1944 the first step was to isolate the PTU. The Progressives had neglected arrangements for proxy representation and were less effective than they might have been. Senator Basner, the guest speaker, started the attack. He quoted from his recent broadsheet, *Wreckers at Work*, saying that the WIL 'and their black supporters are a danger and a menace to the Africans'. By way of contrast he declared that 'the Africans in the last five years were loyal in not striking [*sic*], and in not upsetting the economy of the country'.[17] Makabeni, in his presidential report, condemned the Trotskyists for acting as provocateurs in the strikes and in Alexandra Township, and of ignoring the significant progress in African wages achieved 'by the bosses having to negotiate with the unions' (*Inkululeko*, 14 April 1944). The conference then accepted resolutions saluting the Red Army, welcoming the Yalta Conference, and calling for the removal of all oppressive legislation with the extension of democratic rights to blacks.

Two issues were extensively debated. The first was Koza's resolution that conference convene at an early date

> an emergency all-in Conference of Non-White trade unions in South Africa . . . to formulate policy on the recognition of trade unions [and] . . . on a National minimum wage legislation, and set up a 'Trade Union Centre', to give effect to this demand.

This resolution was adopted unanimously, but a second resolution calling on the trade unions to affiliate to the Non-European Unity Movement and accept its 10-point programme was rejected out of hand. The Conference then elected its office bearers. When it was announced that Marks had defeated Makabeni, and was the new president, the gathering closed in confusion (*Inyaniso*, May 1945). The all-in conference was called for August and all sides prepared for the clashes that were anticipated. Moses Kotane, full-time secretary of the CPSA, was to lead the Cape delegation even though he had no direct link with any trade union. The Pretoria unions from Boom Street were coming but the Natal African unions, which were opposed to the CPSA, do not seem to have been invited.

On 9 July 1945 Xuma wrote to members of his executive saying he had appointed Dan Tloome, who was close to Marks and Vice-President of the TCNETU, as secretary-bookkeeper to the ANC. Tloome's brief was to collect information on Congress membership, finances, branch and provincial activities, and bring local difficulties to the attention of the Executive (*Xuma Papers*, ABX 450709e). At some juncture he gave Xuma a memorandum analysing the interconnection of national and economic oppression of the African people. It was suggested that the task of the ANC was to 'foster a spirit of national consciousness', and 'take up the dual oppression as whole'. Congress should urge all Africans to join a union; monitor unions and combat their weaknesses; organise the training of union officials; and support workers on strike. Finally, migrant workers 'composed comparatively of raw country folk . . . suspicious of trade unionism' should be contacted in the Reserves and Protectorates by members of the ANC and prepared for organisation on the mines.[18]

It is not known whether Xuma had the memorandum when he prepared his address, but he did have a note from Gosani (1 August 1945) with the urgent message that the TCNETU was going through 'a period of crisis, because of the European elements who are interfering in our affairs' (Hemson film). The conference opened in Bloemfontein amidst tension. In the preceding week Makabeni had been involved in a fight with C.R. Phoffu, secretary of the Timber Workers Union and a leading member of the PTU. The dispute ended in Phoffu's hand being broken and was followed by a court action. It was claimed — and denied — that the court action was designed to secure Makabeni's absence from the conference. The two sides gave different accounts of what had occurred and Marks, who took the chair, 'condemned the insincerity and the spirit of rivalry shown by some leaders of the movement along the Rand'.[19]

Dr Xuma opened the conference with an exploration of the aims of African unions, the need for collective bargaining and the right to strike. The economy, he said, kept 'the Non-European worker in suppression for its continued existence', and that was 'a necessary corollary for the suppression of the Non-White'. The objective was to

> commence that struggle for a change of this economy for one that will enable all men regardless of colour to benefit equally from the equal contributions which they make to the country.[20]

In this struggle, said Xuma, the trade unions, teachers' organisations, businessmen and so on would have to co-operate with 'no competition and no antagonism'. He stressed the need for black self-reliance:

> First and foremost, the Non-European workers will have to rely on their own forces and on their ability as a class to carry out the fight for the removal of the iniquities imposed upon them by the employing and ruling classes [*sic*].

The theme of 'race pride' was emphasised:

No race that believes that salvation will come from outside its ranks or through outside leadership is worthy of man's estate. No race that expects others to think for it, that expects spoon-feeding by others, can deserve freedom or liberation. . . .

Xuma warned trade unions against division by political ideologies, or by political parties participating in their running. He spoke of the 'existence of dangerous elements' and condemned the 'mental weaklings' in the unions who 'do not believe in themselves [and] want to have bosses [*sic*] from outside even in leadership'. Such people were 'radio controlled robots . . . agents doing their master's work . . . and traitors to their race'. He hoped and believed, however, that there were none such at the conference. Dr Xuma made one other point: he attacked the SATALC for its failure to help African unions in their fight for recognition and the right of black workers to strike. Nevertheless, he said, a move to set up a national CNETU was premature and would destroy the unity of the conference. He then warned against

chasing ideological theoretical party rainbows . . . [because] it is of less importance to us whether capitalism is smashed or not. It is of greater importance to us that while capitalism exists we must fight and struggle to get our full share and benefit from the system.

It was an address that carried barbs for all but Xuma's closest supporters. His attack on whites had been directed mainly against the WIL, but it contained an implicit attack on the CPSA and a rebuke for those who had invited Basner to open the April conference; and his attack on 'theoretical party rainbows', coupled with his statement that it was 'less important whether capitalism is smashed or not', was an obvious attack on socialism. In this, Xuma undoubtedly condemned both the WIL and the CPSA, although it was the first group which seemed at the time to be the principal target. Edwin Mofutsanyana, who brought fraternal greetings from the CPSA, turned the criticism into a specific attack on the WIL. In a colourful display of invective he condemned 'dice-players, wreckers, disgruntled elements and irresponsibles', and conference got down to work.

The first issue, the recognition of African trade unions, split the conference wide open. Makabeni called for a national campaign for the recognition of African workers as employees under the IC Act, for closer relations between black and white workers, and to secure the support of the SATALC and all progressive organisations (*Friend*, 7 August). Hosea Jaffe, of the Fourth International Organisation of South Africa and the Electrical Workers Industrial Union, contributed an addendum (which was accepted) for the anti-strike clause to be removed from the IC Act, and for 'workers in all occupations [to] have the same rights under the Act'.

Koza moved an amendment for the PTU. He called for the repeal of the IC Act and the passing of new legislation to provide 'proper and efficient collective bargaining machinery along the lines of the National Labour Relations of the USA'. These guidelines gave workers the right to strike, made it mandatory for employers to bargain, outlawed company unions, and set up permanent wage boards. Members of the PTU argued that the IC Act was pernicious. It excluded agricultural and domestic workers, and any union the registrar rejected; it required all unions to disclose confidential information and stopped strikes in all 'essential services' (*Socialist Action*, August 1945). The amendment was lost by 77 votes to 45, and Koza rose to declare that although the PTU believed the decision to be wrong, they would not vote against the motion. Whatever form of recognition was agreed by conference would have to be implemented by a massive campaign, and the PTU pledged its full support (ibid.).

There were differences on other issues. The PTU demanded a national minimum wage of £3 per week, but conference only agreed to demand that sum for the major towns; the PTU call for a 'sliding scale' to ensure increases in line with inflation was flatly rejected. The issue of forming a national body, for which the conference had been convened, was postponed until the last session, and the motion was never put.

James Phillips, treasurer of the TCNETU and member of the CPSA, moved that a National Council be established. His central point was:

> We want the SATALC to become the mouthpiece of all workers in South Africa irrespective of race, colour or creed. So far they have failed, more especially as far as the Non-European is concerned. We want the SATALC to become a real militant workers' organisation. . . .
> By the creation of a national organisation . . . I believe we shall bring pressure to bear on the SATALC to recognise the part we play. We shall strengthen the movement which at present is split and divided (*Friend*, 7 August).

The communists were split; some supported Phillips while others followed the line formulated by H.A. Naidoo, member of the Central Committee of the CPSA, in an article (*Freedom*, December 1945) on the conference. He ridiculed the idea of a separate trade union council for blacks and said that a logical extension would be the formation of trade union bodies by other ethnic groups because of their common political interests. All trade unions should affiliate to the SATALC, despite the reactionary policy of the leadership, because there was sympathy for African demands from many white trade unionists. A policy of militancy inside that organisation could overcome the 'craft exclusiveness [which took] . . . the form of colour exclusiveness'. This viewpoint was endorsed by the CPSA at its next conference (*Freedom*, August–September 1946) and was still upheld by Ray Alexander in 1952 (*Discussion*, December 1952).

The PTU call for a national body was based on different grounds. Dick Mfili, who was reorganising the power workers after the collapse of their union, called for one central body capable of launching a massive drive to put many unions on their feet again, and to bring the unorganised workers into the ranks of efficiently run industrial unions. This was not a task the SATALC would undertake and, being urgent, it required a national body of African unions. A drafting and co-ordinating committee should be appointed, and a conference called within six months to consider a programme and constitution. Other PTU speakers argued that the unions had to be linked with the liberatory movement, and this could only be achieved by a separate trade union council (*Socialist Action*, August 1945). Despite differences of perspective or emphasis, the resolution for a national council had majority support. Those in opposition — including those who followed the official line of the CPSA — tried to prevent a vote, and at one stage most of the Cape Town delegates staged a walk-out. Finally, on the plea that delegates would miss their trains, the resolution was referred back to the TCNETU executive. There was confusion in the hall as delegates were forced to their feet by the singing of the anthem, *Nkosi Sikelele.*

One more scene remained to be played out. The Transvaal Council did not implement any of the conference decisions and there was no sign of any move, let alone a campaign, to set up a national body. The PTU therefore decided to organise 'call back' meetings of their unions to rally workers and inform them of events at the Bloemfontein conference. They were to take place in the market squares of Johannesburg, Vereeniging, Benoni and Pretoria. Some 7,000 workers responded to the first meeting on 19 August to hear reports on the call for a national minimum wage, the recognition of trade unions and the need for a National Council. The workers were enthusiastic, many staying to join one of the unions. There was also a rally at Vereeniging, and this broad mobilisation seemed to foreshadow a serious campaign to build the unions and achieve trade union recognition (*Socialist Action*, September 1945).

The euphoria was short-lived. Koza and Phoffu, the main movers, were summoned to a meeting of the executive of the CNETU and expelled. They were said to have accused Makabeni of misappropriating CNETU funds — a charge they denied; and to have held a factional meeting at Market Square, which was absurd. Unions required no 'permission' from the CNETU to hold meetings, and it seemed to members of the PTU that this was only an attempt to silence embarrassing opposition. The expulsions, however, had an effect. The PTU faltered and did not proceed with its plans. The malaise of the unions, of which it had warned at conference, weakened the whole movement — and a disastrous strike by the timber workers, for which there had been little preparation, destroyed Phoffu's credibility.

The Timber Workers Union had tried to negotiate an improved wage for the industry when the old agreement expired in October 1945. The employers, and in particular the Mine Timber Merchants Association, refused to increase the pay (26*s* plus 8*s* cost of living allowance per week) and the workers came out spontaneously on being told this news (7 October). After a compulsory cooling-off period of 30 days, 1,500 workers again took strike action, only to find that their officials had made no provision for the strike. The union seemed to hope that the Campaign for Rights and Justice would assist them, and rejected offers of help from the PTU. There was a state of confusion in the Timber Workers' office, and in the face of scab labour, mass arrests, and the failure of leadership, the workers went back in disarray.

The leaders of the union had failed miserably and inexcusably. Nonetheless, the defeat of the timber workers had become inevitable when the employers made no concessions, claiming that many of the workers were employed in agriculture and thus were not covered by wage agreements. They were backed by the government, who opposed wage increases, and by the mines, who foresaw rising costs if the price of timber rose (*Socialist Action*, October 1945, January 1946).

The leaders of the CNETU were delighted at the discomfort inside the ranks of the PTU, but in ignoring the fate of the workers they brought no credit to the trade union movement. They also unwittingly cleared the way for the events of July and August 1946, when the steel workers in Vereeniging and then the mine workers on the Rand came out on strike. Their defeat at the hands of the employers in alliance with the state led to the ignominious collapse of the trade union movement.

Notes

1. Some letters written in response to Saffery's booklet are available; similar replies to the CPSA or CNETU publications have not been found. See also the discussion on the booklet *More Money* in Chapter 7.
2. Many points made by Saffery were similar to those of Gordon in reports submitted to the SAIRR.
3. Alex Hepple (1984, pp.277—8) cites the case of armed police dispersing a meeting of iron and steel workers in December 1942 and threatening the same treatment as at Marabastad, discussed below.
4. Muller became a trade union organiser in August 1942; evidence given at Marabastad enquiry by Wilson Malagi (of ICU), reported in *Cape Times*, 7 January 1943. See also *Star*, 10 February 1943.
5. Leo Marquard, teacher and writer, was a member of the Joint Council of Europeans and Natives. He wrote *Black Man's Burden* (under the pseudonym John Burger), a book that had a profound effect on white liberals during the war.
6. See George Findlay's diary for those members, particularly in Pretoria, who supported Browder. Muller's opposition to strike action was reiterated at the Marabastad inquiry, *Inkululeko*, 23 January 1943.
7. Twenty-six letters concerning African trade unions in Pretoria were written by Ethel Binyon to Mrs Ballinger during 1943—4. *Ballinger Papers*, Johannesburg. On the elimination of the CPSA see letter of 27 January 1944; on her *bête noire*, letter of 1 March 1943.
8. Letter from H. Basner to the SATALC and to Xuma, *Xuma Papers*, ABX 421230c. Basner obtained these figures by visiting the hospital with Mampuru, and found them higher than those published in the press. Hepple, p.332, also quotes these higher figures.
9. Evidence of Elias Gordin, of Pretoria Joint Council of Europeans and Natives, quoted in *Star*, 5 January 1943.
10. Reported in *Cape Times*, 5 January 1943. See also evidence of Councillor C.W. Sinclair, reported in *Cape Times*, 20 February 1943, that conditions in the hostel were 'appalling and disgraceful'.
11. For evidence presented at the inquiry, see the *Star*, *Cape Times*, *Inkululeko* and *Guardian*. Evidence on the fatal shooting of Corporal Coetzee is

reported in *Cape Times*, 5 January 1943.

12. This was possibly the Malesela Modiba mentioned ·by Mokgatle above. It was said in an exchange of letters between the SAIRR and the Bishop of Pretoria of 26–27 September that one of the 'responsible members' of these unions had once been a member of the Johannesburg ACDWU. *Rheinallt Jones Papers*. Note that Muller said in evidence that there were twelve unions in Pretoria (*Star*, 9 February 1943).

13. It is doubtful whether many of these unions existed, and there are no indications that workers were ever involved in their functioning. Mokgatle, who worked in the rival trade unions, does not mention them.

14. Letter from M. Ballinger to Z.K. Matthews, 9 March 1943, *Matthews Papers*, Institute of Commonwealth Studies, Reel 2.

15. List of Pretoria unions, August 1946. The Boom Street office had closed, but seven of its one-time unions were listed at a Post Office Box number, and six other unions, with head offices in Johannesburg, were also noted. *Rheinallt Jones Papers*.

16. See Khanhyisa's assertions in *Inkundla ya Bantu*, 18 September 1944. The reply by Umlweli (M. Harmel) is in *Inkululeko*, 7 October 1944. The splintering of the CNETU is discussed in Chapter 14.

17. *Inyaniso*, No. 1, May 1945, CAMP Reel 18b, 2:VA1:85/1; *Inkululeko*, 14 April 1945. *Inyaniso*, which carried the fullest report of the conference, was the organ of the short-lived African Youth League, whose chair was Sam Thule, organiser for the AMWU; the secretary, and moving spirit, was Bethuel Samuel, or Bethuel Nguni.

18. Dan Tloome, 'The African National Congress and African trade unions' (n.d.), addressed to the President General, CAMP, Reel 1b, 3:DA14:89/7. Although Tloome's name is on the document, it is not certain that he wrote it.

19. Detailed reports of the conference appeared in *Socialist Action*, August 1945, written by delegates John Motau and Dick Mfili, and observers B.L[ewis] and B.H[irson]. The *Friend*, 6 and 7 August, reported each session, and carried much of Dr Xuma's opening address. Other reports appeared in *Inkululeko*, August and September 1945, and *Inkundla ya Bantu*, 31 August 1945.

20. All quotations from the address are from the text in the *Xuma Papers*, ABX 450801a. See also *Friend*, 6 August 1945.

10. Rural Protest and Rural Revolt

Urban organisations — rural constituents

Popular ideology . . . is not a purely internal affair and the sole property of a single class or group: that in itself distinguishes it from ideology as 'class consciousness'. . . . It is most often a mixture, a fusion of two elements, of which only one is the peculiar property of the 'popular' classes and the other is superimposed by a process of transmission and adoption from outside.
George Rudé

Ideology, said Rudé in his survey of popular protest, is composed of an 'inherent' element, 'a sort of "mother's milk" ideology' based on direct experience and oral tradition, and a 'derived' element based on structured ideas learnt from others. There was no *tabula rasa* or blank mind on which ideas could be grafted, he maintained, stressing the complexity of the ideas that informed people in their struggles. Ideas adopted by people to confront new problems were a dialectical mix of notions old and new, fused and adapted to meet emerging situations.

An investigation of struggles in South Africa shows that Rudé's analysis is pertinent, provided that it is not applied mechanically: there were times when people in all walks of life took giant steps forward in their comprehension of the difficulties they faced, and there were other periods in which they seemed to retreat, seeking remedies in old customs and archaic beliefs. When they advanced, they brought to the struggle the combined traditions of the old and the new, moving rapidly from old (or preconceived) ideas of what was happening to new methods of struggle. Inevitably, leaders emerged and put their stamp on events — and they too brought ideas, old and new, to inform their followers.

In the South Africa of the 1930s, the imprint of old ideas was strongest in people who had spent their formative years in the rural hinterland. In migrating to the towns, and in their consequent movements between town and country, the fusion of 'traditional' and 'derived' ideologies was rendered more complex by the gulf between the cultures of the societies they inhabited as they went from pre-capitalist subsistence farming to an industrialised society in one giant step. Their move had to absorb the differences in culture and beliefs that apply everywhere across an urban-rural divide. In South Africa they also had to cross the chasm of the colour line, and come to terms with political, social and legal institutions controlled by whites.

Men took to the towns the associations they had known in the Reserves, adapting these to meet new challenges; invariably they were connected with hometown groups that acted as mutual aid societies. They joined religious, cultural and political movements, individually or in groups based on ties of kinship, and some joined trade unions or elected their own representatives to take up complaints at the workplace (as discussed in Chapter 13). They also formed pressure groups to advance the claims of their kin at 'home', and in this way they made contact with aid societies, lawyers, political parties and others.

On returning to the country they spread awareness of the political organisations they had known in the towns. Although they seldom formed branches of those bodies, their local groups did call upon political organisations (as indeed they called upon lawyers, Native Representatives, or other sympathetic persons) when confronted with problems. The organisations established (in town and country) fulfilled definite needs and met the requirements of sectional interests, only rarely those of the whole population. Teachers joined the teachers' (or cultural) associations; workers would form unions; farmers had their own peasant bodies.

These organisations did not always seek publicity, and only when confronted by an emergency did they appeal for support. Such, for example, was the case of the Bakwena-Ba-Mogopa (from Bethanie in the Rustenburg region) who sought the assistance of community leaders in Johannesburg, wrote letters to sympathetic journals, convened meetings that were advertised in the press, sent delegations to the ANC conference, and so on. Others, like the Zoutpansberg Associations (ZBA), found friends in the CPSA and publicised their complaints in the party newspapers, supported trade unions, rented offices and sent out newsletters.

The response in the towns to rural struggles is, at one level, not difficult to explain. Men and women who came from these regions rallied to their kinsmen, rendered whatever assistance was possible, and in the process made contact with lawyers and liberal institutions like the Joint Councils, or with the ANC and socialist organisations. Their contacts with these sources of assistance contributed to the fund of ideas on local and national issues.

The CPSA and the Trotskyist parties were urban-based, but in the early 1930s, in the aftermath of rural struggles throughout the country, the Workers Party of South Africa declared that in the struggle for socialism the land question was 'the alpha and omega of the revolution'. This view did not gain wide currency and the group, centred in Cape Town (and predominantly white), did not establish an organisational base in the countryside. Another call to organise the rural population came from members of the CPSA — but where the initiative came from is not certain. The recruitment of Alpheus Maliba, a pupil at the party night school in the mid-1920s, gave the CPSA access to the Zoutpansberg Associations which he led. It might, on the other hand, have been the 1937 election for a Native Representative in the Senate that turned party attention to the countryside.

Hyman Basner stood against Rheinallt Jones and William Ballinger, and did remarkably well in coming second. The election campaign took him across the OFS and the Transvaal, where he encountered men and women who were bitter over land possession, low wages and official harassment. He also met groups who were still loyal to the ICU, and became aware of the enormity of the struggle in the rural areas. Basner urged that the CPSA organise the rural population, but besides suggestions that a mineworkers' union could be organised by contacting men before they were recruited and entered the compounds, there was little enthusiasm for work in the Reserves. The majority held that it was necessary to concentrate on the organisation of workers in the towns.

The problems of no more than two rural areas are discussed in this chapter, and they are not presented as being either typical or unique. They appear in these pages because their leaders or officials left statements and documents in seeking publicity for their cause. The Mogopas' complaints arose from their demand that schooling be funded by government and taken out of the hands of missionaries; those of the Venda were concerned with land holdings and conditions in the Trust areas. In both regions entire villages entered into conflicts with the administration that continued for years, spilling over into the towns where wider groups of sympathisers were drawn in. It also seems that the campaign of the Mogopa played a part in bringing together men in Johannesburg who were active in urban community struggles, and launched the one new (if transitory) African organisation — the African Democratic Party (ADP).

The Bakwena-Ba-Mogopa committee

The Mogopas' complaints over mission control of schooling were not unique. Since the turn of the century communities had called for state-aided education (Hirson, 1979, pp.20—2). The disaffection arose over the tight discipline maintained in the schools, the poor teaching and lack of facilities, and the inadequacy of the institutions which always claimed to be short of resources. In 1938, the issue came to a head in Bethanie when the government was asked to fund a newly established Bapedi mission school erected by the local community at Makolokoe. The Hermansburg Lutheran mission, which had always provided local schooling, sought the aid of the local administrators to prevent control of education passing out of their hands.

The Bakwena-Ba-Mogopa had a committee, established with official sanction to 'promote the social welfare of the tribe'. Initially it was headed by the chief, but his position was challenged when he sided with the missionaries in the emerging struggle over local schooling. The committee was disbanded by the Native Commissioner in the first phase of the struggle but was reconstituted, and provided the subsequent leadership against the administration. Members of the committee in Johannesburg sought support for their cause in 1942—43 and their case was reported in the *Guardian* (22 October 1942), in a letter to *Socialist Action* (September 1945), in circular letters detailing their complaints (*Xuma Papers*, ABX 421031b/421115a and 430218), and in a resolution moved at the ANC conference in December 1943.

There were three interconnected issues that aroused the people of Bethanie: a conflict with the mission (which is not fully explained); a call for a people's school in a modern building; and a dispute over chiefly succession. In the clash between the committee and the missionaries, the teachers Moses Kan and Philip Machele (who had previously been employed by the missionaries) supported the call for educational autonomy. The missionaries first tried to win over Kan and Machele, but when this failed the Circuit Inspector was called in to examine their teaching performance. When their work was found to be satisfactory, they were accused of working against the Superintendent of the school and transferred to other districts. There were protests from the committee, parents, and members of the tribe — followed by the suspension of the teachers and the dissolution of the committee by the administration. Only after the parents decided to close the mission schools were the teachers returned to Bethanie, with instructions to restore the peace; but they were not reinstated.

Both sides took steps to gain the ascendancy — the missionaries acting in concert with the local Native Commissioner. Tension mounted as the parents tried unsuccessfully, through deputations to both the local and the provincial Native Commissioners, to secure the reinstatement of their teachers. Ultimately the parents moved the children away from the missionaries and placed them in three independent (and unaided) schools. In a series of tit-for-tat measures, the missionaries closed confirmation classes and denied the people the use of church buildings. An independent church was then established, its services initially conducted in private houses. Women also picketed the mission church, preventing the missionaries gaining access to their own buildings.

It seems that in order to secure a more compliant leadership the Native Commissioner deposed the chief, but his successor was deemed by the populace to be 'non-hereditary'. This led to some 28 women attacking the missionary — followed by their arrest and sentences of a month's imprisonment or fines of £4 each. There followed a period of bitter intra-tribal struggle between the new chief's followers (armed with staves and instructed to enforce discipline) and members of the opposition. In March 1940 the chief's men forced open the recently established people's church.

To secure redress, members of the committee called first on Rheinallt Jones (as Senator), and when his petition to Pretoria failed they turned to members of the Native Representative Council and the ANC. Meanwhile, acting independently, young men set fire to the mission church, destroying the furniture and organ. Forty-nine were arrested, and three (including Kan) were given a nine-month sentence; the rest got six months. In August 1941 Kan and Machele were banished under the provisions of the 1927 Native Laws Amendment Act, which allowed for the removal of individuals (or tribes) to a prescribed area if it was believed they would endanger public peace.

The committee appealed against the deportation order and won on a technicality, but knowing they were vulnerable they appealed to several bodies for support. On 15 November 1942 they called a meeting to protest against events in Bethanie and to launch a campaign against the 1927 Act. They invited speakers from the ANC, TATA, the Non-European United Front, African trade unions, CPSA, the Joint Council of Europeans and Natives, and so on. A large audience attended and elected an Action Committee including Self Mampuru, R. Baloyi, Philip Machele (one of the victimised teachers), S.J. Lesolang (the President of TATA) and Dan Koza. Members of this committee took the complaints of the Mogopa to the ANC conference in December 1943 — calling for the reinstatement of the victimised teachers in Bethanie, the appointment of the rightful heir as chief, and the repeal of the 1927 Act. Nothing concrete was achieved, although the Mogopa committee continued sending out letters and statements about the situation. Little was heard of the Action Committee, but its composition indicates that there was a regrouping of political forces in the Transvaal. Baloyi, Mampuru and Koza were involved in the Alexandra bus boycott in 1943–44; and Mampuru, Lesolang and Koza became founding members of the African Democratic Party (see Chapter 11).

Land and land apportionment

> We are looking on you. We know you have details about the land purchase. We complain against dog licence dog tax, dip and grazing taxes which are too much for us to be able to pay.
> We are not able to rebell [*sic*] against the Government.
> Kindly try your best to bring these our complaints before the Parliament. . . . Still people are poor. Owing to the foot and mouth disease. Having lost our big and small stock we are starving. We are not allowed to possess arms and ammunition even when absolutely necessary. We are not told how matters are concerning the land in which we are living (Chief Ngomo Ntiwane).

During the 1930s there were continued appeals from people for more land: their hopes were for intercession with the government because, rightly or wrongly, most believed that they were 'not able to rebel'. Almost one third of all Africans lived on (white) farm land as squatters, sharecroppers or labourers, and another third in regions 'reserved' for them. Dwellers in the Reserves were mostly subsistence farmers, but many were landless. Men moved periodically to the mines or the towns — either from choice, or to find the money for taxes and necessary purchases. The aged, the children, the infirm and many of the women stayed behind.

The Reserves curved round north and east South Africa from the borders of Bechuanaland (now Botswana) to the eastern Cape. Most consisted of infertile, desiccated lands scarred by deep dongas (or pits) due to soil erosion. All were severely overpopulated. These were regions of poverty, malnutrition and high infant mortality: the cash income of the average family from agriculture being little more than £2 10*s* to £5 per year. Families relied on postal orders from their men in the towns to pay a local tax of 10*s* as well as the annual poll tax of £1 paid by each male aged between 18 and 65. The families also paid for compulsory cattle dipping and dog licences, and provided voluntary labour for chiefs and headmen. They did not 'rebel against the Government' as Chief Ntiwane said in 1937, but they were discontented, and their protests surfaced in disputes over taxes and levies, access to firewood, and so on. The bitterness over these issues reflected the disaffection, although the populace did not, or could not, tackle the major issue — that of landlessness.

Prior to 1936 the Reserves measured some 10,546,320 morgen. It was then proposed, under the Native Trust and Land Act, to add 7,250,000 morgen in a ten-year period. Three years later, only 1,500,000 morgen had been purchased, and with the outbreak of war the operation was suspended.[2] The government also transferred approximately one million morgen of crown land, mainly occupied by African squatters, to the Reserves. Other land occupied by squatters was expropriated for settlement by whites, and the African families were transferred to Trust Land. Thus, the immediate effect of the 1936 Act was to further increase overcrowding in the Reserves.

Under the 1936 Act, a region could be proclaimed a 'betterment area' after consultations with local inhabitants. Each location would be surveyed and demarcated for residence, grazing and cultivation. Fencing, irrigation, timber preservation and stock limitation would then be imposed. White agricultural officers, with assistants, would be appointed to allocate the land and 'exercise effective control' — thus usurping the role of local chiefs and headmen. The betterment or 'reclamation' scheme commenced in the late 1930s in the Transvaal, and it was planned to proceed with surveys in Natal and the Cape by 1944. Families complained that they were moved from land they had always ploughed and given four to five morgen (later reduced to one and a half morgen) although many previously had held 20–30 morgen. Much of the allocated land was unsuited for cultivation, and Z.K. Matthews reported that one agricultural officer had said that:

> he did not know whether the Government intended all the African people to turn into monkeys — because of the nature of the land, which was so mountainous, that it would be impossible for the ordinary man to work the land.[3]

There was bound to be resistance, and one recorded centre of action was in the Pietersburg area shortly after it was declared a 'betterment area' under Proclamation 31 of 1939.

'Betterment', and much worse

> The Transvaal, on the whole, knows chiefly the scattered 'location' type of Reserve. Here, however, there are also two remote and inaccessible blocks of Native Land — one known as Secoccoeniland, in the bush-veld between the Pretoria-Pietersburg line and the railway through Lydenburg, the other in the Sibasa [Zoutpansberg] country, the remote and in parts malaria-stricken area towards the Limpopo and the Portuguese border in the North-East (W.M. Macmillan, 1930, p.137).

Conditions in the Transvaal Reserves, as Macmillan observed, were never easy. The Zoutpansberg terrain was hilly, the region overpopulated, and in the early 1930s it was hit by drought, then by foot-and-mouth disease (*Bantu World*, 30 June 1934), and finally by the death of weakened cattle from fodder contaminated by anti-locust poison. There was no government assistance, and requests for maize at subsidised export prices were refused. Few could afford to purchase staples at inflated local prices — and still fewer could pay their taxes. Some 40,000 writs were served in the Pietersburg district in 1937 for non-payment of poll tax — that is, on two thirds of the men liable for tax in the region. Some were four years in arrears, and the taxes and court fine equalled a full year's pay. Many faced dispossession and removal from the land.[4]

After 1936 the Native Trust purchased farms to 'consolidate' the Zoutpansberg Reserve. They were densely populated, rocky and infertile — and gladly vacated by the whites. In 1939 the betterment scheme was proclaimed, the already depleted herds were culled, and families moved to small plots of land (Basner, *Senate Debates*, 26 March 1943, Col. 1021). Maliba stated that after the 1936 Act new families were moved to plots of 4—5 morgen in the Reserve. In 1940 all families were relocated on farms purchased by the Trust, much of it hilly, stony, and unsuited for cultivation, with no compensation for improvements to previous allotments. Taxpayers were allotted two morgen and non-taxpayers (old men, widows and unmarried women) one and a half morgen. In 1941 the allocation was further reduced to one and a half morgen for taxpayers, and nothing for the others. Until then, said Maliba, the peasants had shown remarkable patience, but this was too much.[5]

Families complained over the size of allotments and the regulation forbidding the cutting of trees and gathering of fallen branches for fencing and fuel (for which heavy fines of £5 could be imposed). They opposed the annual grazing fee of 30*s* (payable in advance);[6] and, above all, they complained of the agricultural officers. These men, some of them poor whites, moved families arbitrarily, extorted money for land allocations, and hounded 'hostile elements'.[7]

Conditions worsened. Ploughs had to be abandoned on very stony plots, or on strips where it was forbidden to uproot bushes or trees — but the payment of taxes was tightened, with levies of 2*s* 6*d* on late payments. At a meeting of the ZBA at Piesanghoek in the Louis Trichardt district on 20 October 1941, some 2,000 farmers supported a declaration by Maliba that:

> We, people of the Northern Transvaal, have come together to save ourselves from starvation. We now solemnly decide that everyone of us will plough the land which we were accustomed to plough in past years. We will remove the sticks which the government has set up, and plough our own land. Any person who breaks this resolution is an enemy of the people.
>
> We will send a copy of this resolution to the Native Commissioner and to the Minister for Native Affairs in Pretoria (ZCA circular letter, 7 November 1941).

After the meeting survey pins were removed and many men reclaimed their original land — ignoring the areas allocated to them. They said they would wait no longer, because drought conditions had already made them late for the ploughing (ibid.). Between 60 and 80 men were arrested and the court hearing was set for 13 November. Maliba was charged under the Riotous Assemblies Act with the more serious offence of inciting the people to break the law, but released on bail. The case was never tried: a crowd, estimated at between six and ten thousand strong, marched on the courts and, after an initial postponement, the Secretary for Native Affairs ordered that the charges be withdrawn.

The Piesanghoek meeting was reported in the *Guardian* (20 November 1941) together with a declaration from Paramount Chief Mpefu stating: 'Arrest me! — but let my people go! What they are doing is right. I am prepared to suffer for them!' Yet it was only in 1943 that Basner secured belated publicity for the issue in a Senate debate. He said he had learnt of the demonstration by chance when he appeared for persons charged with gathering twigs for firewood in the Pietersburg district (*Senate Debates*, 12 April 1943, Col. 1821).

Maliba's 'Seven-Point Programme'

There is no indication in CPSA records of any analysis during this period of the land question, and the one document on the subject, issued in the name of the party by Maliba (*c.* 1938), was not Marxist. Maliba addressed himself to the Venda people and included an uncritical appraisal of the chiefly structure 'under the old system . . . [when they were] responsible to the people, and helped those in want'. He wanted better health care and education, improved working and living conditions on the mines and in the towns, and higher wages.[8] He included a 'Seven-Point Programme of the Communist Party for the Northern Transvaal' which called for the mines to become the property of the people, 'to use to their own advantage'; demanded the abolition of poll tax, dog tax, dipping fees, grazing fees, and licences for felling trees 'which serve only to drive people to work'; called for the unity of all tribes in the fight 'against restrictions and oppression'; and demanded that:

> The land must be taken from the rich and must be returned to the people, together with the Crown lands.
> Agricultural schools must be started to teach up-to-date methods of farming, and modern implements must be provided by the government.
> Individual land tenure must take the place of tribal tenure so that competition will be encouraged, and the farm workers will have the incentive to improve their land.

The call in the name of the CPSA for private property, and competition to provide an incentive to land improvement, is remarkable. Yet, if this was not party policy, the printing of this 'programme' in a communist publication suggests that little attention was given to Maliba and his organisation.

The five morgen limit on land

On entering a village Maliba went first to the chief's *kraal*: he made a point of securing support from those who had lost their authority under the new regulations. Without this backing his movements in the district would have been restricted. But the ZBA did not win over many teachers, most of whom joined the local Joint Council of Europeans and Bantu, which organised monthly discussions, eisteddfods and agricultural shows (Documentation Centre holdings, University of South Africa) but avoided discussions of local struggles, resistance and arrests.[9] M.K. Molepo, then President of the TATA, was an exception. He was Basner's translator in the area, a member of the ADP, and stood for the NRC in 1944 (in opposition to Maliba). After investigating allotments on Trust farms, he was removed from his teaching post in June 1944 and, despite the efforts of a defence committee which took his case through the courts, he was deported and only allowed to return in April 1946 (*Guardian*, 8 June 1944; Molepo Defence Committee to Xuma, *Xuma Papers*, ABX 450303d, 450414b, 450425b, 450717c, 460404).

The rejection of the allotments led to mass trials in the Pietersburg court, but charges were withdrawn and the men were instructed by the magistrate to settle their grievances with the Native Commissioner: he, however, could not give them larger allotments (*Forum*, 19 September 1942). According to the same report, thousands of Africans in the region were starving.

In early 1943 it was obvious that the mealie crops had failed, with the yield expected to drop by an average of 30–40 per cent on the white farms and some 70 per cent in the Reserves (*Inkululeko*, 24 April 1943). There was disaffection throughout the region, and on 27 October workers at Messina stopped work when a promised wage increase was not paid. Addressed by the Native Commissioner from Louis Trichardt, they were offered an extra 2*d* a day but demanded 6*d*. Summoned to meet the next day to hear the outcome, they were met by troops with guns at the ready. Those who would not return to work were arrested, and over 80 sentenced to cuts or prison sentences plus fines (*Inkululeko*, 20 November 1943).

In November 1943 police were dispatched from Pretoria to Trust land at Sandfontein, near Pietersburg, where over 2,000 men protested against the five morgen limit, and on 22 November Basner wrote an urgent letter to Xuma, saying:

> I am convinced that the tenants on the Trust Farms will not obey the . . . regulations and I get reports of the gravest nature regarding the actions of the police in the district. One of the organisers of the . . . tenants, has been arrested under the [war-time] Emergency Regulations, and about 40 Africans have been arrested under various criminal charges.
>
> Some of the Headmen of the Trust Farms allege that the police and the Assistant Native Commissioner are travelling around flogging people whom they consider have violated regulations. These . . . will be probed in court in the coming trials which are being handled by the Legal Aid Bureau.[10]

At a meeting of the NRC Dr Moroka, raising the issue as a matter of 'urgent public importance', said police had been sent to Pietersburg to prevent the ploughing of the commonage, and added: 'If my information is correct, the assistance of the Military has been sought and a state of armed warfare exists in the Pietersburg area' (NRC Minutes, 3 December). Members of the NRC asked for a commission to investigate the 'temporary suspension' of the regulations governing Trust farms, and the 'adequacy of land allocated' to the residents. Douglas Smit, from the chair, said he had listened 'with interest and sympathy', but the regulations could not be altered — despite the statement of the Minister of Native Affairs in the Senate on 12 April that in *bona fide* cases men 'would be allowed to occupy land equivalent to that previously worked', but not exceeding 30 morgen (*Senate Debates*, Col. 1775).

Dr Moroka said there was a state of armed warfare in the Pietersburg area, but precisely what happened is not certain. A *Guardian* report of 16 December said: 'It is rumoured that bombers at Pietersburg Aerodrome were told to stand by in case of trouble. One hundred Africans were arrested.' As late as March 1945, James Z. Mdatyualwa, chief organiser of the ADP, and President of the Transvaal Advisory Boards Association, referred to repressive measures in the Transvaal, which he linked with 'the disturbances at Pietersburg where the police, military and aeroplanes were used to intimidate people. . . .' The magistrate at Klerksdorp warned that he would be interned if he maintained his revolutionary and provocative attitude (*Guardian*, 22 March 1945).

It has not been possible to confirm reports about bombings of villages during this period, despite persistent rumours. This matter was summed up, retrospectively, by Basner in a letter to the author (27 May 1975):

> I was involved with scores of struggles on Trust farms and tribal locations about the Native Trust and Land Act, 1936. Cattle culling, squatters, ploughing allotments, chiefly powers versus trust officials were the main issues. Most of the struggles were in the Northern Transvaal, and some were even fiercer and crueller than Witzieshoek, but unreported because only Africans and no police were killed. I received constant reports of bombed villages and had no reason to doubt the reports.

Agitation about the presence of the military grew when, in February 1944, 300 Africans were recruited by the Native Commissioner of Louis Trichardt, ostensibly for the army. Maliba protested in *Inkululeko*, and in a letter to Donald Molteno, and there were also protests from whites about this 'mysterious recruitment of Natives'. The camp was transferred to Hammanskraal, where the men were apparently employed on road work. They had been recruited to act as scabs in the event of the VFP (power) workers striking (see Chapter 13), and when the camp was closed on 27 June a bill for the costs of maintaining more than 2,000 men was sent to the VFP company.[11]

The resistance was extended by women in December 1943, when 43 labour tenants in the Piesanghoek area marched to the local Native Commissioner to complain of brutal treatment by white farmers and being forced to do work usually done by men. The Commissioner dismissed them saying only that they should go with their husbands or chiefs to settle the matter with the farmers (*Inkululeko*, 13 December 1943). There is no further information on the women's actions.

A state of permanent instability

No more land was made available to the farmers. The Reserves added little to Gross Domestic Production, and men were considered mainly as potential workers on the mines or in the towns — although a government report of 1944/5 stressed the need to 'alleviate gross undernourishment', and called for increased food production in the Reserves.[12] Yet agricultural development seems to have been deliberately retarded: piped water was disallowed (because Africans 'were not used to piped water'); the men were required to plough on hillsides because, said the Native Commissioner, 'if they plough on level ground they waste the grass'. The same official said that 'the people in the Native Reserves are too lazy to do anything for themselves and should be sent to the mines to do some work'.[13]

Throughout 1944 farmers in the northern Transvaal were harassed. In February 1944, Maliba reported to Basner that the Native Commissioner had summoned a meeting at Chief Mpefu's location and demanded that all able-bodied men be mobilised to mend the dams and bridges damaged in recent rains. Those who did not come forward would forfeit goats or cattle, in lieu of a fine. Chiefs were instructed to supervise the exercise and control the men (printed in *Guardian*, 16 December 1943). Men from some districts also complained that after being made to plough virgin land a few years before, they had been moved arbitrarily by local officials to new virgin land where they now had to start afresh (*Inkululeko*, 12 February 1944).

Maliba was in constant conflict with the law. In 1944 he organised a May Day demonstration, was charged and fined for holding a public meeting without securing the permission of the Native Commissioner, and had to leave the precincts of Louis Trichardt. In December Maliba was again before the court, charged under the Urban Areas Act for hiring premises from whites in order to build a General Workers Union. He was fined £3 (*Guardian*, 11 May, 28 December 1944). During 1945 persons were deported from several towns in the region, but with little publicity. Maliba maintained a low profile until February 1947, when he sought to prevent the deposition of Ratshivibi Sibasa, Chief of the Bavenda. The matter was taken to the courts, and the ZCA appealed for funds to cover legal costs. The Supreme Court ruled for Sibasa, but the Governor General served a removal order, debarring him from entry to any place in the district without written permission.[14]

The Balemi silenced

By 1945 the people of the northern Transvaal were exhausted. After four years, repression had taken its toll and leading figures had been deported.

The chiefs had also been made to enforce measures or face removal, and this had split some communities. They also faced new catastrophe in the shape of a drought which according to the Society of Friends (Report, 1945) ravaged most of South Africa and 'exacted a huge toll of Native owned stock particularly in the Ciskei . . . northern Transvaal and Zululand'. Malnutrition, said the report, was 'regarded as endemic' in the Reserves.

Hereafter, the ZCA/ZBA seem to have played a smaller role in the region. People tired of open confrontation and sought some accommodation. This was exemplified in a letter sent to Basner on 17 July 1945 by men who led both the Molepo Defence Committee and the newly formed ANC branch in the northern Transvaal. The letter stated that local chiefs and councillors had appealed to the Minister of Native Affairs to consult with them before deporting any of their subjects; and that the proposed removal of some African tribes at Mletzies could lead to bloodshed because people were divided between those who refused to go and others who had taken the advice of one chief and accepted the compensation of 30s per hut. The Native Commissioner, who was supposedly 'sympathetic to the Natives', had set a deadline, and Basner was asked to prevail on everyone to agree to the removal. The letter concluded:

> The Native Commissioner has agreed that we go and hold a meeting before [the deadline]. Please let us repeat that our main object is to facilitate Mr Molepo's chance of returning home. He cannot afford to stay away from his family and property (copy in *Xuma Papers*, ABX 450717c).

Under these conditions there could be no new initiative from the ZCA/ZBA. The body had flourished during the period of struggle and waned after the defeats of 1943–44. Whether there was also pressure on Maliba from the CPSA, in the changing circumstances of the war, or in the light of the opinions of leading party members, is not chronicled. However, there is a diary entry by George Findlay, who appeared in the Pietersburg court in 1944 to argue the case of Molepo against deportation:

> The Platteland [rural] Africans are a secondary area — more propaganda is needed there, not peasant revolts. *Intensify* ideological work — don't water down to 'popular appeal' standards.[15]

Maliba seems to have become a 'non-person' and no more was heard of his activities. Kotane, who had once written glowingly about Maliba's work in the Zoutpansberg, reported in *Freedom*, November–December 1947, on a conference of rural dwellers convened by the CPSA. His list of complaints by delegates was headed: 'We Do Not Know Their Difficulties'. This was absurd. The complaints were well known: removals from 'black spots', low pay, lack of facilities for labour tenants, restrictions on the Trust farms, and objections against obligatory labour for chiefs. The article makes depressing reading on two counts: the plight of rural workers was as bad as ever, with little hope of redress; and the understanding by leading members of the CPSA of rural problems was sub-minimal.

Kotane's report did not mention the rehabilitation scheme, which replaced and tightened the betterment scheme, and was about to lead to new violence in the Reserves (Hirson, 1978). All he offered was a recital of difficulties. Finally, said Kotane, 'The important thing about the Conference is that some start has been made.' In these few words, all the work of Maliba and the ZCA/ZBA was devalued. Three years later the CPSA dissolved itself, and no more was heard of Maliba until 1967, when he was arrested and died mysteriously in a prison cell in Pretoria (Simons and Simons, 1969, p.538).

Notes

1. This chapter includes material from Hirson, 1978.
2. *Senate Debates*, 9 April 1943, Col. 1772. The Minister gave figures for crown land transferred to the Native Trust, but subsequent information provided by government commissions showed these to be unreliable.
3. Minutes of Native Representative Council, 3 December 1943, pp.88—90.
4. See *Spark*, Vol. 3, No. 3, March 1937; and A.M. Maliba (*c.*1938), who estimated the regional population as 300,000 (as against the official figure of some 200,000). There were 223,000 head of cattle in the region — an average of two head to every three people, though in fact ownership of cattle tended to be in few hands.
5. Interview with Maliba by Moses Kotane, *Guardian*, 18 December 1941.
6. Exchange of letters between S.H.M. Soshankana and Rheinallt Jones about conditions in Lichtenburg, September—October 1943, *Rheinallt Jones Papers*.
7. H. Basner, *Senate Debates*, 1943, Col. 1821, said the 'Northern Transvaal was a seething cauldron of discontent' over the methods used by Emmett, a Native Commissioner in the Pietersburg area. It was Basner who drew my attention to the use of poor whites as officials on Trust Lands.
8. There are nine lines on wages on p.5, and workers were urged to join their trade unions. Maliba was critical of 'tribal organisations [that] are usually afraid of politics, and only help individuals who are in need of money', p.9.
9. This was to be expected given the support for the betterment scheme by leading members of the Joint Council, see e.g. Rheinallt Jones, 'Attitudes of the African people towards the government's conservation schemes and relations between their representatives and the administration', manuscript, 1940, copy at Warwick University.
10. *Xuma Papers*, ABX 431122b. Basner made urgent representations and Siboto, the arrested organiser, was released, but after four weeks in confinement he was insane.
11. The account of this recruitment was found in the Douglas Smit papers and quoted by Moodie, *c.* 1984a, pp.42—43.
12. Social and Economic Planning Council, 1945, p.22; also Molteno, *Parliamentary Debates*, 17 March 1942, Cols 3991—2.
13. Report on Native Affairs, 'The living conditions of the people of Sekhukuneland', typescript sent to the SAIIR from Lydenburg district, December 1943, 2pp. *Rheinallt Jones Papers*.
14. Circular letter from Maliba and Muthibe (secretary of the ZCA) appealing

for funds, 7 February 1947, *Xuma Papers*, ABX 470207. See also newsletter of Transvaal Passive Resistance Council, September 1947, CAMP, Reel 27, ET1/1:85/1.
15. Quoted by Haines, 1981. I did not understand the arguments in this paper, but am grateful for the quotations.

ALEXANDRA TOWNSHIP RESIDENTS

YOUR SENATOR H. M. BASNER still in danger of being IMPRISONED. You Know Him. You made him your Senator.

He is being prosecuted because during your Bus strike he found the Native Affairs Police busy stopping you for POLL TAX.
As a leader and your representative in Parliament he could not pass by and not try to find out why this was happening. You can not know what happened when he was trying to find that out until the case is finished.
All you know is that you had a strike and the Native Affairs Department send a Police raid for Poll tax. You know that if there was no police raid for poll tax,

Your Senator H. M. Basner would have never got in to this trouble. Your fight therefore begins in a protest against the poll tax raids.
You will be protesting well if you all go to Court on Thursday this week.
You will all meet at No 2 Square, at 6 in the morning on this Thursday where the Buses will be waiting to take you after your leaders have told you what will be done and how best it can be done.
COME MEN and WOMEN of all ages.

There will be a meeting on SUNDAY 24th, Oct 1943 at No 2, SQUARE, to tell you about the case and plans made for Thursday 28th.

Issued by J. P. Mgoma & Gaur Radebe   Printed by Alexandra Commercial Printers 44, 3rd Ave 4/21/43/10,000

Leaflet addressed to Alexandra residents.

Alexandra — the hope (*c.* 1912) . . .

. . . and the reality (an aerial view in the 1940s).

A.E.P. Fish, arms outstretched, leads the residents of Alexandra on the first day of the bus boycott.

11. Azikwhelwa! — We Shall Not Ride

The road to Alexandra

From its inception in 1905, Alexandra was an anomaly. Proclaimed as a township when white workers were being cleared from the centre of Johannesburg and could neither rent houses nor find the money to purchase newly released freehold stands, land in Alexandra was offered for sale — nine miles from the city centre, and some fourteen or more miles from the nearest gold mines. Its site was inexplicable: the social geography of the town was already established, with white workers tending to live in the southern suburbs, the rich moving ever northwards. Alexandra was situated in the far north-east (Krut, 1980).

The township bordered the road from Pretoria, which in 1905 consisted of a winding dirt track ascending the hills of northern Johannesburg before dipping down to the town centre. Transport to town was by horse-drawn carts, a prohibitively long and expensive journey. Whites would not buy the sites on offer, and in 1912 the owners offered the plots to Africans or Coloureds, with freehold rights, at £35–£40 each (*Agenda, 682nd Ordinary Meeting*, 1943, p.43; Kagan, 1978, p.39).

Alexandra became a miserable slum during the inter-war years. The township consisted of 2,541 stands, 2,185 of approximately a quarter of an acre, the rest appreciably smaller. In 1934 the population was estimated as at least 15,000, growing to some 50,000 by 1939, and topping 100,000 during the war years. A report in 1939 by Dr A.B. Xuma, the Medical Officer of Health, stated that:

> There [were] 1,579 houses, composed of 5,959 rooms, with other 'tenement' houses composed of 10,221 rooms, making a total of 16,180 'habitable' rooms. In addition there [were] 422 shops, 248 stores, 37 churches and 61 classrooms (*Agenda*, 1943, p.44).

Conditions were miserable in this warren of shacks where it was not unusual for entire families to sleep in one room: parents and children, boys and girls, all occupying one or at most two beds. Of the 4,376 buildings in the township, the City Council noted that only 702 were in good order; 1,585 were 'major slums', the rest slums of a lesser order. There were no kitchens, bathrooms or storage places for food. Sanitation was by 'the bucket system', with one pail per stand, and water was in most cases still drawn from shallow wells, 'often liable to contamination' (ibid.). The streets were dirt tracks, pockmarked with ditches and holes; recreation areas were water-filled dongas or polluted rivulets; and two open squares served as bus termini, football grounds, and sites for meetings and rallies. There were few amenities and the annual budget of the Health Committee (which administered the township) never exceeded £20,000; that is, 10s or less per resident. Consequently, there was no gas or electricity, no street lighting, and only one small clinic for the entire population (ibid.; Barry, 1943). Nonetheless, few residents would have gone elsewhere willingly. Alexandra was prized as a haven, free of the permit system and controls of the location, and open to all who could find and pay for a nook to sleep. Also, the existence of some 670 shops and stores, many of which were used as workshops, provided premises for furniture makers, printers, and other small craftsmen.

In the inter-war years, the suburbs of Johannesburg spread outwards, their boundaries extending to within a mile of Alexandra. The white middle class formed the North Eastern District Protection League to campaign for the removal of the township, which they said was overcrowded, lawless, and a barrier to white expansion. They demanded that it be incorporated in Johannesburg and transferred to white ownership. The ruling Ratepayers Association (which the League supported) gave prompt attention to their case. It reached agreement with government officials in 1938 on expropriation, subject to the apportioning of costs between city and government (*Agenda*, 1943, p.44; Hoernlé et al., pp.3—4). Pending removal, the city fathers urged that the Health Committee be given no additional rights, and consequently the Administrator of the Transvaal proposed that the two elected members of the Health Committee (one black, one white) be removed. Stand holders, who held the franchise, protested, and on 14 June 1941 a deputation led by Xuma told the Administrator that

in a special meeting held by the Health Committee with Ratepayers recently, some of the women members stated that they would rather be shot than be compelled to be legislated by a Committee in which they had no confidence. I am not inclined to take this statement as an irresponsible vain threat (*Xuma Papers*, ABX410614).

The anger of the ratepayers encompassed more than the threat to the composition of the Health Committee. From 1921—32 the Committee members had been black, and their removal (on grounds of alleged financial difficulties) had not stirred an electorate which numbered no more than 700, of whom no more than 50 ever voted.[1] At the heart of the protest was the threat of expropriation and removal: the anger this provoked would add strength to the wartime boycott movement when busfares were raised. The Health Committee was not altered, but pressure for the removal of Alexandra continued. In 1942 the Minister of Public Health met city councillors and asked for alternative costs and conditions relating to expropriation or improvements to Alexandra.[2] There the matter rested during the war years, with the threat of removal ever present.

Initially, residents had walked or cycled to work, or used horse-drawn buses at 1s 3d per trip. Then came steam-driven and later petrol-driven buses, but fares remained exorbitant at 1s 3d per trip and 1s 6d at weekends. By 1928 the appearance of more bus owners forced fares down, until they were pegged at 9d per trip by a newly formed Alexandra Bus Owners Association. The service was poor: buses only left the terminus when full, and were sometimes rescheduled to make special journeys to the countryside.[3] Then the Motor Carrier Transportation Act of 1930 was introduced to eliminate competition with the South African Railways. Bus timetables had to be published, unscheduled trips were stopped, and busfares regulated (ibid.). Fares were forced down, firstly by the appearance of 'pirate' taxis (banned in 1941, but always available), and then by regulation of the Road Transportation Board in the early 1930s: the journey to town was fixed at a flat rate of 4d, and 6d over weekends and on Monday mornings. The fare reduction coincided with the mass removals of Africans from white residential areas. Many came to Alexandra, and there they complained bitterly about the lack of buses — only thirteen being available (Koza in *Bantu World*, 14 April 1934). The commuters' position worsened when bus owners shifted the township terminus and raised the fares by 1d, though after representations to the Transportation Board, the 4d ride was restored.[4]

The first boycott

In 1940 the Transportation Board doubled the levy on each bus to 5s per day, allowing an increase in fares to 5d to cover both the levy and the cost of road repairs. A Residents Committee made representations but failed to stop the increase, and after months of protest meetings decided to boycott the buses and walk to work. What happened next is not clear. The daily press carried no mention of the buses, but there was news of street demonstrations; at least two independent sources said there was a boycott. The bus owners then retreated and the fare reverted to 4d.[5]

In October 1942, when expropriation was being discussed with the Minister of Health, the Road Transportation Board raised the bus levy to 10s per day and granted a rise in fare to 5d. Passengers boarded the buses, but only tendered the 4d fare. In retaliation the owners moved the terminus again, leaving passengers a long walk home. The buses were boycotted and pickets prevented passengers from boarding, leading to clashes with bus company officials. Eventually the terminus and 4d fare were restored, pending investigation by the Central Road Transportation Board.[6] E.P. Mart Zulu, formerly of the Alexandra Ratepayers Association and by this time a representative of the Alexandra Workers Union, presented a memorandum to the Board on behalf of the Residents Committee; then he had second thoughts and accepted the 5d fare. A mass meeting, called at Number 2 Square, repudiated Zulu, elected a deputation, and presented its own memorandum. Henceforth, all struggles in the township were organised from this square, where leaders were subjected to popular scrutiny.

New political combinations

The Alexandra Workers Union, which was so prominent in the early stages of the struggle, was the organisation of small traders and craftsmen. Its members had the independence and the initiative to assume leadership in the township. However, the Union included stand holders who were torn between protest over busfares and fear least boycotts interfere with their tenants' ability to pay rentals: hence Zulu's ambivalence over the 1*d* rise.

The prominence of the Workers Union mirrored the weakness of other organisations associated with the presentation of the first memorandum (*Guardian*, 15 November 1942). The ANC did not have an active branch despite the presence of several prominent members, including R.G. Baloyi (national treasurer), C.S. Ramohanoe (Transvaal secretary and future president), and Gaur Radebe. Baloyi, a bus owner, antagonised militants when he opposed their action in 1939—40, and he left Alexandra for several months. Although he said he supported the residents, and accused Ramohanoe (a bus company employee) of siding against the people in their later struggles, his motives were always suspect. The activities of The Daughters of Africa, which had strong ties with the ANC, and the Alexandra Women's Brigade, formed at that time with Lilian Tshabalala at its head, are unknown. The CPSA had a group in Alexandra, and through the Tenants Association and the South African Youth League (SAYL) had been active in the 1939—40 campaigns against fare increases.[7] The SAYL collapsed after Joffe's internment in October 1940: only a few members of the group remained actively engaged in local struggles. The CPSA was further weakened by Gaur Radebe's expulsion (see Chapter 13).

In July 1943 the Central Transportation Board granted the fare increase, to take effect on 1 August. Two days later, following mass meetings at Number 2 Square, the buses were boycotted. At three o'clock in the morning some 15—20,000 men and women began to march down the highway towards their places of work in the city. In the evening they walked home, arriving after dark. The spokesman for the residents was A.E.P. Fish, of the Workers Union. Fish owned a print shop in the township and published the flysheets for the boycott. He protested against the high cost of transport (set against a weekly wage of 27*s*); the iniquity of a flat fare irrespective of distances travelled; and the 'wastages' caused by refusing to replace white inspectors by blacks. He wanted the buses transferred to the Health Committee and all profits used to improve Alexandra.[8]

On the second day of the boycott there were appeals to employers from the CNETU and the City Council not to penalise workers who arrived late; and an appeal to motorists from Basner, the Ballingers, Ellen Hellman and Hilda Kuper of the SAIRR to give lifts to workers. To provide assistance from outside the township Basner also formed an Emergency Transport Committee which included Lilian and Vincent Swart, Paul Mosaka, Gaur Radebe, Self Mampuru, A.E.P. Fish and Lilian Tshabalala — all of them future founding members of the ADP. Other Emergency Committee members were V.C. Berrange, advocate and member of the CPSA, Baloyi, and his bookkeeper J.B. Marks, who used his inside knowledge to denounce bus owners when they claimed to be running at a loss.

Of the few leading members of the ANC on the committee it was said that

'The African people have been frustrated by a Congress leadership which does not organise mass support nor carry on mass action to improve their living standards . . . ' (*Inkululeko*, 18 September 1943). The inactivity of the ANC was obvious, and this precipitated the formation of the ADP. Xuma, who might have provided a lead, was not a man of action, rarely seen at demonstrations, strikes or boycotts. He did not join the walk to town, or speak at Number 2 Square during the boycott, despite the invitations extended to him.

Xuma (and other leaders of the ANC) might have been influenced by another factor. In 1940, when Baloyi's business was floundering, Xuma proposed that the company be refloated under the joint control of Dr Moroka, Baloyi and himself, because he wanted Africans to be successful in commerce, and their companies kept from whites. He felt that bankruptcy would 'reflect badly on us, as a race', and hoped to turn the bus company into a profitable concern.[9] Ramohanoe had also applied for permission to operate a bus in the mid-1930s but had not succeeded (Stadler, 1981, p.234). The ambitions of Xuma and Ramohanoe were not inconsistent with the demands of the ANC on trading rights, but the ownership of buses raised a possible conflict of interests in the struggle over fares. Baloyi had an uneasy relationship with the public when he owned buses, and did not regain their confidence when he said at the Bus Commission that he could operate a service at 4*d*. Xuma's desire to buy a bus company might have been disinterested, but it could have affected his appraisal of the issues involved.[10]

The bus dispute spread to Evaton, near Vereeniging, and to Atteridge-ville, Eersterust and Riverside, all in Pretoria. There were the usual complaints about irregular services, frequent breakdowns and increased fares. In Atteridgeville fares rose from 4*d* to 6*d* (9*d* on Sundays and Monday mornings) and buses were boycotted. Even when fares had not risen, there were rumours of impending changes. Inevitably, employers were becoming impatient: workers arrived late and tired, and wartime production was suffering. For ten days they walked, and only boarded the buses again when the government used emergency regulations to restore the 4*d* fare and appoint a commission of enquiry. Yet fares went up at Eersterust and Riverside on 20 August, and buses were boycotted — with little outside aid, although speakers visited the townships.[11]

Findings of the commission of enquiry

In September 1943 the Bus Commission heard evidence about buses and African workers. Families stirred at 3 a.m., and rushed to get the men aboard the 37 buses that left as they filled between 4 and 5 a.m. There was no further transport until the first bus returned from town. On Monday mornings, when weekend visitors joined the queue, buses departed from 3.30 a.m. (at the weekend fare). There was a daily stampede to board the vehicles in the morning and the evening, and many were injured in the process.[12]

A worker in Alexandra, with an average monthly wage of £5 8*s*, paid 18*s* 9*d* per month on travel before the increase, if he only used the bus on workdays and his family stayed at home.[13] Women who worked as servants or washerwomen were especially aggrieved. They earned 5*s* per 'bundle' of washing, but paid for transport — and had to pay the full fare even if they only went a few stops. Only 'the fastest and strongest' got aboard the overcrowded buses, and they complained of 'injured limbs and ribs trying to run for the buses and squeezing in with men'. In the evenings, when carrying bundles of washing (and they needed as many as they could carry), they would board buses going to town, and pay a double fare to secure a seat going home.[14]

The commission's report (1944, pars. 245, 262) was damning. Quite obviously the issue of bus fares was only part of a deeper malaise:

> The vast bulk of the African workers in the areas covered by the Commission's enquiry were, in 1943, unable from their own earnings, even when supplemented by the earnings of other members of the family, to meet even the minimum requirements for subsistence, health and decency, not to speak of emergency requirements. . . . The actual diet of the African worker is far below the nutritional level of minimum diet. . . .
>
> The . . . policy of segregation and . . . hous[ing] Africans under this policy, away from the space occupied by other races, have created . . . the unique phenomenon that the lowest paid workers have to live farthest from their work. . . .
>
> . . .[T]ransport charges in relation to the worker's wages, or . . . the total family income, are beyond the capacity of the African worker to pay. Indeed it may be said that they cannot afford to pay anything. They certainly cannot afford to pay anything more . . . except by reducing still further their hunger diet.

Yet the report, published in April 1944, recommended a fare increase over weekends on the Alexandra and Pretoria routes, and on weekdays for Atteridgeville; but for the next seven months the fares were pegged. In Johannesburg the Emergency Transport Committee continued its campaign against any rise, but there was no coordination with the residents of Pretoria and Evaton. On 10 November, the government responded to the bus owners' demands by increasing fares by 1*d* under emergency regulations. Workers were told to 'reclaim' the extra cost from their employers, although repayment was not ensured. There was no protection for casual workers, the unemployed, the youth, part-time workers (like washerwomen), or those who shopped in town. Residents rejected the 'scheme' and there were calls for a fresh boycott, particularly from political groups that had emerged during the previous year.

The African Democratic Party

On 26 September 1943 the ADP was launched, its manifesto published under the names of Mosaka, Mampuru, Lesolang, Kuzwayo and Koza. The party was for Africans, but Vincent and Lilian Swart were allowed to join. Basner, the guest speaker at the inaugural meeting, attacked the 'unholy alliance' of CPSA and ANC. On the same day, also in Johannesburg, some fifty whites formed the Socialist Party (SP), with Johanna Cornelius as chair, Anna Scheepers as vice-chair, and Leon Szur one of the secretaries.[15] The new party aimed to fight all forms of racism and fascism, and to struggle for a living wage for all workers, but it was open only to whites, in deference to the demands of the Garment Workers Union officials. It was announced that the party would work among the (white) workers of Fordsburg, Vrededorp, Jeppe and Germiston (*Garment Worker*, September/October 1943).

The programmes of the two parties were liberal or social-democratic. The SP aimed 'to combat all forms of backwardness in our national life', to 'struggle for economic and political freedom', and 'to co-operate with all other organisations and persons who have the interest of labour and general progress at heart'. The manifesto of the ADP was equally nebulous. The problem of South Africa, it said, was basically economic, 'complicated by social and racial issues', and segregation was 'repugnant to the principles of liberty and justice'. Africans were kept as a 'cheap mobile and unskilled labour force', a condition which had to be opposed for 'the greater well being of all sections of the South African population' (paras 23—25). Therefore the ADP demanded a more equitable distribution of land and no restriction on acquisition; a living wage in town and country, and full recognition of African trade unions under the IC Act; adequate educational facilities for the acquisition of skills and literacy to help increase the national income, and to 'more fully enjoy the fruits and benefits of civilisation'; an end to pass laws, ensuring freedom of movement; a share of political power and in 'the more responsible ranks of the administration' (para. 26, points a—e).

The ADP wanted 'peaceful negotiations by leaders whose influence derives from the mass of their followers', and that required the support of whites, particularly those in the SAIRR, Joint Councils, Christian Council, and Friends of Africa. Finally, the manifesto declared, if these peaceful means did not secure change, the ADP would use 'as a last resort . . . the weapon of mass passive resistance' (paras 7—11). The authors said they supported the ANC, but that it was stagnant and disorganised: a new 'dynamic' movement was required to counter the 'imminent dangers' confronting the African people (paras 12—15). In this the ADP was not alone, and it was soon outflanked by the AAC and the Congress Youth League (CYL). The manifesto of the AAC demanded 'full citizenship rights and representation' and the removal of discriminatory legislation, and rejected Native representatives (Karis and Carter, 1972—77, Vol. 2, pp.347—52); the CYL also distanced itself from the ADP with a manifesto calling for exclusive African nationalism and the boycott of all Native representation (ibid., pp.300—8).

Towards the end of the 1943 bus boycott Basner visited Alexandra in the early morning, and there found an angry crowd surrounding African police and men arrested on poll-tax charges. The arrests were highly provocative, and when the police appealed to Basner he advised that the men be released. This led to a charge of aiding men under arrest, which if upheld would have cost his Senate seat. The ADP called a demonstration to coincide with the court case on 15 October, but on the appointed day the leaders were not to be found. The Women's Brigade, formed during the boycott and led by Lilian Tshabalala, Fish, Radebe and others, marched from Alexandra to the court where Basner was found not guilty.

The ADP then faced a crisis when Koza issued a statement similar to the criticism published by Hosea Jaffe (1943) in the name of the Fourth International of South Africa. Moves to expel Koza were countered by his statement that he had the right to appeal to the ADP conference, but the party was saved the spectacle of a public debate on the programme by Koza's resignation.

The next 'initiative' from the ADP came in the form of an advertisement calling for a national day of prayer on 8 January 1944, under the name of Mosaka and Mampuru, and placed in most African papers. The statement read: 'New methods of struggle are needed and a Day of Prayer should be observed: to be known as Atlantic Charter Day.' The authors called on Africans to 'solemnly turn to God' to get their rights, and promised that a meeting would be convened to plan for 8 January. Somewhat fancifully the notice concluded:

> This is our New Year message to the African people. Salvation lies in your own hands. Heaven helps those who help themselves. Observe the African Day of Prayer and fight [*sic*] for freedom.

There is no evidence of any meeting to plan for the day of prayer, or any other mass activity. The leaders of the party visited townships in the Transvaal and the OFS to form branches, but if these were established they collapsed for lack of activity. Nonetheless, the ADP exerted considerable influence in Alexandra, and would play a role in the shantytown which was soon to be built in Orlando.

The fifty day walk

On Tuesday 14 November Basner, David Bopape, Harmel and Dadoo addressed a mass meeting which gave them overwhelming support for a renewal of the boycott and a march to the centre of the city. A policeman at the meeting read a notice banning processions and meetings of more than twenty people from the following day. The next morning lorry loads of police arrived at 3 a.m., but the residents walked to town in groups of less than twenty (CPSA, c.1945; Stadler, 1981). A week later, cars and lorries offering lifts to walkers were stopped by police and accused of using wartime rations of petrol illegally (*Rand Daily Mail*, 21 November 1944). The Emergency Transport Committee organised horse-and-cart transport for the old and incapacitated, and many employers, concerned about the physical state of their workers, bought them bicycles.

A Workers' Transport Action Committee was established containing representatives from township bodies, including the ADP, the Alexandra Workers Union, the Women's Brigade and the CPSA. The Action Committee maintained contact with residents, despite the ban on meetings, by delegating specific action to groups. The Women's Brigade, 'created' by Lilian Tshabalala, consisted of 'formidable churchwomen and beer-brewers who made themselves responsible for the township's solidarity and good order — especially among faint hearted or riotously disposed men' (M. Basner, n.d.). They had to stop the boarding of buses, and did that through seven weeks. After the buses had been withdrawn, attempted resumption of service in the sixth week was prevented when the Action Committee threw a cordon across the only access road to Alexandra, keeping the boycott intact. There was dissension, however. Some pressed for defiance of the ban on meetings, but were overruled by the majority, led by Basner. Koza, the Swarts and Lilian Tshabalala then left the ADP and criticised its actions in *Socialist Action* (March 1945).

Meanwhile railway fares to Orlando/Pimville were increased by 1*d* in September and the workers told that they should claim the extra fare from their employers. When the Action Committee called for a boycott, members of the CPSA also left the body. Despite dissatisfaction, commuters had bought monthly tickets before there was any call for action. When the ADP called a meeting on the issue, their three speakers, Mosaka, Mampuru, and L.P. Kumalo (who was actively engaged in the shantytown movement), were arrested. Subsequently a small group of 20–30 did walk to town but, lacking support, the 'boycott' soon ended.

In November, Labour members on the City Council moved that the city provide a service to its boundary, 1.5 miles from Alexandra, but were vetoed by the Local Transportation Board. They then urged that the city buy the company's buses, but the ruling Ratepayers Association rejected the motion. Finally the Council offered a three months' subsidy of £10,000 to the bus companies, to get the buses back on the road at 4*d*, but the government said the matter lay outside their jurisdiction.[16] The deadlock was broken when the walkers called for a 'sit-down' (or stay-at-home). The CNETU, which was asked to co-operate, suggested a postponement till after the New Year, but the call produced an immediate reaction. The Transvaal Chamber of Industries threatened to fire workers and the City Council defied the government and again offered to subsidise the bus companies. It was proposed that books of coupons, valued at 5*d*, would be discounted and sold at 4*d*, but those without tickets would pay 5*d*, and on weekends, holidays, or Monday mornings the fare would be 7*d* (CPSA, *c.*1945; Stadler, 1981).

The residents supported the radical members of the Action Committee in demanding stage fares, an end to weekend surcharges, and rejection of tickets which involved higher fares for those unable to buy the books. The following day Basner assured residents that it was not necessary to buy full books, and that the Council only needed time to arrange for the transfer of the buses. This did not satisfy the critics, but the residents were persuaded that they had won, and that there was no purpose in continuing the tiring walk. On 4 January 1945 workers tendered their 5*d* coupons, and the boycott was over. But the ADP in Alexandra was shattered. Koza had resigned before the compromise; the Swarts and Lilian Tshabalala joined the WIL; Radebe was back in the fold of the ANC, and was also reported to have returned to the CPSA.

The meaning of victory

There were few who did not welcome the end of the boycott. People were tired and footsore, and during the seven weeks there had been unusually heavy rains. Many reported ill and some lost their jobs; washerwomen had been unable to get their bundles home and were penniless; and many families needed money to buy new shoes. These hardships could not be concealed by the joy of having won against the combined strength of bus owners, employers, the City Council and government. That was no mean achievement, and residents were acclaimed in other townships. In the years to come the 'long walk' became part of the tradition of resistance: that was the legacy bequeathed to those who struggled for better conditions.

Nevertheless, there were misgivings on several counts. By keeping the fare at 4*d* workers had stopped expenses rising by 1*s* per week; yet, although precious, the saving did not appreciably alter the situation of families who lived below the starvation level. There were added fears that after the three months' subsidy ended, fares would be raised again, and that would end the fragile peace. The squabbles seemed interminable. The radical wing, now in the WIL, accused the ADP of betrayal; they, in turn, were lambasted by Basner in a leaflet called 'Wreckers at Work', and by the CPSA. New recriminations were voiced in January when one bus company dismissed three drivers who had sided with the passengers during the boycott, despite assurances that there would be no victimisations. There were also disturbing reports that other bus owners had placed the drivers on weekly notice of dismissal, for fear that the boycott be renewed. Then the buses were all bought by the Public Utility Corporation (PUTCO) — a private company, despite its name — which acceded to the Action Committee's demand that the coupons be scrapped, that the weekend fare be reduced to 6*d*, and that the Monday morning fare be only 4*d*.[17] The centralisation of the buses through PUTCO brought relief to the people of Pretoria and Evaton as well, but the residents had not been brought together during the dispute. There are no indications in any of the reports that the ADP, or the Action Committee, established connections with the other townships during the struggle.

Finally, there was the question of Alexandra's expropriation. Residents were surprised by press reports that Fish, Baloyi and D.G. Nel of the Health Committee were in Cape Town to interview Members of Parliament over the proposed incorporation of Alexandra in Johannesburg. Stand holders were suspected of betrayal, and at a mass meeting at Number 2 Square acclaim greeted a resolution that 'Mr R.G. Baloyi of this Township shall be no more a leader of any class of the African people of this Township until he dies' (*Socialist Action*, March 1945). Alexandra Township was not expropriated, but the stay of execution cannot be attributed directly to the boycott of 1944. Housing in the South West townships had become unbearable, and in 1944 a series of shantytowns were constructed in defiance of the authorities. Under those conditions it was quite apparent that there was nowhere to rehouse the people of Alexandra. The threat of removal had (at least temporarily) receded — except, that is, for those who built a shantytown in Alexandra itself, and were then removed to the Orlando-Moroka area (see Chapter 12).

Notes

1. Rheinallt Jones, reported in Minutes of African Townships Committee, 2 September 1941, SAIRR, A.T.C. 14/41; *Rheinallt Jones Papers*, Johannesburg; *Socialist Action*, November–December 1945.
2. *Agenda*, Johannesburg City Council, pp.46–7. The meeting is referred to in the *Verbatim Report on the Proceedings of the Native Representative Council*, 6th Session, 7–15 December 1942, Vol. 2, p.293; CAMP, Reel 11, 2:AK5/7.
3. R.G. Baloyi, evidence to the Bus Services Commission, 1943, *Xuma Papers*, ABX 430711c. Baloyi was a taxi driver from 1922 to 1927, and then a bus owner in Alexandra. He was National Treasurer of the ANC during the war years.
4. Dr Xuma, Memorandum to the *Commission Appointed to Enquire into the Operation of Bus Services for Non-Europeans on the Witwatersrand and in the Districts of Pretoria and Vereeniging, Xuma Papers*, ABX 430711d.
5. Dr Xuma in his 'Memorandum' spoke of a boycott, but *Inkululeko*, September 1940, only mentioned demonstrations; Saura Woolf, then of the Youth League, was certain there was a boycott and a walk to work (interview, 1976).
6. 'Memorandum representing the Residents of Alexandra Township in Johannesburg, in the dispute over the matter of increased fares between the City–Alexandra Bus Owners and themselves', *Xuma Papers*, ABX 430711a.
7. The Youth League (see Chapter 3), and the Tenants Association were organised by Dr Max Joffee. See *Chain Breaker*, Vol. 1, No. 2, May 1939, Hoover Institute Microfilm, Africa 484, DT779S726, Reel 12. Further information from interviews with Saura Woolf, London, 1977.
8. *Guardian*, 5 November 1942; information on Fish from Miriam Basner, conversations, 1982, Presteigne.
9. *Xuma Papers*: letters 22 January 1940, to Baloyi, ABX 400122b, and to Moroka, ABX 400122a; also letter to D. Mathole inquiring about his shares in the company, 10 February 1940, ABX 400210a, and 15 March 1940, ABX 400315. Shares were not purchased and the company went bankrupt.
10. Although this is only supposition, it is based on an appraisal of the way Xuma acted at a later date, when Sophiatown was being removed and he placed his

own interests above those of the community.

11. Reports in *Inkululeko*, 28 August and 18 September; *Guardian*, 9 September, and the *Star*, 11 August 1943, mentioned Tommy Peters of the defunct SAYL, Mofutsanyana and Marks of the CPSA, and Baloyi.

12. 'Statement of Evidence of Max, a Bus Conductor of Ten Years Standing and a Bus Dispatcher for Five Years', *Xuma Papers*, ABX 430711b.

13. Evidence by Dr Ellen Hellman on behalf of the Alexandra Health Committee, *Star*, 13 September 1943.

14. 'Features of Grievances Regarding the Passenger Transport Operating Between Alexandra Township and the City of Johannesburg', compiled by the Alexandra Women's League, *Xuma Papers*, ABX 430711c. (Also CAMP, Reel 17, 272:WA1:45.)

15. For a fuller account of the ADP and SP, and the personalities involved, see Hirson, 1986, Appendix B. Cornelius and Scheepers were members of the Garment Workers Union Executive, and leaders of the recently formed Independent Labour Party. Szur was one of the leaders of a group that had broken away from the SALP.

16. For the attempted boycott in Orlando see Mampuru, p.20 and *Inkundla ya Bantu*, 30 November and 18 December 1944; for the City Council decisions see *Forward*, 22 November 1944; and for the minority's views see *Socialist Action*, February, March 1945.

17. WIL flyleaf, March 1945, in CAMP, Reel 7B, 2:DW2:84/3. The flyleaf demanded public responsibility for transport, fare stages, and a permanent settlement (which after three months was still not in sight).

12. Umagebule — The Slicer

Orlando, the 'model' township

Throughout the 1930s and 1940s whites and blacks streamed into the towns seeking work, but despite the demand there were always more workers, and particularly unskilled labourers, than industry required. Africans without positions in factories or shops worked as domestic servants, gardeners, night watchmen, 'delivery boys' and road gangers, or took odd jobs. Entry into the towns was controlled, and those 'in excess of calculated labour turnover', were turned back.[1]

Only men employed and registered at the pass office were permitted to stay, with their wives, in the locations. Women had no such rights,[2] and they stayed in the few townships where permits were not required or found jobs in domestic service, living in a room in the back yard. Although this was often little more than a shack with an iron bed and mattress, and adjoining latrine and tap, it could provide shelter (illegally) for husband or friend. Legal barriers did not stop men and women filtering into the towns, and many found ways to subsist through casual employment, petty pilfering, liquor running or beer brewing, illegal gambling rackets, or the more organised criminal gangs. For these people, shelter at night could be a problem, and many slept 'in back yards, in the open yard, on vacant pieces of ground, in shop doorways'[3] or even latrines, transformed by night into doss rooms at a rental of £2 per month (CPSA, c. 1947).

Some slipped in and out of town, and of them the Native Law Commissioner said:

> Natives who have no place where they are legally entitled to live, simply go and sleep in the bushes or on the bare veld, put up shelters of branches, sacks, tins and old sheets of corrugated iron, and in a short while there stands a shanty town. The police are reluctant to interfere, because they themselves do not know where those people can move to. They have, however, broken up some such communities . . . [only to find them rebuilt] one or two miles away. . . . [The] real nucleus of squatter's villages outside town generally consists of people who are employed in the town, but who have been excluded from the towns because the extension of the location has not kept pace with industrial expansion.

To writers of these reports it was natural that there were set places where Africans were 'legally entitled to live'. Otherwise, there was no place to live legally, because the locations had not been built, or had not expanded, to absorb the growing working class.

The restrictions on residential areas did not leave Africans much choice in the towns, but they preferred the back yards or the slum quarters, despite the lack of amenities. This allowed an escape from the prevailing controls and surveillance of the fenced-in location system. Yet when Africans in locations or townships did campaign for more housing, or set up shantytowns, there was no overt call for an end to the location system.

Orlando Township, eleven miles from the centre of the city, was Johannesburg's contribution to 'Native housing': its design decided by competition in 1930 with a £500 prize for the best layout of a new 'model township'. Yet, as Eberhardt (1950, p.12) was to say twenty years later, 'the basic stipulations of the competition made it practically impossible for a model township to emerge'. Rows of two roomed houses were built, on stands 50 by 75 feet, without floors or ceilings, kitchens or bathrooms, electricity, gas or water, and dependent on buckets for sewage disposal.[4] Many houses were built over anthills and the houses were infested with these pests.[5] To overcome the reluctance to move to Orlando, Prospect Township 'was demolished in 1937 . . . and the inhabitants transferred *en masse* to Orlando. Shortly thereafter the population of the Malay quarter in Vrededorp [predominantly African despite its name] were dealt with in like manner.'[6]

The number of Africans entering Johannesburg increased sharply during the first years of the war, when drought in the countryside coincided with increased employment in the war industries. The demand for housing was so great that the townships of Alexandra, Sophiatown and Newclare could absorb no further residents; yet, claiming that there was a shortage of building materials due to war needs, the authorities built no new houses. Instead, regulations prohibiting lodgers, or the sub-letting of dwellings in the locations, were relaxed, and an increasing number of families squeezed into the two- and three-roomed houses.[7]

The householders of Orlando could retain their houses whilst they were gainfully employed, and elected four members of the Advisory Board. The sub-tenants had no rights, being in the house and location on sufferance. Ultimately it was these rightless dwellers who took action. The pioneers of the movement built the first shantytown near Orlando, to be followed by groups in other locations, townships, and even compounds: workers of the Vereeniging Brick and Tile Company, protesting against intolerable living conditions, set up shacks near the new Sharpeville location.[8]

According to the Moroka Commission Report (1948, p.22) associations formed by sub-tenants in the locations or townships set up the squatter camps. Their leaders controlled site allocation and provided amenities, had their own 'strong-arm' corps, meted out justice in courts, levied fines and floggings, and controlled entry to the camps. Their followers paid a weekly toll and food vans could enter only on paying a fee. All monies were in the hands of the leaders, to be used at their discretion. The rank and file obeyed instructions and, in return, got their squatter 'rights' and protection against intruders — including the alien city authority. Women were among the group's most devoted members: widowed, deserted, young unmarried, or newly arrived women faced ejection from the townships if discovered. In the shantytowns they enjoyed a new freedom, and were beholden only to the leader.

The Sofasonke ('We Shall All Die') Movement

Several men emerged in 1944–45 as shantytown leaders, but it was James Sofasonke Mpanza who initiated, inspired, and planned the greatest shantytown of all. Born in 1890, he was an interpreter and clerk at the age of 18, but was imprisoned for fraud in 1910 and sentenced to death in 1912 for murdering his employer, an Indian trader. He was reprieved, and spent the next thirteen years in gaol. In 1918, said Mpanza, he 'had a vision: was converted to the Lord . . . and was born again', and was allowed to preach to prison inmates. On release he continued to preach, and then arrived in Johannesburg in 1930 where he taught at a 'private school'.[9]

In Orlando, Mpanza was a trader or hawker, and a householder, which allowed him to be elected to the Advisory Board. No evidence is available on his policies prior to 1944, the year in which he took action on the housing situation.[10] He sought allies for an *ad hoc* civic body and approached the CPSA and the ADP (whose members had been defeated in the last Advisory Board election by communist candidates). The CPSA group in Orlando stayed aloof, playing no part in the events that followed (Mampuru, 1945, pp.19–22).

The civic body called meetings in Orlando, and on the night of 25 March some 500 families met on the location outskirts with Mpanza. He was dressed in the regalia which he wore throughout this period, part 'chief' and part commissionaire. Mpanza announced that they were about to cross the River Jordan, and led them to a strip of bare veld which he named Sofasonke Village. Entrants paid 6s (being membership fee of the Sofasonke Party, and qualification for living in the camp), 2s 6d for admission to the site, and then 2s 6d per week for administration and policing of the village (*Moroka Report*, 1948, p.24). Sofasonke Village was built of cardboard, flattened biscuit tins, hessian, poles and even mealie stalks. In most cases the structures gave minimal protection from the rain and the cold, and many squatters suffered severe discomfort, illness, and death in the coming months (Huddleston, 1956, p.54). The City Council chose initially to ignore the move: offering no assistance, but not intervening. Within a matter of days, some 3,500 families had gathered in the camp (Mampuru, report, April 1944).

At this stage the ADP worked with Mpanza, and Basner and Mosaka were guests of honour at a meeting within the first week of the move. Miriam Basner, in a letter to the author, writes:

> . . . it [was] a dramatic occasion, culminating in us being escorted down the hill on our way back by the whole population, by torchlight, dancing and singing, with the red dust high in the air. The numbers were so great that I swear the earth jumped underfoot to their stamping!

Hyman Basner acted on behalf of the squatters in negotiations with the City Council, and [?] Nchee, a paid organiser of the ADP, was named Deputy Leader of the new settlement (Mampuru, 1945). The ADP, however, exercised very little influence on Mpanza and his followers. In part, this can be ascribed to their policy of 'peaceful negotiations'. They were on course when the idea was first mooted: that is 'to bring the situation to the notice of the authorities', but were distressed by the tough measures used to keep the settlement in order, and could not cope with a leader who wanted to be a 'Messiah-cum-Chief-cum-Gangster Boss and wanting housing for everyone . . . . Mad or sane, he was cunning and brave, dedicated and grasping, all at once' (M. Basner, letter).

The police would not intervene, saying it was a civil issue between municipality and squatters, and the City Council could not prosecute because, they were advised, this would fail if no alternative housing was available. Consequently, the Non-European Affairs Department announced that they would not prosecute, provided the influx into the camp stopped. Squatters employed in Johannesburg could remain, pending the provision of housing, and meanwhile water and sanitary services would be provided (*Moroka Report*, 1948, pp.25—7). Mpanza accepted the services but did not stop new squatters, and the Council appointed a white inspector and thirteen special African policemen to prevent further entrants. Four thousand breeze-block shelters were commissioned (*sans* windows and *sans* doors)[11] and squatters could rent them for 5s per month if they demolished their shanties (without compensation). The City Council took over the administration of the shantytown in June, and members of the ADP, now in disagreement with Mpanza on the committee, welcomed the change.[12]

It was mid-winter, bitterly cold, and the City Council set up a soup distribution centre at the camp. The Mpanza family intervened, declaring: 'We have not come here for soup. We want houses', and Mpanza's wife Julia was said to have wielded a *sjambok* and knobkerrie to stop anyone taking a portion. There was a fight and John Mpine, one of the squatters, was killed. James, Julia and Julia's father were arrested, but there was no charge to answer and the family was released (Kros, 1978, quoting *Bantu World*, 2 January 1954). Mampuru condemned the Mpanzas, maintaining that their hostility to the Council arose from the loss of shantytown revenue.[13] But Mampuru failed to understand Mpanza's followers. They saw him as a saviour, in both the religious and secular sense, and believed he would get them homes. Anyone who broke ranks (even to take soup), was weakening the cause, and it was bitterness over this that lay behind the fighting (*Moroka Report*, 1948, Conclusion). At the trial women from the camp packed the court, and when Mpanza was released on bail his message to his supporters, despite its pretensions and absurdities, was hailed with enthusiasm:

> The position of the chieftainship is given to me like Jesus. Many people thought I was arrested and I was not. The same as with Jesus. Many thought he was dead, and yet he was not.[14]

A Vigilance Committee, opposed to the Sofasonke Party, was formed after the split over the shelters, but the two groups formed a joint Independent Committee, which was recognised by the superintendent — and usually bypassed! Complaints about rentals and allocations of the shelters were ignored (only the Advisory Board, on which squatters were not represented, being consulted). When the Committee pressed for the right of squatters to trade in their own shanty stores, a temporary market building was built on the outskirts of the shantytown, and licences given to non-residents. The squatters persisted in patronising their own traders, who were prosecuted for being without a licence to sell.[15] Mpanza and his friends outflanked the Vigilance Committee in December 1944 by winning Advisory Board seats on a Sofasonke-ADP slate.[16] Their manifesto called for opposition to the City Council's plan to impose passes on women when (as rumoured) they gained control of pass distribution; and for rejection of the expulsion of the homeless from Johannesburg as a 'solution' to the housing problem.

In October 1945 the 4,042 shelters and 73 blocks of communal latrines were completed and the shanties demolished. Some 20,000 persons were moved and the City Council, alarmed at the new call to house a further 30,000, took steps to remove the one man who personified the squatter community — James Mpanza. The conflict between Mpanza and the Council extended over several years. The Labour Party, which took office after the first shelters were commissioned, never controlled or defeated its *bête noire*. In their clash with Mpanza, the councillors perceived only a crook or a charlatan, living off the proceeds of the squatters' rentals: like Mampuru, they underestimated the reverence accorded him by his followers.

Mpanza was a consummate showman who taunted and ridiculed officials at meetings, and mixed political pronouncements with 'prophecy' to prove his superior powers. He was proved correct when he announced at one meeting that the approaching rains would cover the veld below, but would not touch a nearby hill; and also when he said that the Manager of the Non-European Affairs Department would not arrive at a meeting because the roads would be washed away. These 'prophecies' were probably based on knowledge of local natural phenomena, but that did not detract from Mpanza's 'prescience' and councillors felt less able to cope with the challenge he presented.

Council antipathy increased when (it is alleged) he said he would lead the people off the land if a racecourse was built and he had control of the tote. Mpanza's passionate interest in horses was well known — he rode through Orlando on his favourite brown steed, followed by his entourage on foot — and he might have wanted his racecourse, but he was no Pied Piper, and the squatters would not have surrendered the land they occupied. It is also possible that his 'offer' was a jibe at his white opponents, but Colin Legum (and other councillors) believed him capable of any chicanery and were resolved to remove him (conversation with Legum, 1976).

The press disclosed plans to remove Mpanza in December 1944, but the deportation order was served only after several confrontations between squatters and officials, which all believed to have been engineered. On 23 January, Mpanza, Xorile and L.P. Kumalo demanded that the Council provide tents for the sub-tenants, or make land available for building houses.

Four days later, Legum and W. Light of the Council, and L.I. Venables of the Non-European Affairs Department addressed a meeting and requested thirty days in which to attend to the matter. The next day a thousand families arrived at the Orlando superintendent's office saying they had been expelled by householders and had nowhere to go: some occupied, and others camped around 61 partly completed or vacant houses (earmarked for others) (*Socialist Action*, February 1946).

Some Council officials wanted deportation warnings to 'instigators', the eviction of families who had occupied houses, and their removal to tents.[17] But it all failed. The tents acquired from the government were unsuitable, and without accompanying poles could not even be erected; the government opposed the removal of the families; and the steps taken against L.P. Kumalo, Xorile and Mpanza, deemed to be the instigators of the new squat, misfired. L.P. Kumalo and Xorile were only warned that they would be deported, and Edward Kumalo, another 'instigator', was removed only to reappear in August 1947 as the leader of a new squat (see below).

Mpanza was ordered out of Johannesburg but invoked the (archaic) Exemption from Native Law of 1865, which applied to 'detribalised Natives' of Natal, proving that he was exempted from the provisions of the Native Administration Act. To celebrate his victory he slaughtered an ox and distributed the meat ceremoniously. The people marched past him as he sat in state, and a praise-singer lauded him as King of Orlando. Despite the many charges proffered against him, Mpanza always won, and even when the (Natal) letter of exemption was withdrawn, he was not prosecuted because each case only enhanced his status! (*Moroka Report*, 1948, pp.35–43; Stadler, 1979).

Before the hearing of his appeal against the deportation in September 1946, the squatters' movement spread to Alberton, Kliptown, Vereeniging, Pimville, Albertynville and Alexandra: all regions of high population density, and all acutely short of housing. The 119 families who squatted on the commonage at Alberton, just outside Johannesburg, got short shrift: their shelters were destroyed, and they were moved sixty miles away to Hammanskraal and placed under canvas (*Socialist Action*, May 1945). On 3 February 1946 similar action was taken in Orlando when the location superintendent used emergency regulations to order squatters out of the occupied houses. They moved, but took possession of the Orlando Communal Hall and camped in its grounds. Others joined them, and within days hundreds of hessian shacks were erected, containing 300–500 families.

On 18 February the Council, with ministerial permission, drafted 400 white armed police and 350 municipal (black) police and labourers to remove these families. The squatters were given 15 minutes to quit, and dragged their belongings into the veld. There they stayed, huddled under the trees, some 50 yards from the hall, and forbidden to erect any shelters. On 8 March, in heavy rain, they defiantly erected shacks which the municipal workers, against police advice, were ordered to destroy. In the melée that followed, a municipal policeman and a squatter were killed, and many others injured. The squatters drove the labourers and police into the Communal Hall and, ignoring Mosaka's intercession, only agreed to release them the following day.[18] An uneasy peace followed: only after a third squatters' movement appeared later that month did the councillors agree to meet Mosaka and Mpanza. Land was offered at Jabavu, on which residents shown to be employed in Johannesburg could erect rent-free shelters some two to three miles from the hall. Transport, water taps and latrines would be provided by the Council.

The Council tried at the last minute to switch squatters and 'legitimate' sub-tenants; the latter to be sent to the new shelters at Jabavu, and the squatters shifted back to sub-tenancy in Orlando. But existing sub-tenants feared scrutiny, and squatters would not return. The plan was therefore dropped and finally, of the 1,538 families who had squatted, 1,062 were taken to Jabavu, 174 disappeared before they could be charged, and 80 were charged under the Urban Areas Act and deported.

The 'Slicers'

James Mpanza was hailed as *Magebule*, the Slicer, by his followers, because he had sliced a new piece of land for them from the Council. In fact, it was the thousands of men, women, and children who set up their shacks on the veld, in the face of a hostile Council and government, and withstood all attempts at removing them, who had carved out the land. Mpanza, in leading these people, put himself at the head of the biggest social and political upheaval of the war years.

Mpanza attacked all political parties except the ADP, but the latter was snuffed out by the shantytown movement. Mosaka and Mampuru were committee men, not activists, and their participation in the bus boycott and in Orlando extended them to the limit. Their dark suits and ties marked them as strangers in the midst of hessian shacks and cardboard shelters. The colourful dress of Mpanza, his 'prophecies', religious pretensions and fierce independence, were somehow more appropriate to shantytown than the measured tones of his ADP allies.

The ANC's relations with Mpanza appear to have been those of mutual antagonism. The ANC condemned all independent initiative, and Mpanza would brook no rivals. But there was criticism inside the ANC. 'Kanyisa', writing in *Inkundla ya Bantu* on 27 February 1947, said:

> Congress has shilly-shallied and missed a golden opportunity to crystallise the shantytown movement into the spearhead of the African's fight against oppression and the discriminatory land policy. Shantytowns grow every month around Johannesburg and to this day Congress has no plan of how to deal with them.

There was a point at which the paths of Mpanza (an Africanist in deed) and A.W. Lembede, the philosopher of that ideology, joined in an attack on communism. Mpanza, astride his horse, arrived with his followers at a meeting of the Orlando branch of the ANC in July 1945, and L.P. Kumalo led the group into the hall. Chanting 'Communist Jew' they demanded that elections to the branch committee be reopened. Lembede, who had been silent, joined the Sofasonke group in their attack on the platform, but Dan Tloome, from the chair, stopped them (*Inkululeko*, 28 July 1945). The two men might have met again — but they were on different tracks: Lembede had no record of practical work in the community and Mpanza had no overt political philosophy. Nonetheless, despite their meeting that day being a coincidence, their agreement was in keeping with a broad sympathy of outlook and a shared hatred of the CPSA.

New squatters, new leaders

One of Johannesburg's worst locations was Pimville (previously Klipspruit), an area near Orlando. Built as a temporary township in 1904, it bordered a sewage farm and was condemned as a residential area in 1920, but still had 12,500 residents in 1938. The houses were either semi-cylindrical corrugated iron tanks, placed on the earth like roofs without walls, ceilings, floors, or windows, and with no facilities for cooking or washing; or consisted of wood and iron rooms that were described in an official report as providing 'a rather primitive type of accommodation'.[19]

In 1943 residents were informed that they would be moved to Orlando West and their houses demolished. Then the plan was shelved and sub-tenants were told that they would be allocated twelve out of every fifty houses built in Orlando West. Only a few of the houses had been built when Mpanza crossed his River Jordan, and in December 1945 his followers occupied them. After that all new houses were given to Orlando residents: Mdatyualwa reported that in 1945 Venables appealed to Pimville sub-tenants to wait. When more squatters appeared in Orlando, the Pimville Sub-Tenants Association pressed for homes and were assured by councillors that 36 of the first 150 houses would be allocated to them. Shortly thereafter houses were available, but the Council's decision to make the allocations were disputed by the Sub-Tenants Association. On 24 March Abiel Ntoi, their chairman, declaring that only those who broke the law got houses, led a group of some thirty men and sixty women to Orlando West. There they squatted, and grew in number to some 1,500—2,000. On 12 May they were given seven days to return home. After demanding that their rentals be fixed by the Rent Board — which the Council rejected — the squatters refused to move, until eventually 456 families were transported to the new Jabavu site and 437 who could prove local employment were permitted to erect shacks (Mdatyualwa, 1946).

Squatter groups appeared in and around Johannesburg in 1946, as living conditions grew increasingly impossible. On 2 September 1946 L.I. Venables, manager of the Non-European and Native Affairs Department, reported that in Newclare,

Inhabitants were being exploited by unscrupulous landlords. In many cases they were living in crowded rooms, in stables, and in verminous and greatly overcrowded structures of all kinds. . . . In some cases as many as nine or ten people were living in a room 12 [feet] square — people of all ages and of both sexes. There was no room to walk between the people, and sanitary facilities were inadequate. . . .

Small groups of 25–50 families erected shacks near the Newclare station but were dispersed by police before they could settle in. Other Newclare residents went in truckloads to Orlando, but were told to move on and eventually camped at Albertynville (their story is told below). Despite the dubious legality of squatting, none crossed the segregatory boundaries, or threatened the social structure of the towns. The action was unruly, and even rebellious, but went no further, and the state found no need for drastic counter-measures. One medical officer even stated that:

Something had to happen to relieve the strain both on accommodation and on family incomes. . . . Squatters' camps have sprung up, where up to the present, no rentals have been payable. Thus the squatters have more to spend on food. Hunger is less tolerable than life virtually in the open air, and indeed, life in the open air is, for most days in the year in South Africa, more tolerable than life in an overcrowded, ill-ventilated, slum dwelling. . . .

. . . [A]dequate nutrition is even more important for health than is good housing. For this reason . . . even the squatters' camp[s] may not be an unmitigated evil if they help the inhabitants to tide over the present period of high food prices.[20]

'Life in the open air' was a remarkable prescription for good health from doctors who retired to their well-fitted houses every evening. However, the belief that this would save money which could be used for food was a misreading of what was happening. The Albertynville families had first squatted at Volkshaven, and then moved to a site nearer Johannesburg which they 'purchased' from Ebrahim Moonshi. Unfortunately the land was not Moonshi's to sell and when he died shortly thereafter the squatters had to pay for the right to erect dwellings:

It is about ten or twelve miles from the centre of the city . . . on a particularly bleak and barren piece of veld. The land is owned by an individual who charges rent to each squatter electing to build his shack there. Amenities are almost entirely lacking. It is just a conglomerate of lean-to corrugated-iron and mud-brick dwellings, with water of a kind, not too far away (Huddleston, 1956, p.39).

Edward Kumalo, expelled by the Council from the Orlando shantytown, moved to Albertynville and assumed leadership of the squatters. There were nearly 2,000 persons on the site by mid-1947 and there they lived, a forgotten group, until six years later a tornado left 'forlorn bits of wreckage that had been "houses" — the old iron tins and biscuit boxes, the mud (bricks) crumbling into slime, the timber from packing-cases. . .' (ibid). Following an appeal from the Mayor of Johannesburg the families received money, clothes, and provisions. Within weeks a new shantytown was built, and the *status quo ante* restored. In 1956 the camp had grown to 15,000 when all were ordered to quit and move to the fast-growing Orlando complex where plots were provided on the basis of 'site and service' (tenants to build their own shacks, standpipes and latrines being provided). All but

110 of the family heads were employed in Johannesburg, and they received sites. Seventy men and women who had served the squatters as traders, tailors, carpenters, cobblers, coal dealers, herbalists, and so on — or as washerwomen, or part-time domestic servants — were told to obtain accommodation for their families by taking up employment as farm labourers.[21]

A priest at 'Tobruk'

On 7 September 1946, some 800 families, led by Oriel Lotuma Monongoaha of the Pimville Sub-Tenants Vigilance Committee, occupied the land on which the worst houses stood before demolition. Within a few weeks there were 2,400 families. Most were forcibly ejected by the police and squatted on an adjoining site; a minority returned to their previous homes. The camp was forced to move again, and 1,500 families squatted in Orlando. There the community grew to between 3,000 and 5,000 families, the majority led by Monongoaha, a smaller group following the lead of a Coloured ex-serviceman, Samuel Komo (*Moroka Report*, 1948, pp.65—6).

Komo was a chief interpreter during the war and had joined the Springbok Legion, as had his main associates. They called their camp Tobruk, a name that symbolised stubborn resistance, but it was like most camps in practice. The residents paid the fees and the leaders arranged latrines, rubbish disposal, water, law courts, and so on (Scott, 1946, pp.164—8; Davidson, 1952, p.130). The Tobruk camp split and one faction invited Michael Scott, fresh from his participation in the Natal Indian campaign against discriminatory laws, to straighten out the administration of the camp. Scott (p.158) went in with evangelical fervour to oppose the 'gangsters who ruled Tobruk' and place control in the hands of the Congregational Church of Christ. At first he triumphed. Komo was removed, a new constitution was drafted, and Scott chaired the committee overseeing the services of the camp.

Komo and his followers launched a counter-attack, with raids on shacks and harassment of church followers. Finally, they burnt down the hessian church. Komo did not want Scott, and the police concurred: Scott trespassed by living in a Native area, and was prosecuted. In the middle of court proceedings there was an outbreak of smallpox in the camp and Scott was released to tend the ill. This was followed by cases of typhoid, and again Scott was needed. Shortly thereafter the case was dropped. Although he no longer slept in the camp, Scott visited the site daily. Komo and 28 others were also tried, for assault on Scott and his Christian followers, but the charges were withdrawn because the assailants could not be identified.[22]

Communists at the tail end

Communists rejected Mpanza's invitation to join the original shantytown, partly because they mistrusted the man, but mainly, said Hilda Watts, because:

VOTE FOR

L. P. KUMALO   J. G. MOPHIRING
J. S. MPHANZA   G. G. XORILE
Official Candidates for the African Democratic Party

The ADP-supported candidates for the Orlando Advisory Board elections, December 1944 — posing for an advertisement which appeared in Basner's *Socialist Review* (Mpanza in regalia).

(Leon Levson/IDAF)

The Tobruk leaders, ex-servicemen and still in uniform, 'inspecting the guard'.

Opposite: The playing fields of Orlando. Over a Jordan like this one Mpanza led his followers to found Sofasonke Village (Africana Museum, Johannesburg).

A shanytytown structure.

'Breezeblock' latrines provided by the municipality.

How *Socialist Review* saw the shantytowns, June 1945.

Backyard kitchens Prospect Township.

The forced removal — Prospect Township, 1948.

A shop in shantytown.

Moroka street scene.

The building: 'site and service' construction in progress.

The breaking: a family looks on helplessly as their shanty comes down.

Police raid. Anywhere, any time, South Africa.

(*Star*, Johannesburg)

it was generally agreed [after discussion in Johannesburg groups] that the party could not have been so irresponsible as to send thousands of people to set up hessian shanties at the beginning of winter, with all the resultant dangers, particularly to the children (*Freedom*, November–December 1946).

Watts said the CPSA offered assistance to the squatters, but 'actively discouraged' the setting up of the camps. Shantytowns could not solve the housing question, and ultimately they would just become part of the townships. Watts also condemned the extortion of money by unscrupulous leaders who looked upon the squatters as a source of income: the correct procedure was to campaign against the land laws, and for higher wages so that workers could obtain their own houses.

The matter was somewhat more complicated than Watts indicated. The CPSA had lost the initiative in the townships while trying to win the support of the whites and raise funds for Medical Aid for Russia. Members of the CPSA, particularly among ex-servicemen, complained about the direction of party activity, and warned:

it is more important for the Communist Party to win every election in the location than to win four thousand votes from the Europeans in Hillbrow and Yeoville, and lose every Advisory Board to the Trotskyists [*sic*].[23]

One month later the CPSA was severely embarrassed when Franz Boshoff, a lawyer achieving prominence in party circles, accepted a brief to appear for the state in the action against Mpanza. Coming so soon after the defeat of CPSA candidates in Orlando, this collusion between a party member and the state against a shantytown leader caused considerable discomfort. Boshoff was suspended, and no more was heard of him (*Inkululeko*, March 1946). The CPSA had further cause to revise its policy when Tobruk was established by members of the Springbok Legion, an organisation with which the party had close ties. Then came the shantytown of Alexandra's sub-tenants, under the leadership of Schreiner Bhaduza, Abner Kunene and Mark Ramitloa, all committee members of the CPSA in the township.[24]

The first Alexandra squat started in November 1946, when 78 families of the Alexandra Tenants Association occupied land adjacent to the township. The police demolished the shacks, dispersed the squatters, and arrested Bhaduza (chairman) and Kunene (secretary), who were charged under the Native Trust and Land Act but released. On 29 November 100 families set up a camp, but dispersed after the Native Commissioner and members of the Alexandra Health Committee addressed them. A few days later a much larger group from Alexandra under Bhaduza's leadership assembled alongside Tobruk and set up a camp of 600–800 shacks.

The City Council moved the families back to Alexandra (under a court order) on 3 January 1946, taking with them some Orlando squatters. A camp was opened on two of the public squares and there they were joined by new families, until there were over 6,000 persons (*Moroka Report*, 1948, pp.70–1). All three squares were soon filled, and the health and hygiene problems were intractable. 'A stench hung over the camp,' and there were cases of smallpox and typhoid (*South African Builder*, April 1947). The City

Council, in urgent consultation with the government (over finances) set aside land for site-and-service plots to accommodate 10,000 squatter families immediately and 10,000 more when necessary. The Council would provide water, pit latrines, administrative buildings and clinics; the government would secure building materials, including cement and water piping. The residents would have sites measuring 20 feet square, on which to erect a single room structure, without any partitions, no larger than 14 feet square.[25]

The squatters from Pimville, Orlando and Alexandra were all transported to the new township, named Moroka. This was no more than an elephantine, official shantytown, on which families were given sites to occupy (if they were employed in Johannesburg) at an exorbitant rental of 17s per month. This was the end of the autonomous and self-controlled squatter camps, at least for the time being, and despite the smallness of the sites, many families constructed their own houses of brick, mud brick, or just mud. The average cost of a house was £10 (*South African Builder*, February and September 1951).

When the Johannesburg District Committee of the CPSA met in January 1947, it was confronted with an emergency following the mineworkers' strike, raids by police (on the party, the trade unions, the *Guardian*, and the Springbok Legion), the trial of leading members after the strike, and then the arraignment of eight members of the Central Committee of the party on a charge of sedition (see Chapter 14). The committee resolved that its earlier appraisal of the shantytowns had been wrong, and that as the camps had grown in size, the movement had matured in wisdom and political consciousness. The resolution continued:

> The demand for land is the most profound national aspiration of the oppressed African people . . . [and the shantytown movement constituted an] important contribution towards the struggle for the national liberation of the African people.[26]

The CPSA also reported in *Inkululeko* (January (2), 1947) that 'the leaders of the most important shantytowns from Alexandra, Orlando and Albertynville met and formed the Johannesburg Joint Shanty Towns Co-ordinating Committee'. Bhaduza was chairman, Monongoaha was treasurer, and Mofutsanyana (who previously opposed the squatting, and condemned the leaders as 'less politically advanced'), was the secretary. The committee was formed by the CPSA, in belated recognition of the social significance of the squatters' movement, but it was too late. Within six months all squatters' camps, except those in Albertynville, were moved to Moroka and lost their group identity. Bhaduza and Bokaba were deported to Hammanskraal, and Kunene and Ramitloa (the writer Modikwe Dikobe) were placed in houses in Orlando to keep them away from their former constituents (*Inkululeko*, January (2), 1947).

A rent strike and riot: the end of the road

In May the Co-ordinating Committee protested against the application of emergency regulations to the proposed new camp; the powers given the superintendent to make each resident prove that he was a 'fit and proper person to reside in the camp'; the restricted size of each site; and the rental of 15s per month — in contrast to 17s 4d for a two-roomed brick house in Orlando and 10s in Pimville (*Inkululeko*, May (2), 1947).

Monongoaha also issued a statement on 29 April 1947 as 'the leader of the squatters'. He demanded plots of 30 by 50 yards, to allow residents to keep horses, cattle, cars and trollies, and a rental of 7s 6d per month (comprising three sums of 2s 6d for water, sanitary charges, and lodger's permit). He wanted emergency regulations replaced by municipal regulations under the Urban Areas Act; rejected the Council's statement that Moroka would be a temporary camp for five years; and wanted 99-year leases, 'or at least 50 years' (*Xuma Papers*, ABX 470429). Monongoaha claimed that his memorandum was 'the leading power of the aim and objects of the squatters'. He forecast a camp population of 9,000, requiring 180 stalls; that is, 60 each for groceries and provisions, butcheries, and eating houses. A further sixty would be required for shoemaking, tailoring, hairdressing and so on, and each stall would pay a rental of 15s per month. He also wanted a 'West Orlando Squatters Transportation Co-operation', for 'Native Transporters'. There would be an entrance fee of £10 which would be for bursaries to 'eventually contribute to the financial development of the African people as a whole'.

Although much of the memorandum was unrealisable, Monongoaha had thought out some of the problems more thoroughly than the municipal officials. The residents were discontented, and their complaints were stated in the memorandum of the Moroka Vigilance and Tenants League: the sites were tiny, the rents exorbitant, the lack of privacy in the small shacks unbearable, and the superintendent's powers (to remove residents, prohibit meetings, stop collections, and even decide if a dog could be kept) unacceptable.

According to the City Council (as quoted by Stadler, 1979), the rents had to be 'high enough to deter householders from joining squatting; not so high as to result in boycott of camp and mass squatting on free ground; not so low as to result in occupants refusing to move to temporary housing when ready'. That is, the squatters' movement had to be stamped out. But they were not easily intimidated, and refused to pay any rental. There were 1,750 householders registered in Jabavu, and of these, 43 paid rent in May 1947. Two paid rent in June (ibid.). Residents had been told there would be no rentals in Jabavu, and led by Ntoi and Peter Lengeni (who organised the Asinamali, or 'No Money' Party), took the matter to the courts. They lost the case, however, and faced the prospect of paying up or being removed.[27]

The residents were angry when, as non-rent payers, they were debarred from voting in Advisory Board elections. They also complained about liquor raids, and were bitter over the allocation of trading licences for 26 stalls in Moroka (*Moroka Report*, 1948, pp.80–3). The question of trading arose in the first squatter camp organised by Mpanza, and surfaced again in Moroka and Jabavu. The issue did not concern traders (some of whom were also householders) alone: the stalls were a potential source of income which could be used to finance some of the community services, and a source of emergency supplies for residents. The procedures announced by the City Council in calling for stall holders also angered the squatters. The successful applicants had to show connections with a commercial wholesaler, demonstrate literacy and ability to keep books, and possess capital resources. There were 243 applicants, including 26 from the camps; but only three squatters were offered stalls (*Moroka Report*, 1948, p.5).

A demonstration against the stalls was called for 30 August, but it is not clear who made the call or how many responded. Ellen Hellmann stated that only 150–200 (out of a population of 60,000) were involved in the riot that followed – but there is little information on how many joined the demonstration. What is clear, however, is that a small number did attack the stalls, and that there was considerable looting.[28] The police were summoned and fired into the air. Stones were thrown in response and, in the barrage, three policemen were killed. The crowd then scattered, and 21 were arrested. Thirteen were found guilty on various charges, and received gaol sentences ranging from six months to ten years (*Moroka Report*, 1948, p.10).

Although the riot was provoked by the setting up of the stalls, and there was antagonism against the new traders, the issues transcended the matter of trade. The squatters were furious at the way their demands were dismissed, but they were also undoubtedly aware of the collapse of the original community spirit. The shantytown groups were breaking up inside the large, faceless camps controlled by the superintendent and municipal officials. They still lived in makeshift shacks, but without the sense of self-governance which made the earlier (and less comfortable) camps more bearable. The stall holders, who appeared to be the creatures of officialdom, bore the brunt of their anger, and that anger spilled over when police arrived bearing arms. For some, *Sofasonke*, We Shall All Die, became all too apt a name that day. Nevertheless, shortly afterwards, rents were reduced (retrospectively to the beginning of the camps) to 10*s* per month. Whether it was a result of the riots is not known – but it was seen as a victory by those who took part in the events of the day.

The shantytown movement had lost its impetus, but the mood of resistance which governed the men and women who walked or squatted, in bus boycotts or shantytowns, was part of a groundswell which impelled the political movement forward. The struggle was cruel, and it devoured people and political groups. The ADP, which seemed to ride so high, disappeared because it was not ready to meet the challenges – then or later. The CPSA missed the main opportunity, and could not capitalise on the growing militancy, because passivity in the face of popular action had become part of its hallmark.

The squatter leaders were scattered: some had been banished, others faded into obscurity or left the centres of struggle, and James Mpanza alone remained. He still rode his horse 'into battle', breaking up meetings. When he disrupted the White City Residents Association in January 1948, he declared from the saddle that he was King of Orlando. He still won elections to the Orlando Advisory Board, and although he changed the name of his organisation to the Magebule Party, the name by which he was always known was Sofasonke, and he remained on the Board until his defeat in June 1955.[29]

The mood of resistance and anger was translated by the Congress Youth League into the rhetoric of their programme, but the failure of the ANC to participate in the major township events of Johannesburg left it small and relatively powerless. The ANC was the only organisation to survive the collapse or banning of political groups in the early 1950s, and that ensured its future activity — but it had failed to bring substantial sections of the townships (in the Transvaal) into its ranks, and it lacked a base inside the organised workers' movement. That lay in the future: but the process of collapse, particularly of the trade union movement, took place in the aftermath of the war. It is this collapse which is discussed in Chapters 13 and 14.

Notes

1. This is from the *Report of Native Laws Commission*, 1948, p.5, but it could refer to any year in the 1930s or 1940s.
2. Widows and single women who lived in locations faced ejection, and that was a factor in their support for shantytown leaders during the 1940s.
3. Assistant Manager, Johannesburg Non-European and Native Affairs Department, reported in *Minutes of a Conference on Urban Juvenile Native Delinquency*, Johannesburg, 1938.
4. Eberhardt, c. 1950, p.14; 500 houses were built in 1932, and by 1939 there were 4,088 two-roomed houses and 1,801 three-roomed houses, with one standpipe for every twelve houses. All plots were of equal size. See also R. Kantorovich, 'Planning', in Connell et al., 1939, p.104.
5. Electioneering flysheet for Advisory Board elections, L.P. Kumalo, J.S. Mpanza, J.G. Mophiring, G.G. Xorile, December 1944.
6. Eberhardt, c. 1950, p.14. The factual tone of this official publication conceals the trauma of the removals. J. Wells, 1982, pp.267—8, describes the cat and mouse game played by families who occupied houses as others were evacuated, and had themselves to be moved before Prospect Township (near the city centre) could be demolished.
7. Annual Report of the Manager, Non-European Affairs Department, December 1944 to June 1948, CAMP, Reel 16, 272:BJM:61/1.
8. The shantytown was built in 1942. Families were promised houses as soon as building materials arrived, but were removed to the Old Location in June 1944, where they established their 'new' shantytown, *Guardian*, 8 July 1944 and 14 August 1944. See also Hirson, *Workers Voice*, June 1944, Hoover Institute Microfilm, Reel 9.
9. Mpanza provided these details in *African Sunrise*, March 1946. This journal, for jazz fans, is not available, but extracts are quoted by Roux, 1949,

pp.331–3; Roux also provides information on the journal, p.357. 'Sofasonke' (We Shall All Die), was used by Mpanza as a personal name and as the name of his organisation.

10. Self Mampuru, Report to Friends of Africa, April 1944, *Ballinger Papers*, Johannesburg. Mpanza said he meant 'to bring the situation to the notice of the authorities'.

11. Breeze-block slabs were eight parts ash to one part each of sand and cement. They were porous.

12. Mampuru, Report to Friends of Africa, May–June 1944, *Ballinger Papers*.

13. Mampuru, Report to Friends of Africa, 20 July 1944, *Ballinger Papers*.

14. Quoted by Stadler, 1979, from the Johannesburg City Council Supplementary Memorandum to the Moroka Commission.

15. Anon ('By a Resident African'), 'What is happening in Shanty Town', *Democrat*, 20 October 1945. I have found no further details on the Vigilance Committee.

16. There were two candidates from each party: James Mpanza and Lucas P. Kumalo, and J.P. Mophiring and G.G. Xorile (who all won). Their opponents (who lost) included E. Mofutsanyana and S. Moema, members of the CPSA and the Anti-Pass Council.

17. L.I. Venables, 'Annual Report of the Manager, Non-European Affairs Department, for the period December 1944 to 30 June 1948', CAMP, Reel 16, 272:BJ7:61/1.

18. For the evictions see *Moroka Report*, 1948, pp.51–2; Cross, 1946; and a report by J. Mdatyualwa, organiser for the ADP, 1946.

19. Johannesburg City Council, *Non-European Housing*, 1951, p.2; CPSA, c. 1947; Kagan, 1978, pp.98–107; Maud, 1938, pp.135, 355.

20. 'Annual Report of the Department of Public Health, year ended 30th June, 1946', UG18, 1947, p.2 (thanks to Shula Marks for this reference).

21. Memorandum by Ruth Heyman, legal representative for the 110 families, *Heyman Papers*, SOAS. The fate of the 110 is not known.

22. Except for a short account in the *Moroka Report*, 1948, p.72, I have had to rely almost entirely on Scott's account. He offers no satisfactory explanation for the invitation into the camp, for the split, or the violence and counter-violence in the camp.

23. B. O'Brien, 1946. Hillbrow (represented by Watts) and Yeoville were middle-class suburbs. All opponents were dubbed 'Trotskyists' and O'Brien was undoubtedly referring to the ADP.

24. Alexandra committee members were announced in *Inkululeko*, 24 August 1944; leadership of the squat in *Inkululeko*, July (2) 1947. See also Modikwe Dikobe, 1979a, pp.109–14.

25. *Moroka Report*, 1948, p.74; *South African Builder*, February 1951; Moroka Vigilance and Tenants League Memorandum, 1947, *Xuma Papers, ABX 470831a*.

26. *Inkululeko*, January (2) 1947; CPSA, c. 1947; M. Harmel, 'Johannesburg squatters movement', *Freedom*, Vol. 6, Nos 1 and 2, 1947.

27. Ibid., p.37. G.G. Xorile broke with Mpanza and joined the Asinamali Party, indicating that there were tensions (of which we have no details) among the leaders of the squatter movements.

28. Report on meeting of Joint Council, 8 September 1947, SAIRR.

29. The White City report from *Guardian*, 19 February 1948; party name

from *Bantu World*, 4 December 1948; Mpanza's defeat in *Golden City Post*, 9 October 1955. See also Todd Matshikiza, interview with Mpanza, *Drum*, May 1955.

(Bob Gosani)

James 'Sofasonke' Mpanza ('the Slicer'), riding his favourite horse, in the 1960s.

13. Organising the Migrant Workers

Egoli, the golden city

In the 1930s, 300,000 men or more came by rail or road to Johannesburg every year to work in the gold mines. They were taken first to the headquarters of the Witwatersrand Native Labour Association, WENELA, and then dispatched to mines along the Rand. The trains carried kinsmen and friends from the rural districts, and new arrivals learnt about conditions from those with experience: the mines that were preferable, the compounds to avoid, the managers and *indunas* (headmen) to be feared (First, 1983, p.96). The migrants were seen in the vicinity of the railway station, herded by mine police through the streets, strangers from 'another world', some blanketed, others in ill-fitting clothes, all 'peasants' and seemingly uneasy in the city. Those who watched saw an alien, seemingly unfathomable people, come to work on the mines (see Abrahams, 1968; Patel, 1975, p.5; Williams and May, 1936, p.85).

The sheer size of this labour force, concentrated in one industry, was an indication of the centrality of gold in the South African economy. There were 235,134 African mineworkers in 1921 (as against 203,776 employed in all industry and construction) and 388,894 in 1936 (as against 276,013 in other sectors).[1] Consequently, the mines set the pattern — in terms of wages, treatment, and control — of the African working class. Industry paid only marginally better wages, and controls on other workers, although less stringent, were shaped by regulations initially designed to meet the needs of the mines. Although the work force was so large and so concentrated, it was divided ethnically (as shown in Table 13.1). This was nurtured by mine management and thrived on the myth that some ethnic groups were more suited to particular tasks: Sotho for development work, Mpondo for rock drilling, and so on.

The workers did not stay in eGoli (or Joni), as Johannesburg was called, but were dispersed across the 40-mile arc that constituted the Witwatersrand. They were housed in compounds on mines with complements of 2,000—10,000 black workers, several miles outside the towns that served the mines (F. Wilson, 1972a, Table 3).

The men were allocated to mines after bargaining based partly on the men's requests and on the preferences of compound managers — most mines establishing an ethnic composition which became the accepted pattern. Men from each province or district chose particular mines, and each fresh wave of immigrants reinforced this selection, bringing with them ties based on age groups, gangs, or associations. Like all hometown groups these provided contacts with home areas; aid for the needy and the sick; money for burials, and so on.

Table 13.1
Source of labour force employed on the mines (per cent)

	1910	1920	1930	1939	1946
South Africa					
Cape	26.0	26.7	35.3	33.9	27.8
Transvaal	7.5	5.2	7.2	7.8	7.6
Natal/Zululand	6.7	2.1	2.8	4.9	4.4
OFS	0.3	0.2	0.7	1.5	1.5
Protectorates					
Basutoland	3.2	7.3	13.2	15.0	12.5
Bechuanaland	0.4	0.8	1.4	2.7	2.3
Swaziland	1.5	1.6	2.2	2.1	1.8
Mozambique	52.0	55.6	37.1	26.1	31.5
Tropical	0	0.4	0.2	6.0	10.6
Total (000)	**179**	**173**	**222**	**323**	**305**

Source: Legassick and de Clerq, 1984, Table 7.6

Considerable coercion, nevertheless, was involved in the recruitment of mineworkers, and its intensity depended in part on the territory from which the men came. The policy of forced labour (or *chibalo*) in Mozambique, although not the only factor, ensured that the quota of men agreed with WENELA would always be forthcoming. First (1983, p.183) found that by the 1930s compulsion was not the only determining factor:

> Peasant families became dependent on wages from mine labour for their very reproduction; that is, for the purchase of the basic necessities of everyday family life . . . [and] of essential instruments of production like ploughs, working oxen, grain mills, even hoes for agriculture. Likewise artisan skills and crafts [depended] on mine wages . . . [for the] purchase of sewing machines, carpentry and building tools. . . .

The men constantly returned to the mines, taking only 'long leave' between contracts. They had become proletarianised, and took with them the value systems that were deeply rooted in family, clan, and ethnic group (see Chapter 10). This rural—urban bridge is described by William Beinart (1984) in his study of 'M', a migrant worker of the 1940s who came from the Bizana district in Pondoland. The Mpondo youth belonged to age group associations that provided a range of activities for men with common educational attainment. They included in their activities the 'conquest' of local girls and a propensity to some criminal activities. They remained loyal to their organisation as they shuttled between Reserve and sugar fields or mines; dressed distinctively; spurned adult control; and were hostile to the white administration and the more literate youth (who never entered the mines). That is, they constituted a self-conscious sub-culture, and built parallel groups on the mines with structured activities that regulated their leisure hours.

Other Mpondo gangs, originating in adjacent districts in the eastern Cape, operated on the mines — arranging job allocations, directing criminal activities and supervising homosexual pairing. All these groups, part 'welfare' societies, part gangs, reinforced ethnic identities and 'helped anchor [them] in local politics and culture', playing a role not unlike that of the 'friendly societies' in eighteenth- and nineteenth-century Europe. But, unlike the friendly societies, these gangs did not necessarily provide a bridge to urban trade unions.

Compound organisation

Throughout the contract period the mineworker slept in the compound and ate at the canteen. He expected no luxuries and he did not get any — but he demanded a minimal standard and complained when this was not forthcoming. He knew what controls could be imposed on his leisure activities and that 'misdemeanours' could be reported to the manager. This was irksome, and men protested, but living in a compound was part of the contract and was accepted. It was here that men formed their dance groups; played and drank; and found catamites by choice or by necessity. This was 'home', and their lives were structured by the groups they entered, and the dormitories in which they were housed.

Dunbar Moodie has examined another network through which the workers operated, perhaps overlapping or even coinciding with groups like the one to which 'M' owed allegiance. Workers in each dormitory elected *izibonda*, who were mediators amongst the men, or acted as their spokesmen. The *izibonda* were unpaid and distinct from the management, and in the first instance took the workers' complaints to the *indunas*. In complaints against *indunas*, the *izibonda* of several rooms gathered with their men outside the manager's office and there they would sit 'until noticed' and seek redress (1984b). In some cases these representatives from entire sections of a compound would gather outside the manager's office, or outside the general manager's office (if the compound manager was implicated). These gatherings cut across ethnic divisions, except where the complaint was against the *induna* or police 'boy' who was appointed from within an ethnic group (1984a, pp.12—13).

Complaints that went through the *izibonda*, or were mediated through 'hometown' associations, involved work conditions or relations inside the compound; assaults on workers underground; cuts in rations, or shortages of food in the mess; cheating at the local mine store; bullying by *indunas*; brewing of beer, and so on. More specific complaints about work conditions, and about pay, were usually raised by the *izibonda*, and many disturbances recorded during the 1930s and 1940s were probably led by these men. Thus the *izibonda* were the 'voice' of the workers, but their 'powers' extended beyond making formal complaints. Yet we still know little about them. What contact, if any, did some of these men have with the mineworkers' union? Were they also migrants, or were some of them *tshipa* (literally, absconders from home), that is, proletarianised urbanites? And if some were *tshipa* (and not in the union), did they have links with those *tshipa* who were actively involved in propagating the mineworkers' strike in the week before it took place in August 1946? (See Moodie, 1984c, p.70.)

The management, of course, maintained a hierarchical structure that controlled every compound. It extended from the mine and compound managers, through the police 'boys' and the *indunas*, with the worker at the bottom of the pile. Men could also be divided ethnically in dormitories, and this was usually accepted, and even welcomed, even though work and leisure activities cut across such division. Over and above the mine's formal structures, however, the workers gave their allegiance to the associations they knew at home. From his interviews, Beinart found that

> In M's compound, at least, it seemed that internal organisation depended on networks such as those described, which were other than those of the [trade] union. These were associations of people becoming proletarianised, and through which worker action could be organised, but were not essentially class-conscious worker organisations.

Whatever the answer to these questions, when the African Mine Workers Union (AMWU) was formed, it had to compete with several established networks for the allegiance of the workers. It had to contend with both the 'popular ideology' of the groups to which 'M' and his friends belonged, and the 'mine compound ideology' associated with the complaints procedure and the *izibonda*.

Organising the 'unorganisable'

> The gold mining industry of the Witwatersrand has indeed been fortunate in having secured, for its unskilled labour, native peasants who have been prepared to come to the Witwatersrand for periods of labour at comparatively low wages. But for this fortunate circumstance the industry could never have reached its present stage of development . . . (*Report of the Witwatersrand Mine Natives Wages Commission*, 1943, para. 70).

> The value of [mining] production was sixty-six million pounds in 1939. It employed 480,139 workers: 55,008 European, 850 Indian and 424,281 African.
> The Gold Mining Industry alone employs over 348,000 African workers . . . recruited from landless, poverty stricken, heavily taxed and backward [sic] peasants in the reserves.
> In 1939 these . . . workers helped to produce gold valued over £54,000,000 which gave the shareholders a profit of more than £19,999,000. But they only received an average wage of £2 17s 1d per month: 685 died as a result of accidents, and 1,498 died of disease. . . . Every year thousands more die of miner's phthisis contracted on the mines, and in most instances the dependants receive no compensation (Moses Kotane, *Freedom*, September 1941).

T.W. Thibedi, veteran communist and organiser for the Non-European Federation of Trade Unions in 1929—31, first enrolled workers in a mineworkers' union in 1931, but was then expelled from the CPSA. He formed a Communist League of Africa (Opposition) and re-established several unions amongst laundry workers and municipal employees (at the Doornfontein City Power Compound). He also gathered the nucleus of a miners' union at City Deep Mine and Crown Mines (*Militant*, 6 August 1932). He worked alone, recruiting mineworkers until at least 1936 (Simons and Simons, pp.424—512), and then stopped. He seems to have ceased all political work until 1945, when he briefly joined the Workers International League, but by then he had lost all contact with the trade union movement.

Attempts by white socialists to contact blacks in the mines in the 1930s usually misfired. Heaton Lee, a mine surveyor and member of the Workers Party in Johannesburg, sold *Spark* in the mine through his 'bossboy', until discovery by management led to Lee's transference to another mine: the 'bossboy' was dismissed. That ended the contact: shortly thereafter Lee left for Britain, where he became an organiser in the British Trotskyist movement (interview, 1967). Max Gordon also tried: he enrolled mine clerks in the General Workers Union, preparatory to launching a mineworkers' union.[2] He also gathered information about management policy, obtained by emptying the office wastepaper baskets. This file was kept and handed to the union when it was relaunched in 1941.[3]

The CPSA conference of March 1940 met primarily to discuss the war, and the only document published was Morkel's 'The War and South Africa'. Ray Alexander (Simons) presented a report on the trade unions for the *Politburo*, and criticised the Johannesburg District Party Committee (DPC) for having no influence on African unions and neglecting the mineworkers. She claimed that in Cape Town the CPSA's activity among dockers and railwaymen led to improvements that would be a stimulus to all workers, and particularly to blacks. The organisation of African miners would provide an even greater stimulus, and this was the most urgent task in Johannesburg:

> It is not impossible. It can be done. It must be done. All obstacles must be overcome by Bolsheviks. We must get a bridge to them, find out their position and train leaders to work among them. If necessary we must send in a member of the DPC to work among miners.

Morkel, speaking for the Central Committee, said that the party did not want to antagonise the white workers. The Committee was not certain whether there was a basis for workers' unity, and was not clear (his words) on the issue of blacks demanding the right to fill any post of which they were capable, therefore he could give no directive. Morkel was fudging an issue that was to be expressed more forthrightly later, when it transpired that several members of the Central Committee were opposed to the formation of separate black unions.

Ray Alexander thought that African trade unionists accepted Ballinger as their representative, but was corrected by Johannesburg delegates. Willie Kalk, veteran trade union organiser, and Edwin Mofutsanyana (interviewed by Bob Edgar), a one-time miner who had some contacts on the mines, pointed to Gordon as the main influence, and said that it was the Trotskyists who were able to call meetings of 10,000 workers. Harmel added: 'It is not impossible to contact the African miners. It has been done by one of Gordon's organisers . . . . We are in contact with a man who goes into the mines . . . .'[4] He proposed that the party approach white mineworkers with whom they were in contact. These men were pro-war, he said, but they had some good ideas, and it was the opinion of the DPC that white miners, who had the necessary facilities, should organise the Africans.

However, at the national conference in April 1941 Harmel reported that the DPC had failed because the party's resources were too small (A. Brooks, 1967, p.69). Yet the CPSA was determined to organise a mineworkers' union, its policies at the time being directed at embarrassing the government and undermining the war effort. Mofutsanyana proposed that contacts on the mines be formed into a trade union, and a mineworkers' office be opened (ibid).

Then, on 22 June 1941, German troops marched into Russia and the party reversed its war policy. This had not been foreseen at the April conference, and plans already afoot for the launching of a union went ahead. Gaur Radebe, who was at the CPSA conference in 1940 when it was planned to organise the miners, was also 'Secretary for Mines' in the Transvaal African Congress, and used his position to call for a mineworkers' union (Roux, 1949, p.342). Radebe argued that this would greatly encourage African trade unionism and would also benefit white miners, whose pay packets would be protected if Africans got higher wages. Furthermore, shopkeepers and traders would benefit from the increased purchasing power of the mineworkers.[5]

Radebe invited Dr Xuma to preside over the meeting to launch the union, but in an angry rebuttal Xuma maintained that such issues should be handled more covertly, and also that letters sent in the name of the ANC should be approved beforehand by the provincial secretary.[6] Xuma's response was obstructive, if formally correct. He probably saw the hand of the CPSA behind the plan, and was opposed to the party using the ANC platform. Furthermore, he was not a keen supporter of trade unions and wanted funds for the ANC from the Bantu Welfare Trust, which had close connections with the Chamber of Mines (Karis and Carter, 1972–1977, Vol. 2, p.86).

Eighty-one delegates met on Sunday, 3 August, representing trade unions, branches of the CPSA, the NEUF and the SAIRR. S.P. Matseka of the ANC took the chair, but despite its sponsorship there were few delegates from the ANC. Those present decided to launch the union, which would recruit members in the mines and in the rural areas. A committee of fifteen was nominated to raise funds for the AMWU and contained at least seven members of the CPSA, including Mofutsanyana, Eli Weinberg and J.B. Marks. Radebe, who gave the keynote address, was chairman. Gordon and Koza were on the committee (*Guardian*, 25 July 1941) — the former presumably because of his contacts on the mines. A. Msitshana was the secretary. Apart from a few letters, however, there is little evidence of activity during his term of office.

James Mojoro, who had been a miner with Mofutsanyana, was deputy-secretary, and proved invaluable. He was a leading member of the Mine Clerks' Association, a body of some 500 clerical workers which was recognised by the Chamber of Mines after agreeing to limit its membership to certain categories of employees (excluding Coloureds, *indunas*, etc.), not to raise the dismissal of any clerk with the management, and not to act as a trade union.[7] The clerical staff had its own wage structure, but on requesting a cost of living allowance in 1942 was told that legislation explicitly excluded all mine labourers. The clerks' association thereupon joined the AMWU, providing the union with members who had access to the compounds. Mojoro was sacked in 1942, when he made representation on behalf of the clerks (evidence to Industrial Legislation Commission, 1950), but access to the compounds was maintained.

Organising a miners' union was difficult. There was no money with which to appoint full-time staff, and subscriptions at 6*d* per month were barely enough to pay for essential union requirements.[8] For some time the AMWU had only an office and unpaid officials. The union's first step was to request the extension of cost of living allowances to all miners. The only official response was interrogation of union officials by the police.[9] Workers joined the union, but there is little information about the number of recruits, or of paid-up membership. In October 1945, when the AMWU claimed a registered membership of 20,000 and was at its peak, the secretary of the union informed the executive of the CPSA that there were about 2,000 paid-up members.[10] But whether the number was 2,000 or 20,000, this was infinitesimal in an industry that employed 350,000 black workers.

Migrant workers and the VFP

I work for a Political Company which in conjunction with the mining houses seeks to obtain control of the souls as well as the bodies of their wage earning dependents . . .
(D. Ivon Jones, letter, March 1913).

The Victoria Falls and Transvaal Power Company (or VFP) originally planned to supply electricity for the mines with power generated at the Victoria Falls and brought overland to the Witwatersrand. The project was too costly and instead the company built a coal-fired station at Witbank to service the gold mines on the Witwatersrand and the local colliery (Katzenellenbogen, 1975). In 1935 the mines needed two million kwh (equal to the total requirements of Johannesburg, Cape Town, Durban and Bloemfontein over a five-year period).

The VFP's approach to its labour force was identical to that of the mines. Africans were migrant (although not recruited),[11] almost entirely unskilled, and housed in compounds; wages were comparable to those of the mines. The company was opposed to trade unionism, but nonetheless, in the late

1930s, power workers were recruited into Gordon's General Workers Union. The workers' complaints were wide-ranging: rations were unsatisfactory, wages at 2s per shift plus 8d cost of living allowance were insufficient, and there was no paid leave. Furthermore they were only paid after completing thirty shifts (or every five weeks) and they were excluded from Wage Determination No. 105 (for unskilled trades).[12] All workers lived in compounds and there were no married quarters. Altogether there were 2,536 black labourers employed, of whom nearly four fifths received only the basic pay (*Star*, 12 October 1943).

When Gordon was interned the General Workers' Union collapsed and power workers were left without a union. In late December 1942 a deputation of workers to the compound manager at the Rosherville power station, just outside Johannesburg, was rebuffed, and the workers called for a strike. The VFP management called in officials of the Native Affairs and the Labour Departments to prevent the strike, but the workers were unmoved. The officials then invited leaders of the CNETU, who had 'no connection with the workers concerned', according to Gana Makabeni, to intervene.[13]

The leaders of the CNETU co-operated with government officials in stopping the strike. There were no concessions from the officials: only the 'right' to form a trade union which was not afforded recognition and whose function was to act as a strike breaker! The CNETU approach was explained by Makabeni in 1944:

> We have endeavoured for over a year to hold the workers back from striking . . . it is the accepted policy of the trade union movement to support the government in its war effort and to avoid anything which will embarrass them. We are still determined to pursue this policy in the future . . . but there must be a contented working class.[14]

The workers were in 'a dangerous mood', said Makabeni, and persuading them to call off the strike involved a 'considerable risk'. He continued:

> . . . on the understanding that the Management of the firm together with the two Departments, were prepared to consider the case of the workers, the officials of the Council . . . succeeded in persuading the workers to call off the strike, and to leave the matter in the hands of the Council.

The CNETU officials met with management and the government departments, but 'it became obvious that the Management had little to say'. The government officials were more forthcoming:

> 1. They regard the VFP as part of the mining industry;
> 2. The consequence of any increase in wages given to the Native workers concerned would be serious in its repercussions in the mining industry, i.e. it would unsettle the Native mine force, as some of the VFP installations are on mine property.
> A few days after the announcement that wages would not be increased, the workers unanimously decided not to take food; for a second time, the authorities were at a loss.
> The officials of the Council were therefore again asked to come forward, and the trouble was again averted by the same council.

The workers at the VFP were little different from the mineworkers. They had their own organisation (probably through elected *izibonda*), and contacts between power stations were maintained before Makabeni intervened. The men appointed a deputation, met to decide on means of struggle, and stood firm against all the arguments of management and government officials. Despite management statements that they were not ready for trade unions, their grasp of organisational tactics was not inferior to those who were brought in to 'lead' them.

Officials of the CNETU formed a trade union, and the majority of workers enrolled — but despite representations by union officials and W.G. Ballinger to the Minister of Labour, their claims for 35s per week, two weeks' annual leave, and the provision of married quarters were rejected (Friends of Africa Report, January–July 1943, *Ballinger Papers*). It was this action at the VFP, followed by stoppages at mines, that led to the setting up of the Mine Native Wages Commission. Initially the Minister had said he could not allow a Wage Board inquiry, or an arbitrator, in the case of the VFP, because of its close association with the mining industry (Moodie, 1984a). When the workers again threatened to strike in July, however, the government ordered that the claims of the VFP workers be submitted to the Mine Native Wages Commission. The workers at the VFP might not have fared better without formal trade union organisation, but they could hardly have fared worse. Their union officials achieved little and they did not obtain wage increases through the efforts of the newly constituted body. However, there was a union, and the workers remained loyal to its officials.

The Witwatersrand Mine Native Wages Commission

The threatened strike at the VFP was preceded by a stoppage at the Langlaagte Estates gold mines between 1 and 9 January. Some 500 workers struck work, objecting to double and even treble shifts, the use of a measuring string with drills, compulsory recitation of work regulations by the numbers of the paragraphs (with assaults until word perfect), and the compound manager's failure to obtain redress.[15] The police used considerable force in breaking the strike, and arrested some 500 men. Of the 48 described as 'ringleaders', 25 were badly beaten by police and had to be admitted to hospital (*Guardian*, 21 January 1953).

The court case which followed was remarkable for the line pursued by the lawyers, Messrs Festenstein and Baker, both members of or close to the CPSA. According to party journals, the defence persuaded the workers to plead guilty to contravening War Measure 145 because this would allow them to return immediately to production! It was claimed that 'Stormjaers' and others associated with the pro-German Ossewa Brandwag incited the men to strike to hamper the war effort, and that Africans who objected had been assaulted by white miners and kept underground for three consecutive shifts (ibid; *Inkululeko*, 20 February 1943). The Africans' world was being stood on its head: white (nationalist) miners were urging them to strike! Finally, ten of the defendants received light sentences with the alternative of a fine, and the Communists got them back to work.

The complaints by mineworkers did not go away because their 'champions' supported the war effort, and the Langlaagte affair was barely over when men at the Nourse mine downed tools (*Rand Daily Mail*, 23 January 1943). This time there were no 'Stormjaers' to blame, and the AMWU was reported in *Inkululeko* to be 'making desperate efforts to secure wage increases' — by demanding a Wage Board inquiry! In February Madeley set up the Witwatersrand Mine Native Wages Commission (or Lansdown Commission), excluding all reference to the VFP workers. The workers were not mollified by the announcement and continued their agitation for higher pay. On 23 February, 200 workers at the Durban Deep mines in Roodepoort stopped work. Police detachments were sent into the compound and workers demanded their passage home. Only after some parleying, and the offer of a pay increase of 1*d* per day, did they return to work (*Inkululeko*, 5 March 1943).

The appointment of the Commission was not without its problems. There were conflicting interests in the state, and the government had already taken steps to draft troops into affected areas to dampen the rising militancy. It seems that neither the mines nor the government had any intention of allowing a general wage increase in the industry, and that the appointment of the commission was a delaying tactic. In February 1943, the editor of the *Mining and Engineering Journal* wrote:

> We immediately asked ourselves: what is behind all this? Can it be, we mused, that the authorities want to disclose just how well off the mine labourer is by comparison with other natives? Reluctantly we were forced to recall Eliza Doolittle's classical reply: Not bloody likely!
> Reading between the lines, we came to the conclusion that this might be a first step towards an expansion of the purchasing power of the Natives as envisaged by the progressive, if somewhat idealistic, reformer.
> We made enquiries from one of our behind-the-scene politicians, who informed us airily that 'the whole thing's fixed: the Native worker will receive an additional 4*d* a day'. We made a rapid mental calculation. Where we asked, is the extra £2 million a year coming from? Our informant shrugged his shoulders. 'There will be a remission in taxation', he suggested (Weinberg, 1944).

The commission's members went to work, as did those who prepared memoranda and submitted evidence: the SAIRR, ANC, Friends of Africa, CPSA, trade unionists, mine management, the VFP, and others.[16] Meanwhile workers were urged to be patient while the position was being considered.

The report was published in April 1944, more than a year after the commission was constituted, and like most reports (at that time) contains a wealth of information about the misery of the migrant worker, on the mines and in the Reserves. But there was little consolation for the miners in the recommendations. It was proposed that surface workers get an increase of 5*d* per shift, and underground workers a 6*d* rise. To this should be added a 3*d* cost of living allowance, a boot allowance, overtime and Sunday pay, and two weeks' annual leave for permanent employees. The VFP workers, it was suggested, should be covered by the wage determination for unskilled workers and receive 25s per week, plus two weeks' paid annual leave. The commission felt that Africans should be allowed some form of collective bargaining, but endorsed the Chamber of Mines' contention that African miners had 'not yet reached the stage of development which would enable them safely and usefully to employ trade unionism as a means of promoting their advancement'.

It soon transpired that the 'behind-the-scene' politician and informant of the editor of the *Mining and Engineering Journal* had been correct. Surface workers were only given a rise of 4d, and underground workers got 5d extra per shift. Overtime pay was agreed, but other recommendations were rejected. Furthermore, the mines were given a tax remission, as anticipated, to pay for these miserable concessions. The VFP workers were given a rise of only 4d per shift, and in the year that followed their union was smashed.

Action and reaction: Strike One!

The VFP workers were impatient and, after Makabeni had presented their case to the Lansdown Commission, Dick Mfili, the union secretary, asked the Minister of Labour to appoint an arbitrator under the provisions of War Measure 145. The government did not respond, and the workers instructed the union to give thirty days' notice of intention to strike. Union officials warned the Director of Native Labour that they could no longer restrain the workers, and still there was no official response. In January 1944, the workers in five power stations came out on strike.[17]

The government had been preparing for this since the strike threat in January 1943. The compounds were isolated and surrounded by police and armed forces backed up by armoured cars, contrary (as the VFP union stated) to the recommendations of the Marabastad riot inquiry. The union claimed that workers did not allow themselves to be provoked, but that compounds were isolated and the union could do little. Units of the Native Military Corps were sent into the power stations to work the turbines, but turned out to be reluctant workers and were used as cleaners. The stations continued working because the white workers scabbed, disregarding instructions from the South African Electrical Workers Association and the Joint Mechanics Union. Union officials were kept away from the workers and only when men at the Brakpan compound categorically refused to end their strike without consulting union officials was a meeting arranged. The union called off the strike after insisting that the workers' return required that the recommendations of the Lansdown Commission be implemented immediately, and that the increase in wages be backdated to 1 January 1944.

After the strike the police interrogated the workers individually and, fearing victimisation, Xuma, in consultation with Makabeni, Mfili, Selope Thema and Paul Mosaka, saw Piet van der Byl (Minister of Native Affairs) and the Minister of Labour. Van der Byl said that the strike was illegal . . . and he could not see how anything that was illegal could subsequently be made legal. The workers and their leaders had given evidence before the Lansdown Commission and had no option but to wait for the report.

. . . If the strike had proved effective it would have struck a blow at the industrial and economic life of the Witwatersrand . . . . Nothing was left for the Government, as an emergency step, to prevent a threat to the community but to resort to public authority purpose [*sic*].

[Furthermore] . . . the strike was instigated, because if they had waited the natives might be satisfied with the recommendations of the Commission report, and would find it difficult to induce the Natives to strike.[18]

Xuma added his own note: 'this despite the actions of the Council of Non-European Trade Unions in persuading the workers to return earlier'. The VFP workers would have accepted the 25s per week recommended by Lansdown, low as it was, and in that respect Van der Byl was correct. He was probably aware, however, of the government's intention to impose a much lower wage increase, and his contention that workers would be satisfied with the outcome was absurd.

In April the VFP workers again decided to strike, and said that they would not be deterred by penalties imposed under War Measure 145. Basner, who informed the Senate of this decision (*Senate Debates*, 26 April 1946, Col. 1650), added that the workers had been prevented from taking strike action only because he and the union officials had intervened. Thereafter the union collapsed; the militants were weeded out and discharged, and the workers thrown back on their own resources. Mfili broke with the Makabeni group of unions in 1945 and new attempts were made to organise the union — but despite the continued loyalty of the workers, there was only limited success. Recognition of the right to organise a union was withdrawn and, to reach the workers, organisers positioned a public address system behind the compound and played *kwela* (popular) music. Workers gathered behind the compound fence: after being addressed, they slipped their sixpences through the wire mesh in exchange for union cards. But enthusiasm could not be sustained and workers stopped coming. There were complaints at meetings of harassment from management, and the union collapsed.

Action and reaction — approaching Strike Two

The similarities between work conditions on the VFP and the mines, and the connection between the industries, meant that the workers were controlled in like fashion, and also that the methods used against 2,600 strikers in 1944 would be repeated in 1946 when some 70,000 men refused to go underground in the gold mines. Nonetheless, the difficulties that faced compound workers on strike — described and circulated by the VFP ('Statement on strike', 28 January 1944) — seem to have been ignored by officials of the AMWU. The two strikes were separated by a period of two and a half years, and conditions in the world, as well as in the trade unions, had altered radically. The war in Europe was over. At home, the African unions were in disarray, making the organisation of a sympathy strike more difficult.

The strike, when it came in August 1946, was not unexpected. Even before publication of the Mine Wages Commission Report in April 1944, workers had called for a strike throughout the gold fields, or taken action in compounds over working conditions, wages, or food. Month after month there were disturbances, some reported but most ignored by the press (see Burford, 1946). They are recorded in the minutes of meetings of the Chamber of Mines on the subject of 'Native labour' over the period December 1945 to August 1946.[19]

There is no indication of the extent of union influence on the mines. There was some initial success in enrolling members in mines near Johannesburg, particularly amongst the clerks, but the union had few resources and no money. By November 1942 the membership was approximately 1,000, and six months later had edged up to 1,800. The AMWU needed some success to win workers' confidence and was apparently waiting for the report of the Wages Commission, hoping to announce a victory. Finally, in early 1944, union officials launched a campaign of meetings on mine property which extended over eight months and brought a surge in recruitment. The drive was brought to an end in October by the promulgation of War Measure 1425, which banned meetings of more than 20 persons on proclaimed mining ground.

The new initiative coincided with the unease expressed in CPSA papers over the delay in opening the Second Front in Europe. In January 1944, at its annual conference in Johannesburg, the CPSA decided to recruit members and embark 'on a new phase of struggle for liberation from the oppression of the colour bar system' (Bunting, 1981, pp.183–90). J.B. Marks, president of the AMWU, claimed later in an interview with T. Karis that he had decided 'to take the bull by the horns . . . and the first meeting was held outside the Robinson Mine', but his tactic was obviously determined by the changing policy of the CPSA. It was following the party conference that Marks and Mojoro started visiting mines, demanding 'better wages, better food and better living conditions'. By July 1944 the AMWU claimed a membership of 11,000 (see Moodie, 1984a, p.48) and it is clear that the two men were well received by the workers. In a typical speech Marks declared that 'South Africa cannot afford to have these mines stand still for 24 hours' and would grant the workers' demands if they were well organised (ibid.). He threatened 'action' but cautioned against strikes. This was the hallmark of the union through the war years.

On 30 July 1944 the AMWU held its annual conference in Johannesburg. The gathering was more like a rally, 700 men being accorded delegate status with a further 1,300 present as rank and file members (*Inkululeko*, 17 August 1944). The report of the Wages Commission was considered, and delegates were angry. Many called for an immediate strike, but were urged by the executive not to take any action which would hamper the war effort (O'Meara, 1975, p.159). In the end the conference resolved to accept the increase as a step in the right direction, but maintained that it was totally inadequate. Delegates demanded a Wage Board inquiry, and resolved to continue the struggle for the union's recognition (*Inkululeko*, 26 August 1944; Simons and Simons, 1969, p.572).

Despite the success of the gathering, the union had little time left. War measure 1425 was gazetted in October: meetings near mines were effectively stopped, and organisers could neither address workers nor collect subscriptions. Furthermore, organisers were arrested, even when trying to disperse workers who had unwittingly broken the law. The recruitment of members almost ceased, and the income of the union plummeted from £120 to £30 a month.[20] In the compounds, a campaign of intimidation was under way: compound managers, mine police, and Native Affairs officials did all they could to discourage workers staying in the AMWU. Any clerk or key worker associated with the union was dismissed within 24 hours.[21]

The union lost contact with many compounds, but that had little effect on the growing number of disturbances on the mines. Short rations during 1945, when there was a food shortage in the country, was a major source of complaint. It led to clashes with police in 1945 at Crown Mines and at Modderfontein,[22] and even to a spontaneous hunger strike at Crown Mines which only ended after a number of men collapsed (*Forum*, 24 August 1946). A large number of incidents that lasted only a few hours, or a day, received no publicity, but clearly the situation was combustible. On 17 December there was a disturbance at Vogelspruitfontein over food, and similar conflicts on a dozen mines over the next seven months. Most were over food, but there were also complaints about wages and taxes. Police were summoned in several instances, there were arrests and shootings, and some workers were killed (Chamber of Mines, minutes: see note 19).

Mine managers reported that the leaders in many of these disturbances were Mpondo, Sotho and Mozambicans. The role of Sotho workers in many struggles probably arose from wartime conditions. Recruitment from Basutoland, Swaziland and Bechuanaland had stopped after the British High Commissioner intimated that young men were required for the army (*Report of the Witwatersrand Mine Native Wages Commission*, 1943, p.5), and although the Sotho had still taken jobs in the mines, their ranks were depleted, and they lost their claim to be the shaft sinkers. The Sotho, moreover, were angry over taxes, which had risen from 25s to 28s per year in 1942, and to 34s in 1946, plus an additional 25s per year for every wife after the first wife.[23] The discontent was so marked, said the general manager of the Native Labour Organisation, that Sotho officials on the Reef were asked to deal directly with these men, and for the time being not to request mine officials to help collect the increased tax (Chamber of Mines, minutes).

Protests were rife throughout the compounds, with the initiative in the hands of some ethnic groups and their associations, or the *izibonda*, and the AMWU seems to have played only a minor role in the events preceding the strike. On 14 April 1946 the AMWU's annual conference was attended, it was claimed, by over 2,000 delegates. In some respects the proceedings were unremarkable. Marks urged patience, but demanded adequate food rations in the mines and a minimum wage of 10*s* per day,[24] in line with the new policy of the CNETU. The demand appeared for the first time in the agenda circulated on the mines in preparation for the gathering (Moodie, 1984c).

The real surprise came from the platform oratory of Louis Joffe, who appeared with Issy Woolfson (a prominent trade unionist and fellow communist). Joffe was reported as saying:

> I am not telling you that when you go out of here you should go and make a strike, but I do say that you should prepare yourself first if you want to make a strike. I believe that one of these days you might be compelled by your suffering to act and I assure you that the Communist Party will stand with you (ibid.).

Joffe assured his audience that the gold they dug was theirs, and that people who did not work had no right to take it away from them. He ended with the call to 'unite to fight for your rights'. There could be little doubt that Joffe was in fact calling for a strike and, linked with the new call for 10*s*, the result was explosive. The miners called for strike action (against the advice of Marks and Mojoro who urged restraint) and for an end to the spate of spontaneous strikes. They also urged the union to write to the authorities drawing attention to the miners' grievances (*Forum*, 24 August 1946).

One week later workers demanded 10*s* a week, and from 23 April to 6 May there were demonstrations or stoppages affecting at least five mines and involving over 7,000 workers. The workers met with management, or were confronted by police; over 100 were arrested and charged, and several were injured. The strikes were of short duration, and there was no sign of external organisation. In some cases workers referred to the whites who said that they would get 10*s* — or, as two compound leaders told the Native Commissioner, 'The decision to demand 10*s* a shift was reached after the Union meeting had been exhorted thereto by two Europeans' (Moodie, 1984c).

The workers were defeated in every case. Their actions had been called from within the compounds, sometimes after hearing of action on adjacent sites, but all ultimately inspired by the speech of Louis Joffe. There is no evidence of what led to his call to strike (however veiled the language), but it followed close on Churchill's Fulton speech, which could only have caused concern for many Russophiles among the party faithful.[25] Whatever the reason, his speech sparked off precipitate action amongst the mineworkers, and after their defeat in April/May they did not respond to the strike call four months later.

In May the General Council of the union met and again called for strike action, but the leadership only urged that they write to the authorities (*Forum*, 24 August 1946). In May 1946 Basner was told by Marks that 'he could not hold the position any longer', and that the workers were determined to strike. According to Basner, they were bitter over the 'refusal to implement the recommendations of the Lansdown Report', and when they met in conference in July/August 1944 they demanded immediate strike action. He had appealed to them from the platform to 'hold their hands' until further representations could be made to the government, but his attempts to secure concessions through a group of Native Representatives had failed.[26] After his interview with Marks in May 1946, Basner warned Colin Steyn, the Minister of Justice, that there could be a strike in the next few days, but even that had no effect. All concessions were ruled out, and nothing was done to placate the workers.[27] The leaders of the AMWU must have known of these attempts, and they temporised: the workers either did not know or no longer cared.

We have no knowledge of preparations made by the AMWU for the inevitable clash. The officials wrote letters to the Chamber of Mines and the government. They also kept the CPSA, the ANC, the Organising Fund Committee (see Blaxall, 1965, p.61) and others informed about the situation. The CNETU, of which Marks was president, was also called upon to help, and in June 1946 resolved unanimously to call a sympathy strike if the miners downed tools (*Inkululeko*, June (1) 1946). However, it is doubtful whether this decision could ever have been put into effect. The CNETU was in disarray after the expulsion of Koza and Phoffu, and there was a coolness between Makabeni and Marks that extended back to the change in the presidency.

On 4 August, mineworkers met in special conference at the Market Square, Johannesburg. With 1,000 workers present, once again it was more like a rally: the workers called for a strike, the leadership urged caution. Finally it was agreed to give the Chamber of Mines one week to meet their demands: if these were not met they would strike from 12 August. The Chamber did not reply, but prepared for the strike. Its committees found time to discuss and confirm a plan, agreed with government in July, to place workers under the direct control of the Native Affairs Department and not the Department of Labour. It was also decided by management that during the week contact would be maintained between the police and compound managers. The workers at the VFP and at the African Explosives and Chemical Industries (who had been on strike at the Lenz and Modderfontein dynamite factories in June and August 1945 respectively)[28] would be transferred to the NAD as soon as staffing arrangements made this possible. That is, they would be permanently denied the rights of trade union organisation (Chamber of Mines, minutes).

That mine owners and government ministers, when a strike was imminent, should calmly discuss who would ultimately exercise control over the mineworkers (when staffing permitted!) can only be regarded as a sign of confidence by the employers that they could defeat the union. Indeed, the administration was ready, and certain of full government support.

Notes

1. *Union Statistics for Fifty Years, 1910–1960*, 1960, A–33. Africans on the gold mines numbered 179,800 (1921) and 310,000 (1936), Katzen, 1964, Table 1.

2. Minutes of the CPSA conference, March 1940, CAMP, Reel 3A, 2:CC1:32.
3. I owe this information to Hillel Ticktin, who met Gordon in the 1950s.
4. Minutes of 1940 CPSA conference. Simons and Simons, 1969, mention this debate but do not cite the minutes, and do not credit Gordon with organising mineworkers.
5. Circular letter from Radebe, 9 June 1941, CAMP, 2:DA21:41.
6. Letter from Radebe to Dr Xuma, 2 July 1941, and responses from Xuma, 5 July. *Xuma Papers*, ABX 410702a, 410705a, 410705b.
7. Report of conference of the Association, CAMP Reel 15A, 2:XC9:30/74.
8. Letter from Mojoro to Xuma, appealing for money, 30 May 1942, *Xuma Papers*, ABX 420530a.
9. See résumé of AMWU activities: 'The impending strike of the African miners: a statement of the African Mine Workers Union', mimeo, 1946.
10. Evidence of J.H. Simons at the Sedition Inquiry, reported in *Cape Argus*, 13 February 1947.
11. T.G. Otley, General Manager VFP, evidence to Mine Native Wages Commission.
12. Statement read by Makabeni to Mine Native Wages Commission. He referred to an earlier union 'which did not specifically cater for their interests', *Ballinger Papers*, Cape Town, BC 347 C5 X15.
13. See Simons and Simons, p.570. Their account is incorrect, and ignores Makabeni's evidence to the commission, which is the source followed here.
14. 'Statement by African Gas and Power Workers Union on the strike at Simmerpan, Rosherville, Brakpan, Vereeniging and Klip', 28 January 1944, mimeo, Hemson film.
15. *The Star*, 18 January 1943, trivialises the complaints. Moodie, 1984a, pp.12−16, provides more comprehensive accounts from archival sources, but misses the sequel (provided below).
16. For commentaries on the report, see Roux, 1949, pp.344−5; Simons and Simons, 1969, p.571; O'Meara, 1975.
17. '4,000 workers on strike for a living wage', leaflet issued by the union, January 1944. The company stated that the number of black workers was just under 2,600 (see above) and there is no independent source to determine how many workers there were. But they were all on strike!
18. 'Interview on VFP strike', memorandum by Xuma, 2 February 1944, *Xuma Papers*, ABX 440202b.
19. I was fortunate in being shown copies of these minutes. The Chamber of Mines does not normally allow inspection of its records.
20. Evidence of Dr Robertson, treasurer of AMWU Fund Organising Committee, at sedition trial, reported in *Inkululeko Daily Trial Bulletin*, 19 June 1946.
21. The union's problems are detailed in 'Statement on the trade union organising disabilities of the African Mine Workers Union', n.d., *Ballinger Papers*, Johannesburg; O'Meara, 1975, p.159; J.B. Marks, evidence to Industrial Legislation Commission, reported in *Star*, 12 April 1950.
22. Report of provincial secretary of Transvaal ANC, 29 September 1945, CAMP, Reel 3B; 2:DA21:30/3.
23. Proclamation No. 10, 1946. See Lord Hailey, *Native Administration in the British African Territories*, Part 5, HMSO, 1953, pp.90−4.
24. AMWU, 'The impending strike', cf. Bunting, 1975, p.130, for a different chronology.

25. Joffe's close adherence to the 'Moscow line' was the subject of many jokes in Johannesburg in the 1930s and 1940s, and the effect of Churchill's words about the 'growing challenge and peril to civilisation [from the] Communist fifth columns . . . [and of] a return to the Dark Ages, the Stone Age . . .', and his call on the US to guard its superiority in nuclear weapons, and uphold the peoples of eastern Europe against Communism, would have provoked a response from this speaker. (See the comments on reactions to Churchill's speech in Deutscher, 1974, p.565.)
26. Evidence by Basner at sedition inquiry, reported in *Cape Argus,* 12 February 1947.
27. A similar account, taken from the typescript on the strike by L. ('Rusty') Bernstein, is in the Benson Papers, SOAS, London. Bernstein could not find a copy of the document for me.
28. The strike and settlement at Lenz, *Guardian,* 21 June 1945; at Modderfontein, *Guardian,* 2 August 1945. The demands of the African Explosives Workers Union are found in a letter to the Minister of Labour, 21 March 1945, *Xuma Papers,* ABX 450321. Government agreement was reported to the Chamber by the chairman (Chamber of Mines, minutes).

14. The 1946 Miners' Strike

August 1946

The mineworkers' strike, called for 12 August, led to stoppages on over 30 sites, and involved between 70,000 and 100,000 men over five days. It was an action that aroused intense passion at the time. For the future, it was a clear sign that the black working class was a force which could, and would, play a leading role in the assault on the state. Nevertheless the strike also signalled the eclipse of the CNETU and the industrial organisation of black workers in this period. In the coming decade, their organisations weakened if not smashed, the workers would play only a subordinate role in the struggle against the state, and the political initiative would be grasped by the petty bourgeoisie inside the ANC.

The constraints imposed on the mineworkers by the AMWU during its five-year existence, the premature demand for 10s which led to the April/May strikes, and the failure to campaign on the issue of food — all these bungled opportunities now ended in a resolution that the strike take place within one week. The leadership had persuaded the workers on so many occasions to 'hold their hands' that they could no longer counsel restraint. They were now confronted with the almost impossible task of organising a strike in an industry that employed over 350,000 workers, in just one week, without a strategy or even so much as the means to get a strike message to workers, most of whom had never heard of the AMWU.[1]

In the week 5–11 August union officials visited the more accessible mines and delivered a simple, unrealistic, but telling message: 'if you are not paid 10s a day, don't go to work'.[2] In the mines nearest Johannesburg, where the AMWU had its strongest following, active union members (usually *tshipa*) and presumably those that attended the conferences in large numbers, spread the message that there would be a strike if 10s was not forthcoming (Beinart, 1984, p.70). The union printed thousands of leaflets and — with the assistance of the CPSA and volunteers drawn from the ANC, the Indian Congress and student groups — got them into the compounds. The message was simple and direct: all men were entitled to 10s per day, to good food, and to good housing, and if these were not granted, men would refuse to work. The leaflets were read by the literate to their friends, and although the origin of the leaflets was not clear to many recipients, the message was welcomed as expressing their demands (ibid., pp.66–8).

Yet, although the call was for a strike, there were no instructions on how the struggle was to be organised or conducted, and ultimately it was the hometown associations or the *izibonda* who brought many of the workers out. One worker recalled:

> On the Sundays they were drinking with men of the other tribes they were talking about the money. . . . In the room they were talking about this, having meetings about it — they decided in the rooms, not outside where they were drinking with others. In each room, two men were deputed to go to all the rooms with the message: 'Tomorrow, no work. Monday, not going to work'. So everybody in the compound knew. The men they chose were men whom they trusted: it was the *isibonda* and the assistant (ibid., p.67). [Note: *isibonda* is singular, *izibonda* plural.]

Another worker provided a similar account:

> The *izibonda* went from room to room telling the people that on such and such a day we will get dressed but we won't go down to work. The rooms made the decision and then it was discussed at a meeting of the *isibonda*. He was the one who told the *isibonda* that he must tell the other *izibonda* that people must not go down. No one told him they heard from the other compounds, and then they discussed it in their room — and they told the *isibonda* to tell the others (ibid., p.68).

Members of some hometown associations also came out, although they remained outside the AMWU. It is not clear whether these groups came out together or left the decision to individual inclination.[3]

There were real difficulties in getting into the compounds that the union had never overcome, but other lapses in organisation were inexplicable. The support of other unions was needed, but Marks failed to summon the CNETU executive to lay down contingency plans during the crucial week before the strike. On Tuesday 13th, at a meeting of the working committee of the ANC — attended by Dr Xuma, C.S. Ramohanoe, E.P. Moretsele, and the trade union leaders Makabeni, Tloome and Gosani — the latter said that the CNETU 'had not been properly informed of the strike, and this had created much confusion'.[4]

Naboth Mokgatle, a member of the CNETU executive, was also confounded:

> The day before the strike I was summoned to be in Johannesburg to attend the executive committee meeting the next day to plan what was to be done to see the strike through (pp.251—2).

The meeting, said Mokgatle, had to find ways of contacting the workers, who also needed money for food: nothing had been planned. This ineptitude was compounded by the failure of the executive to recognise the threat posed by detectives who interrupted the meeting in mid-morning and questioned Marks. He blithely informed them that the meeting was discussing the strike. After their departure the meeting continued, breaking only for lunch, without taking any steps to avoid the inevitable reappearance of the police and arrest of Marks — after which, said Mokgatle, the executive was 'over-come by confusion' (p.252).

The confusion continued. The CNETU had no plan for the sympathy strike that had been agreed at conference, and James Phillips, a member of the executive of the Council, said he was summoned from his place of work (interview). At CNETU headquarters, feelings were running high following news of police brutality and the death of miners. The executive set up an action committee with Phillips in the chair, despite his protest that he was inexperienced and that Makabeni would be a better chairman. A resolution of the action committee was read by Phillips to a meeting that had meanwhile assembled, pledging support to the mineworkers and promising to 'do everything to alleviate their suffering'. This was rejected by Basner and others as meaningless. Ambrose Makiwane of the ANC called for a general strike within two days and this was accepted unanimously — but there were few offers of help, and it is doubtful whether there was much support from trade union officials. Handbills and leaflets were printed and distributed, with the help of Communists and sympathisers (ibid.).[5]

The Johannesburg City Council took the strike threat seriously, and sent a deputation to the committee requesting that essential services be exempt.[6] This reversal of roles, in which civic leaders visited the CNETU's headquarters, was testimony to what Phillips called the 'electricity in the air' and the obvious anger of the black working class at police brutality. The sympathy strike was called for Thursday 15th, but the response was patchy. Without previous preparation, and with only 36 hours available to the new committee, few workers were contacted. It was reported that some tobacco workers stopped work, and that groups of workers in Industria, just outside Johannesbug, had marched in protest towards the city centre. They had been ordered to disperse, and then beaten up by police ('Strike Bulletin, No.4', *Ballinger Papers*). A mass meeting called for Thursday at the Market Square was reported banned by the Minister of Justice,[7] and when the speakers arrived they found some 600 police, the blacks armed with *assegais* (short spears) and knobkerries, the whites wielding *sjamboks* and rifles. Phillips and Makabeni, who were to officiate, were given five minutes to disperse the crowd: though there were calls to defy the order, the majority left. That was the end of the sympathy strike, and a few days later Makabeni, Phillips, and perhaps Koza decided to disband the committee.[8]

Strike!

Despite the shambles at trade union headquarters, men had joined the strike and for four days maintained their action against bloody repression. The figures released by the police, although undoubtedly understating the situation, indicate the breadth of worker responses. Over 75,000 miners were involved and at least 21 mines were affected, eleven wholly and ten partially. On the Monday some 46,000 men came out, 65,500 on Tuesday, 50,000 on Wednesday, then 21,000 on Thursday and a few thousand on Friday.[9] There were 1,600 white police involved and an unknown number of blacks. Over 1,000 miners were arrested, some 1,250 injured, and at least 13 killed.[10]

The pattern of events varied from mine to mine, and partly reflected the recent experiences of the workers. Many of those on the west Rand who had come out in April and May continued working, although some did strike. They were relatively few in number, and were soon forced back to work after small groups were arrested or hounded out of the compounds by police. On the east Rand some mines closed, and on others some miners refused to go underground. Some mines only joined the strike on Tuesday or even later, and tactics altered from compound to compound, ranging from sit-ins to the occupation of a mine dump or a railway embankment. There were marches to the local police station in Benoni to demand the release of arrested workers, and a march of at least 4,000 to Johannesburg to demand the return of their passes so that they could go home (see Moodie, 1984c). It is not known whether the AMWU or its members provided any leadership, but it does seem that much of the activity was locally inspired and organised. In any event the mines were isolated, and communication between the workers and the union almost entirely blocked: the AMWU had failed to learn from the experiences of the VFP workers.

If the AMWU and the unions generally were unprepared, and worker organisation deficient, the same could not be said about the Chamber of Mines, the government, or the police. Committees of the Chamber, meeting daily, were in direct contact with the government; and the latter used the police to drive the workers back to work. Compounds were sealed off by the police and men were driven down the stopes or off the mine dumps at bayonet point. The marches were dispersed; the men assaulted and then arrested, or sent home. A memorandum by Michael Scott (1946) based on statements by miners taken immediately after the strikes stated:

> At the City Deep . . . police went down No.1 shaft with the African miners and assaulted them underground and . . . chased the Africans in all directions assailing them with their batons even to the doors of the hospital where they ran for protection.
> At Robinson Deep it appears . . . that the police carried out carefully prepared plans . . . three groups of police appear to have driven the Africans from their living quarters. The fourth group intercepted them at the gates when they tried to escape. Eventually many of the miners appear to have taken refuge at the top of the mine dump consisting of broken rock . . . they were persuaded to come down by a number of Natives claiming to be members of the Union . . . to hold a meeting . . . on another dump which consisted of fine sand. They were then attacked by the police and those who ran to the top of the dump were chased and assaulted, and were seen falling down . . . to the bottom of the dump. . . .
> 'The police were attacking anyone they could catch', said a witness at City Deep. 'Many people were unconscious afterwards. They were hitting the people as though they did not care whether they killed them. . . .

Some workers hid in locations and never returned; others, less fortunate, were found and returned to the compound, or railed home.[11] By Friday the strike was over, and workers who were not awaiting trial or facing dismissal were back at work. The defeat of the mineworkers was unconditional, and no concessions were made by the government or the mines. Workers in commerce and industry, angry over reports of police brutality but lacking the organisation or preparation necessary to take action, had also experienced defeat. That only weakened their trade unions further.

The AMWU was shattered, and although the union might have retained the loyalty of some of its members, the base for recruitment was undermined by defeat. Accounts of the mood amongst the mineworkers, as collected by Moodie (1984c), indicate the extent of the demoralisation. Mpotsongo Mde of the Van Dyke mine said:

> They never struck again. They were still waiting for that money. They never spoke about it amongst themselves in later years — nobody ever talked about it. They had been defeated.

Ncathama Mdelwa said at the end of his account:

> Everyone was talking about it but after a couple of weeks none spoke of it because nothing happened; they got no money. All they used to speak about was to work and then go home. . . (p.69).

Congress and the strike

Behind the scenes the behaviour of Xuma added to disenchantment with his leadership of the ANC. Relations between Xuma and the AMWU had never been easy, and had not been improved when Marks (its president) replaced Makabeni at the head of the CNETU. An open break had been avoided, but the events of August led to a breach. In June Marks met the working committee of the ANC to discuss the threatened strike of the mineworkers, and apparently assured the committee that 'no action would be taken for a considerable time to come, and that Congress would be furnished with a prepared statement for its information long beforehand'.[12] This assurance, said Dr Xuma, had not been honoured, and only on 10 August had he received a statement detailing the negotiations leading to strike action.[13] Although this might have been formally correct, the strike decision had not been anticipated by Marks, and Xuma was not providing a complete account of what had happened in the preceding weeks.

Dr Xuma was invited to the AMWU meeting on the morning of 4 August at the Market Square, where the strike decision was taken, but did not attend. Marks said of him in a subsequent interview: 'he just didn't show any interest'. Several members of the Congress Youth League (CYL), including Oliver Tambo, Nelson Mandela and Anton Lembede, had seen Xuma 'to try to persuade him', but had no success. This, concluded Marks, 'was the beginning of the end as far as they were concerned. They felt he would never do'. Even more remarkably, Bunting (1975, p.132) claims that Xuma, Moretsele and Ramohanoe, all members of the ANC working committee, appeared that afternoon at the same square, at an anti-pass rally. Marks was on the platform and, with many miners in the audience, it is inconceivable that the decision to strike was not mentioned.

The events surrounding the 1946 strike were not the sole cause of the disenchantment noted by Marks, but they must have contributed to the rift in 1949, when Xuma was ousted as president of the ANC. The CYL, still feeling its way in 1946, was not noted for its encouragement of the working-class movement, nor did its members conceive of the African worker as central to the struggle in South Africa. They supported the miner's fight because it was part of the African's struggle against white domination, and on those grounds they quarrelled with Xuma: it was not central to their decision that he 'would not do'.

Precisely what Dr Xuma did during the strike is not clear. His immediate aim was to end it, and his contribution to the miners' cause was a telegram to Smuts protesting against the use of force and intimidation, and urging immediate negotiations between 'Government representatives, the Chamber of Mines, African trade unions and the ANC'.[14] The CYL contribution was a leaflet (Karis and Carter, 1972—77, Vol. 2, pp.318—19) stating:

> The African Mine Workers had risen in revolt against the most brutal, callous and inhuman exploitation of man in the history of mankind. Their struggle is a challenge to the whole economic and political structure of South Africa.

The exaggerations are understandable and reflect the anger felt at the time. But this was not yet a revolt, and not yet a challenge to the whole structure of the country. The leaflet called for active support for the miners and then, in words which could not have helped the workers much in their struggle, called on 'spiritual forces' (against the guns?) to lead the men to victory:

> The African Mine Workers' struggle is our struggle. They are fighting political colour bar and economic discrimination against Africans.
> Then Brethren, on to the struggle! Although we are physically unarmed yet we are spritually fortified. We are struggling for a just cause, the very fundamental conditions of human existence. We must remember that in all spheres of human activity it is the spiritual forces that lead the WORLD.
> We demand a living wage for all African workers!!!!

The political focus moved to Members of the Native Representative Council (MRCs) when they suspended the Council's meeting indefinitely on 15 August (see Roth, 1983). This move had been initiated by Xuma in July, following the government's cavalier rejection of the anti-pass petition. He had called on MRCs to support a motion of adjournment and non-cooperation unless the government agreed to abolish the passes; recognise trade unions under the IC Act; and repeal the repressive measures under the Urban Areas Amendment Act and other legislation allowing the removal of African leaders without trial.[15] Now MRCs, angered by news from the mines, linked their action to the strike although, as Z.K. Matthews said (1946), the adjournment was not 'the result of a sudden decision brought about solely by the mine labourers' strike'.

In October, Xuma convened an 'Emergency Conference of All Africans' in Bloemfontein, attended by over 500 delegates, including several MRCs. They condemned the Representation of Natives Act of 1936 as 'a fraud and a means to perpetuate the policy of segregation, oppression and humiliation'. There was also a call to boycott all future elections under the Act,[16] with some equivocation over the use of the boycott tactic. Lembede's call for the immediate resignation of all MRCs was rejected. The adjournment of the Council was approved. Police brutality in the strike was condemned, and delegates observed two minutes silence in memory of the dead and wounded.[17]

On 26 August 1946 52 members of the CPSA, the ANC, and the CNETU were charged under the Riotous Assemblies Act and War Measure 145: 46 were fined nominal amounts for aiding an illegal strike. In November eight members of the CPSA Central Executive Committee were charged with sedition, and the case continued till May 1948 when the defendants (now numbering nine) were discharged (Simons and Simons, 1969, pp.583–7). In October 1948, the National Party finally withdrew the charges, and two years later outlawed all left-wing movements under the Suppression of Communism Act.

Unions in trouble

The anger in the townships and factories over the treatment of the miners could not, and did not, lead to a general strike, despite the resolution passed unanimously at the conference of the CNETU. With a few notable exceptions, there were no stoppages on the Witwatersrand ('Strike Bulletins' 1–5, *Ballinger Papers*). The call for a general strike in a period of relative political quiescence, without preparation, and when trade union membership was falling sharply, was unrealistic. The debacle of August also marked the end of the wartime trade unions. The decline had set in as early as 1944: the long fall in morale in the unions had been (in part) the cause of the bickering within the CNETU, and had been masked by those conflicts. Only a resounding victory for the workers could have reversed the position, and in retrospect it seems that after the retreat over the milling workers' struggle, there was little hope of altering the situation. Each reverse thereafter only led to further demoralisation.

One of the first casualties was the WIL, whose members had been working in the trade unions and in the PTU. This led them to believe that they could overcome the inertia inside the CNETU, but there were doubts: the unions were not making significant progress in securing better conditions for the workers, and even the 'militant' unions seemed to be as bureaucratic as those they criticised. The collapse of the Timber Workers Union strike was a blow to members of the WIL. Phoffu, the secretary of the union, had ignored the advice of the PTU, and had not prepared for the inevitable strike.[18] Some leading members of the League now argued that work in the trade unions was fruitless, and gave this a theoretical cloak by claiming that the new industries were bound to collapse in the face of post-war competition. After a long and bitter internal debate, the League decided to withdraw from all trade union activity, with only a small minority dissenting.[19] By mid-1946 the WIL had disintegrated and, with its collapse, the PTU (already severely weakened by the debacle of the timber workers' strike) all but ceased functioning.[20]

The collapse of the unions was widespread, as an account from Pretoria shows. The twelve unions of Boom Street and the Federation of African Unions simply disappeared. In 1947 Mokgatle found that he was the only survivor of the Pretoria unions and made several attempts to rebuild a Distributive Workers Union and a General Workers Union. In the latter organisation his main efforts were directed at fighting cases for men who had been 'refused entry' to Pretoria (under influx control regulations). This was obviously the one factor that drew many men to the union, and service was provided for these 'members' if they paid a two-year subscription amounting to 50s 6d — which is approximately what a lawyer would have charged. There is no indication that Mokgatle carried out any other trade union function in Pretoria (see Mokgatle, 1971, pp.255, 264–6).

Disintegration of the unions

On 30 August 1947 the CNETU met in conference, but for most delegates the proceedings did not get beyond the report of the credentials committee. Thirty-six unions were represented, but only six had paid affiliation fees, and eight unions were not affiliated to the Council. The delegates agreed that all the unions be represented, but the right of the eight (non-affiliated) unions to vote was in doubt. Only the six paid-up unions and members of the executive had the constitutional right to vote, and they decided against the eight. This led to a walk-out by the majority, which included Koza, Phoffu, Mfili and their one-time antagonists, Makabeni and Jacob D. Nyaosa of the Bakers and Confectioners Union (Anon., c. 1948). The defectors set up a Transvaal Council of African Trade Unions and issued statements condemning communist control of the CNETU. The new Council never functioned, and Makabeni and Nyaosa returned to the CNETU, where they were later appointed president and secretary. Koza also resigned from the new Council, and stayed aloof from both federal bodies.

The issue of voting rights precipitated but did not cause the split. The unions had reached breaking point and several other issues may have persuaded delegates to join the walk-out. There were at least three distinct groups among the trade union leaders, giving rise to shifting alliances. There were those in the CPSA together with their supporters; the former members of the PTU; and the 'nationalists' (for want of a better word) who differed from the Communists on many points, but usually voted with them. The one overriding issue the trade unions faced in 1947 was the vexed question of registration. Now, however, the question was no longer hypothetical, and the conditions were far worse than anyone had foreseen.

In 1947 the Smuts government published its Industrial Conciliation (Natives) Bill, proposing recognition for African unions (excluding mineworkers, domestic servants and farm labourers). Any body not registered under the Act would not be allowed to carry on trade union activities or collect subscriptions. Officials of the unions had to be South African nationals. Their election had to be supervised by a government-appointed registrar and was subject to veto by the Minister of Labour (*Inkululeko*, June (1) 1947). All disputes had to be settled through a Central Mediation Board (also appointed by the state) and strikes were illegal (with a penalty of £500 or three years in jail). Furthermore, Africans could not belong to trade unions in which other ethnic groups were organised, and trade unions registered under the IC Act were required to expel all Africans. The CNETU (or at least part of the Executive) rejected the Bill, and at a rally on 1 June called upon the government to withdraw the measure (*Inkululeko*, June (2) 1947). The issue was taken to the ill-fated August conference, and those that remained rejected the Bill. However, Nyaosa and other union officials argued for acceptance, saying that registration would at least provide the unions with a base from which to operate (Interview with Nyaosa). At the break-away conference, this was one of the issues discussed: no vote was taken, but it was reported that the chairman had summed up 'opinion as being in favour of acceptance subject to modification' (*Rand Daily Mail*, 13 October 1947).

Yet most former members of the PTU had opposed registration under the IC Act, and Koza stated subsequently that it was not the chairman who said that the new Bill could be accepted, but a member of the audience.[21] He also said that he rejected the Bill as dangerous — because it placed African unions in the hands of civil servants who could regulate wage claims and disputes as they wished. Koza broke away from the new Council, but whether he spoke for others is not known. The issue became even more confused when Nyaosa and Makabeni, who did not change their views on registration, and did not drop their criticism of Communist control of the unions, returned to the fold of the CNETU. Dick Mfili, the spokesman of the break-away unions, condemned the CNETU for 'acting undemocratically and against the interests of the African trade unions', itemising occasions on which the executive had either failed to call meetings (even during the mineworkers' strike), or nominated delegates to the Dakar Conference of African trade unions without consultation, and so on. All were valid complaints but skirted the issues of Communist control and registration, which found no place in this report.[22]

The government withdrew the Bill but in 1948, when the Nationalist Party won the election, the unions faced an administration that would not countenance an organised black working-class movement. An Industrial Legislation Commission was established, and all secretaries summoned to appear and provide information on the state of their unions. Koza alone refused, noting that the ACDWU rejected the principle of segregation in the organisation of workers and demanding the right of all workers to enter any occupation without discrimination. Koza also declared that the 'economic struggle of the African worker [was] indissolubly bound with the struggle of the African people' (*Guardian*, 15 December 1949).

When the Commission was given the power to make trade unionists give evidence and present minutes and financial books, Koza had to appear, but he refused to co-operate. In a letter to the Commission he stated that the subject of African trade unions can only be considered properly by representatives of the African trade unions' own choice, and, because of the absence of such representatives from the membership of your Commission, this union has no confidence in its deliberations (*Torch*, 1 May 1950).

This note of defiance, correct as it was politically, was otherwise without effect, because of the actual weakness of the trade unions. In his address to the Joint Council in 1947, Koza was minuted as saying that

Since 1943 there had been a great recession owing to decreased [trade union] activity and the government's policy of wage ceilings. The Iron and Steel Workers Union, potentially the largest, had an income of £500 per month in 1943, but was now practically non-existent. A similar decline had taken place in the Municipal Workers and Brick and Tile Workers Unions. In the Commercial Distributive Union the membership had been 10,000 and was now 1,500—2,000.

But Koza was looking ahead. He believed that the future of trade unions was bound up with the development of secondary industry: the search for an expanding market would provide a forceful argument for higher wages and increased purchasing power. Once again expressing his conception of the unions' political role in the struggle for liberation, he continued:

To enable the unions to play their part, the right to organise and bargain with the employers must be granted. The trade union movement must become a wing of the political movement for national liberation.

Facing the future

African workers were ill prepared to face the problems confronting them in the post-war years. Their trade unions were in a state of disarray after a series of defeats in nearly every industry; union members had dropped out and even those unions that survived were almost penniless; and the federal body was weak and split.

In the immediate future there seemed little chance that the unions would revive. This was not because of incompetence or lack of will (although both failings could be detected), but because the black working class faced redundancy in the post-war period. Production had tended to be labour-intensive owing to the difficulty, or impossibility, of importing modern machinery, although some advanced techniques and skills had been developed for the armaments and import substitution programmes (Innes, 1984,p.167). During the war that had not mattered much, because the government was the major buyer and the factories had not been concerned to meet competition. But in peacetime the small, underdeveloped workshops were priced out of the market. Even in the mid-1950s, workshops were under-capitalised, technologically undeveloped, and too small to effect significant changes. In 1953/4 65 per cent of all industrial firms employed fewer than nine workers, and 92 per cent employed less than fifty. After 1945 war production had come to an end, and local firms could not meet the new competition from imported goods.

During the war manufacture had absorbed an increasing number of workers, and the number of blacks employed had increased by 74 per cent, from 143,069 in 1938/9, to 248,785 in 1944/5. But although manufacturing after the war contributed 17 per cent to the Gross Domestic Product, making it the biggest contributor for the first time,[23] gold was still strategically the pivot of the economy because of its high contribution to state revenue. With four new gold fields about to be developed (and large investments needed to get them operational), the major capital resources were directed to gold. This starved other industries of necessary capital and also led to new, more stringent controls on labour to keep costs down (Innes, 1984, pp.144—5).

South African firms bought extravagantly, and unwisely, in an effort to acquire the more up to date technology that had come on the market. Exports lagged far behind imports, there was a Balance of Payments crisis in 1948/9, the South African pound was devalued, and large numbers of workers were discharged (ibid., p.170). In this climate of economic insecurity, it would have required a remarkable effort by viable trade unions to have slowed down the erosion of the workers' position in industry. A defenceless black working class, faced with an antagonistic government, was unable to refurbish its organisation.[24]

Conditions in the locations also deteriorated as the state took drastic steps to remove the unemployed from the towns, and tightened pass and liquor laws. The locations were combed to remove 'surplus' population, but nothing was done to alleviate living conditions, provide relief for the unemployed, build more houses, or extend education. Inevitably, there were riots across the country,[25] and on the Witwatersrand these took place at Krugersdorp, Randfontein, and Newlands (Johannesburg) in November 1949; in Newclare (Johannesburg) and Benoni in January 1950; in Newclare, Sophiatown and Benoni in February; and at the Bantu Sports Ground (Johannesburg) in March during a liquor raid (*Survey of Race Relations*, 1949—50, p.19). Then came a call by the CPSA, the rump of the CNETU, and the Transvaal Congress to stay away from work on 1 May 1950. There was an uneven response, some regions experiencing stay-at-homes of up to 60 per cent while other areas barely responded. In the evening police confronted demonstrators, and there was shooting at Orlando, Moroka, Sophiatown, Newclare, Alexandra, Benoni and Brakpan. At least 18 Africans were killed and 30 wounded. Bus shelters, cinemas, railway stations and trains were attacked: some were destroyed, others stoned or set alight.[26]

The May Day demonstrations were called by organisations to mark 'Freedom Day' and in opposition to the Suppression of Communism Bill. The confrontations at the end of the day were an expression of hostility between crowds and police, and the leaders were anonymous — whether drawn from the ranks of the ANC or not. The pattern of earlier riots was unmistakable. Workers who participated were unorganised, had no immediate demands, and merely expressed frustration at the oppressive way in which they were being treated. The trade unions had lent their name to the action, but there were few indications that the working-class movement had yet learnt the need to co-ordinate action at the workplace with that in the locations. The slogans were couched in the language of national liberation, not of workers' solidarity. This pattern was to become dominant in the 1950s, but it had been set in the 1940s.

Notes

1. Moodie, 1984c, found that the miners who were interviewed, and were on the mines in 1946, had not heard of the AMWU before the strike.
2. A 'bossboy' at Brakpan mines in 1946, recounting his experience, quoted by Moodie, 1984c, p.64.
3. Beinart, 1984, records that 'M' was not involved in workers' organisation, but said of 1946, 'we struck work, and we refused to go underground'.
4. Minutes of the ANC working committee, August 1946, found in the *Molema Papers*.
5. The wording of the resolution is given as Phillips remembers it. During the interview, Phillips was referred to the account of the events surrounding the 'sympathy strike' in Simons and Simons, 1969. He rejected their account point by point.
6. Phillips, interview. See also 'Strike Bulletin No. 3' issued by the AMWU, 14 August, for a brief report on the meeting. The committee agreed that water and hospital services would be exempt from the strike call. Copy in *Ballinger Papers*, Johannesburg.
7. 'Strike Bulletin No. 4' states that reports that the meeting was banned could not be confirmed, and there was uncertainty amongst the strike leaders. Copy in *Ballinger Papers*.
8. Phillips interview. Phillips could not confirm the presence of Koza, as suggested by Simons and Simons, 1969.
9. The published figures claim an accuracy to the last digit. This gives a false impression of accuracy, and I only quote round numbers.
10. Schedules 'A' and 'B' presented at the subsequent trial; Moodie, 1984c, pp.39–40.
11. Moodie, ibid., pp.38–63. See also 'Strike Bulletin No. 4', *Ballinger Papers*; Simons and Simons, 1969, pp.575–7; Roux, 1949, pp.347–8; *Star* and *Rand Daily Mail*.
12. Statement by Dr Xuma as minuted at the meeting of the working committee, 13 August 1946.
13. Minutes of the working committee of the ANC, 13 August 1946, Dr Xuma's statement.
14. Letters confirming the telegram, 14 August, *Xuma Papers*, ABX 460814b.
15. Circular letter from Dr Xuma to all MRCs, 26 July 1946, *Xuma Papers*, ABX 460726a.
16. *Inkululeko*, November (1), 1946; letter by Xuma to W. Champion, 14 October 1946; *Xuma Papers*, ABX 461014.
17. See the scathing comments on the boycott issue in Tabata, 1950, pp.135–6; also Karis and Carter, 1972-77, Vol. 2, p.95.
18. The criticism in *Socialist Action* was an expression of the anger felt by

members of the WIL at what they considered a betrayal of the workers by one of their allies.

19. See S. Kruger, 1945, CAMP, Reel 7B 2:DW2:85/1 and 2:DW2:41 for the debate in the WIL, and the author's resignation as secretary of the League in protest at the majority decision.

20. 'Report on the split in the African trade union movement, Johannesburg', mimeographed, *c.* January 1948. My thanks to Mark Stein for a copy of this document. The report mentions the WIL, but does not describe the events that led to its demise.

21. Minutes of Joint Council of Europeans and Africans, 8 December 1947. Koza had been invited to attend and address the body. *Xuma Papers*, ABX 480202b.

22. I have not been able to ascertain who drew up the report on the split, and do not know how accurately it reflects Mfili's views. The report claims to be impartial and includes replies by an official of the CNETU. I questioned Nyaosa on some of these issues, but except for his assertion that he had been correct in wishing to accept registration under the Bill, he had little to add.

23. Agriculture contributed 13 per cent, and mining 19.9 per cent to GDP.

24. It is doubtful whether the Smuts government would have been less severe in its handling of the black working class, but that is beside the point. The Nationalists were in control and they used all the resources of the state to stifle opposition.

25. The account given here is restricted to the Transvaal. There is therefore no attempt to discuss the most tragic of all the riots, that of January 1949 in Durban, where Zulus attacked Indians, and police shot both. Nor is there any attempt here to give a comprehensive account of the riots. That would require a separate study.

26. Ibid. The events were widely publicised, and this account is taken from *Torch*, 8 May 1950. Reports in other papers differed only in details.

15. Conclusion

In February 1933, after South Africa had gone off the gold standard and ensured thereby a rapid recovery from economic depression, the two major parliamentary parties joined a coalition cabinet, and then a year later fused to form the United South African National Party (or United Party). Although there were disagreements inside the new ruling party on such issues as the country's flag and anthem, there was broad consensus on 'Native policy' (including the disenfranchisement of Africans in the Cape, a further and 'final' delimitation of land, and tighter regulation of labour in the towns) and on 'neutrality' in foreign policy.

The foreign and military policies of the South African government during the 1930s need to be viewed against the storm then breaking in Asia, Europe and America. With the 'world-out-there' struggling to extricate itself from the effects of a world depression, and fascism advancing inexorably across Europe and Asia, the western powers pursued a policy of appeasement in the face of Nazi aggrandisement. Consequently, South Africa's pre-war policy of 'neutrality' in the event of war was acceptable to all but a minority of the white electorate. All over the country there was an eruption of 'shirt' movements in imitation of the fascists of Europe. These groups aped their German and Italian counterparts in their virulent racism, and they won recruits from a widening public during the centenary celebrations of the 'Great Trek' in 1938. There was in these movements a racism with local roots, coupled with a pro-German ideology, that fed into the thinking on the approaching war. Sections of the National Party agreed with the objectives of these groups, and joined with them in opposing the government after 1939.

When war did break out in September 1939, the cabinet was split, but Deputy Prime Minister Smuts called for intervention, and won a majority, first in the cabinet and then in Parliament. The country went to war but with a voluntary army for service abroad. Smuts joined the British war cabinet, repeating the role he had played in the First World War, but his support for the war was not disinterested. This he saw as his opportunity to advance South Africa's claims to a sub-continent dominated by white settlers — a programme he had outlined in 1929 in his 'Rhodes lectures' at Oxford University.

Although removed from the centre of world politics in the 1930s, South Africa, as the world's largest gold producer, occupied an important position in the west's economic system. As the country emerged rapidly from the depression after leaving the gold standard, mines prospered, new businesses and industries were established, and towns on the Witwatersrand grew or were rebuilt. The resultant prosperity accrued mainly to a small section of the population, but did provide new opportunities for employment and the working class gained, albeit marginally. The new industries served the country well during the war years, particularly as military suppliers, while the expansion of the economy brought an even larger working class into existence.

The new prosperity of the early to mid-1930s led to further demands that black labour be channelled to the mines and farms, and in part this was why Hertzog's Native Bills were placed before parliament and approved. African opposition to the new measures was ineffectual: the All-African Convention convened by African leaders to plan resistance to the Native Bills temporised and then compromised, leaving its followers in disarray. Yet despite this failure of leadership, the period produced two important organisational or political initiatives. In the Transvaal a beginning was made to the formation of industrial unions for Africans, while nationally anti-war/ anti-fascist agitation developed. The latter started in earnest with spontaneous protests by blacks against the Italian invasion of Ethiopia, and continued with protests against fascist aggression in Europe. This 'war-against-war' clamour inevitably merged with calls for greater democracy in South Africa and the ending of discriminatory legislation, and this set the scene for the struggles of the 1940s and beyond.

The Second World War generated a sense amongst South Africans, although removed from the main war zone, that change in the direction of greater democracy was inevitable. It was not just the likelihood of victory that led to this optimistic belief, but also the emergence of the USA and the USSR as allied 'superpowers'. They were perceived as providing alternative (or even complementary) models for post-war political, social and economic change. Their philosophies rubbed off on political parties in South Africa, although there were also countervailing influences from the fascist powers. A sizeable section of the National Party drew inspiration from Germany and at least one abortive pro-Nazi coup was planned during the war. The influence of the USA grew when Roosevelt endorsed both the 'Four Freedoms' and the Atlantic Charter. The twin concepts of 'freedom' and 'democracy' became the slogans of the western powers, and educational programmes for the mainly white South African troops were designed to highlight these ideals. Both black organisations, the African National Congress and the All African Convention, drafted (or changed) their programmes to claim the franchise — and this call for the vote pointed for the first time to majority black rule. What was less certain was the nature of the society that would be created when the vote was won. The programmes were open-ended, and could have been applied in a reformed capitalist society, or by a country in which radical social change was envisaged. It was a time of political fudge, and the African movements were not alone in being unable to define the society they wanted. Some members of the Communist Party of South Africa (CPSA) followed Earl Browder, the American Communist leader, in believing that, if Stalin and Roosevelt could settle problems amicably at Yalta, the era of class struggle was over. South Africa was bound to follow suit and wartime sacrifices would produce a better and safer post-war country.

Most members of the CPSA uncritically accepted sharp changes in Soviet policy, switching from an anti-Nazi position in the mid-1930s to support for the Nazi-Soviet pact, and then, after a short period of indecision, to an anti-war stance. It was with relief that these same people could once again switch and support the war after the USSR was invaded. Now it was again possible to combine Russophilism with support for the war against Nazism. There was admiration for the exploits of the Red Army, and collecting money for Medical Aid for Russia became an important (and respectable) political activity.

The radio brought the war into virtually every household (or at least every white house) in South Africa and in that respect the war was made somewhat 'democratic'. This led, for example, to urgent demands in the CPSA's press for the opening of the 'second front' in Europe to support the Red Army. There was less talk about class war, and more propaganda for building a democratic South Africa. The defence of Stalingrad and the rolling back of the German armies lent increased credence to this standpoint: never again, said the pundits, would South Africa be allowed to sink back into the bad old days of segregation. The new popularity of the USSR and CPSA rubbed off in some electoral victories; in Johannesburg, for example, a Communist candidate won a seat on the municipal council. The CPSA's new supporters came mainly from the middle-class whites but, because they abstained from, or condemned, industrial and township struggles, it did not win significant numbers of African followers.

Africans were used as non-combatants in the army even though the government had little cause to fear the black nationalist movements. Both the ANC and the AAC supported the war effort, and the former deplored all strikes. The CPSA seemed for a brief period capable of organising dissent, but it surrendered its class role after Germany invaded the USSR and it switched to support the government's war effort. Only the Indians in the Party remained disaffected. They found conditions in South Africa intolerable, and many were supporters of Gandhi and the 'Quit India' campaign. Leading figures in the South African Indian Congress who opposed the war experienced detention and imprisonment — only after the invasion of the USSR, when they declared their support for the war, did the harassment lessen. All other socialists were pro-war and although a small group (gathered around the Socialist Party) were key figures in the Alexandra bus boycott, their opposition to the state was subordinated to their stand on the war. Only the Trotskyists remained anti-war and they had a limited presence in the Cape and the Transvaal. In their ranks were Max Gordon (interned in 1940) and the Workers International League (1943–46) which was active in the trade union movement and in the bus boycott. Nevertheless, the anti-warites gained few recruits on these grounds.

Although African workers on the Witwatersrand were eager for industrial organisation in the early 1930s, the existing trade union federation refused to accept them as members. After several false starts, it was the patient winning of small demands, often for individual workers, that led to the growth of a viable trade union movement. Workers were persuaded of the utility of trade unions when wage increases were won, by submissions for improvements before the Wage Board, and then through industrial action to get the Wage Board's decision implemented. The use of official state machinery to secure improvements was not without its difficulties. When minimum wages were gazetted, the unions flourished, but when the government opposed further increases in 1943, they went into decline.

When war came the government gave *de facto* recognition to the burgeoning unions. In their hour of need, with the allied forces in retreat, the government allowed trade unions space within which to grow and by 1943 they claimed a total membership of 150,000. The organisation of African workers in the shops, factories and townships was often achieved with the help of political groups. It must remain a moot point whether they could have achieved more had they not been influenced by such pressure groups. The fact is that in almost every case of struggle there was contact of some kind — close or peripheral — with one or other of the movements that offered assistance. Workers turned to (or were wooed by) one or more of the Institute of Race Relations, the Friends of Africa, the CPSA and the WIL, the Socialist Party and its black counterpart the African Democratic Party, and the ANC. It is not possible to generalise about the influence of so diverse a source of contacts; and there is no possibility of comparing organisations that wanted to stop all strikes with those which encouraged such activity through the war years. What can be said is that the trade unions would have been less successful if Max Gordon had not participated in their organisation, and that the bus boycott, which rested on Alexandra's community organisations, would not have fared as well had it not been for the support of Socialist Party members and the WIL. Ultimately such discussions are academic and only deflect attention away from a more fundamental question: the importance to be ascribed to the class nature of organisation and the type of struggle such bodies entered.

For Gordon and for the WIL the prime task was the formation of trade unions and their conversion into a base for a working-class movement. They failed in the attempt, but that does nothing to lessen the importance of that perspective. Other trade unions, whether supported or not by outside parties, were no more successful. Most crumbled before the refusal of the government to allow any further wage rises — but government intransigence was not the only cause of their demise. During the war those movements that supported the war effort either opposed strike action, or urged the workers to exercise restraint. None went as far as the Ballingers and their organisation, the Friends of Africa, in deprecating all strike action, but, in the case of the VFP workers who had no formal organisation, trade union leaders were used by government officials as strike-breakers, and during the war mineworkers were prevented from striking by their union officials. Yet even this is not the entire story. Compound workers were not easily organised in the 1940s and wartime regulations were promulgated to prevent the union's functioning. In so far as there was organisation on the mines, the *izibonda* (or room leaders) were probably more important than union officials. When ultimately the unionised workers would brook no further delay, the African Mine Workers' Union was totally unprepared, and only the action of the *izibonda* prevented the 1946 strike action collapsing ignominiously. Even so, it ended disastrously with the collapse of the union — and, with it, much of the wartime union movement.

Struggles in the community were more successful, but in this case the government had fewer means by which to control popular outbursts — short of bringing in troops. The Smuts government was not beyond such action, as it showed in Marabastad and Moroka, but it was obviously more effective to contain dissent by less draconian means. The issues were patched up and the basic problems left untouched, but still the communities could claim some victories. They walked for weeks in the case of the bus boycotts and prevented the rise in busfares, or camped out in the open in shantytowns in defiance of police action, municipal pressure and inclement weather.

In the building of industrial and community organisations, African workers engaged in two arenas of struggle: at the place of production (or distribution) and inside the wider community. There was nothing exceptional in their being involved in two distinct centres of conflict. Both were important in the fight for better living conditions — whether it was on the economic front or related to social conditions. But what was lacking was the merging of the two — an essential strategy, given the narrow base that factory workers occupied. This was understood by the inhabitants of Alexandra during the bus boycott, but despite the appeal to the trade unions to bring their members out in support of the struggle, they received no organisational assistance. It was the authorities who realised the potential strength of a community struggle backed by trade unions — and they gave way in order to avert the danger.

The trade unions also faced other issues, some of which were to surface again forty years later — the question of trade union registration and the formulation of minimum demands over wages or work conditions; the issue of centralising trade union organisation, and the relation to political movements. New protagonists argued these same questions afresh in the late 1970s, seemingly unaware of the fierce debates of 1944–45.

What then was the legacy of the struggles of the 1930s and 1940s? Leaving aside the riots, which provide no measure for organisation and no prescription for advancement, what can be learned from the political agitation over impending war, the demonstrations against the pass laws, the trade union struggles, and the boycotts and shanty town movements? Clearly this was no passive working class but a fighting body of people prepared to struggle for better conditions. Nor was this only a 'man's' struggle. Without the women there could have been no success in the bus boycotts and the shantytown movement would have collapsed. Other campaigns against lodger permits, against pick-up patrols and beer raids, depended on the resolution of women in the face of police harassment and imprisonment. They were also in the front rank in trade union protests. They marched at the head of the workers when Koza and one of his organisers were arrested, and they were prominent at strikes in the commercial trade.

Why then did the struggles end in defeat? This is a loaded question because defeat must always be a relative term. The workers notched up some victories — in wage increases, better work conditions, and in their communities. No one defeat could take that away from them. But in the 1940s the African workers were at a disadvantage, fighting not from strength but from weakness. Their position in the towns and in the factories was far from assured — either economically or politically — and their unions never received legislative sanction. After the war the situation worsened: they faced displacement when soldiers returned and were demobilised, and they faced a second threat when there was a downturn in the economy after the war. In fact, they had begun to face repression as soon as the government sensed it was on the winning side in the war. Pass laws had been intensified by 1943, and wages were pegged (with very few exceptions) after 1943. All the bravery displayed at the power stations and on the mines (and by workers everywhere) could not prevail against a government that had decided to curtail the development of their unions, and was preparing post-war legislation to that end.

Nonetheless, tens of thousands of workers had been organised, and even more had taken part in rallies, demonstrations and strikes. Some unions won notable victories and a tradition of struggle was established. Across the country, workers set out to form trade unions, and some of their stories are in this book — Lawrence Mlambo, the domestic worker who organised a union in Parktown North (Johannesburg); Willie Bosiame of the irrigation supply store in Oliphantshoek who enrolled 31 workers in their own union; Jacks Ngwenya, a teacher at Oranjeville, who was asked by labourers at a nearby airfield to help them form a union. These initiatives came to nought, partly because organisational assistance was not forthcoming, but they represented a stirring that was part of a larger movement to secure better conditions for newly urbanised workers.

What was the perspective of those who participated in these struggles? There is no simple answer to this question, because these people were not a homogeneous mass with one objective, but rather men and women at different levels of incorporation into (or of alienation from) the society they had entered. Although they were mostly workers (from mine labourers to domestic servants), there were also petty traders, craftsmen, teachers and nurses: some were literate, others totally illiterate. Some still thought of villages in the reserves as their homes, and owed allegiance to clan or age groups. They brought with them the tribal customs to which they were accustomed and attached; they still visited the herbalist, or sought the 'medicine man' when in trouble. Others had moved away from their rural kin and knew only the towns and cities as their home. For all these diverse groups the struggles were over wages, better conditions of work, more houses, or against rising bus fares, but their appraisal of these campaigns must have differed in accordance with their understanding of the life they had now entered. That is only one part of the story. These men and women came to the towns hoping to adjust to new demands and integrate themselves in the society they encountered. They were appalled at the conditions they found (on the mines, in the townships and in the backyards where servants were housed) and they hated the police presence, the pass, tax and beer raids, the overcrowding in houses, the poor schooling, and the privileges accorded every white. There was no offensive against the system as a whole, and instead they found ways to exist inside an unbelievably ugly world. More houses were demanded, albeit inside segregated townships; rising fares were resisted (on buses and trains), though there was no call for integrated transport; higher wages were demanded by workers confined to segregated jobs; they asked for better schools, but not for integrated education. Even backyard accommodation in the towns, so miserable and uncomfortable, was prized by servants and their friends.

This was not yet a revolutionary crowd that threatened the system, and stuggles were usually constrained by reformist demands. Could a more militant leadership, by focusing on political struggles that affected African workers, have achieved more? If, like other similar questions, that must remain unanswered, it is more certain that such leaders were not found, and that the political parties of the period failed to offer a way forward. For this failure of leadership African workers were to pay dearly in the years to come.

Bibliography

Abbreviations

ASI	African Studies Institute, Rand
CAMP	Co-operative African Microfilm Project, Chicago University Library
CUP	Cambridge University Press
ICS	Institute of Commonwealth Studies, London
ISMA	Institute for the Study of Man in Africa
JSAS	*Journal of Southern African Studies*, Oxford
NUSAS	National Union of South African Students
OUP	Oxford University Press
Rand	University of the Witwatersrand
SAIRR	South African Institute of Race Relations
SALB	*South African Labour Bulletin*
SOAS	School of Oriental and African Studies, London
SSAC	The Societies of Southern Africa in the Nineteenth and Twentieth Centuries, ICS
UCT	University of Cape Town
Wits HW	University of the Witwatersrand History Workshop
WUP	Witwatersrand University Press

A. Primary sources — unpublished

Ballinger, W.G. and Margaret, papers, UCT and Rand/film ICS.

Benson, Mary, papers, SOAS.

Bunche, Ralph, diary, 1937, transcript, ICS.

Carter, Gwendolen and Karis, Tom, *South African Political Materials* (CAMP) film, ICS.

Champion, A.W.G., papers, UCT/film ICS.

Cope, R.K., papers, Rand/film Borthwick Library, York.

Fabian Colonial Bureau, papers, Rhodes House.

Findlay, George, papers, Rand.

Goodlatte, Clare, papers, South African Library.

Hemson, David, film, University of Warwick/ICS.

Hoover Institute Microfilm Africa 484, DT779S726, Rhodes House.

International Labour Organisation, papers related to South Africa.

Jones, David Ivon, letters, National Library of Wales.

Jones, J.D. Rheinallt, papers, Rand/fiche ICS.

Lazar, Ruth, papers, SOAS.

Luthuli, Albert, papers, film ICS.

Matthews, Z.K., papers, Rand/film ICS.

Molema, S.M., papers, film ICS.

Saffery, Lynn, papers (two collections), Rand.

South African Department of Justice, files, Pretoria/film SOAS.
South African Trade Union Movement, records as found in the archives of the Trade Union Council of South Africa, film ICS.
University of Warwick, Sociology Department, photocopies of archive papers from South Africa and elsewhere.
Vigne, Randolph, papers, SOAS.
Woolf, Saura, album of press cuttings (private collection), 1938—40.
Xuma, A.B., papers, Rand/film ICS.

Official publications

I. Municipal authorities

Durban
Annual Report of the Medical Officer of Health, 1932, 1935.

Johannesburg
Minutes of a Conference on Urban Juvenile Delinquency, 10—12 October 1938.
Annual Report of Manager, 1 July 1938—30 June 1939.
Survey of Reef Locations, 1939.
Survey of the African in Industry within the Municipality of Johannesburg, June 1939.
Agenda, 682nd Ordinary Meeting, 26 January 1943, City Council.
Non-European Housing and Social Amenities, November 1951, mimeo.

II. Union of South Africa

Parliamentary Debates (1937—44).
Senate Debates (1937—47).
Verbatim Reports on the Proceedings of the Native Representative Council (1940—43).
Annual Reports of the Department of Public Health, 1938—46.

Listed chronologically in year of publication

Report of Native Economic Commission, 1930—32, UG 22, 1932.
Interim and Final Reports of the Commission of Inquiry on certain matters concerning the South African Police and the South African Railways and Harbour Police, UG 50, 1937.
Report of the Native Farm Labour Commission, 1937—38, GPS 9523-1940-400, 1939.
Social and Economic Planning Council Report No.1: Re-employment, Reconstruction and the Council's Status, UG 9, 1943.
Report of the Witwatersrand Mine Native Wages Commission, 1943, UG 21—44, 1944.
Report of the Commission of Inquiry into the Operation of Bus Services for Non-Europeans on the Witwatersrand and in the Districts of Pretoria and

Vereeniging, UG 31 1944.

Social and Economic Planning Council: The Future of Farming in South Africa, UG 10—45, 1945.

Report of the Commission of Enquiry into the Disturbances at Moroka, Johannesburg, on the 30th August 1947, An.145, 1948.

Report of Native Laws Commission, 1946—48, UG 28, 1948.

Geographical Distribution of the Population of the Union of South Africa: Population Census, 7 May 1946, UG 51, 1949.

Report of the Commission on Native Education, UG 53, 1951.

Report of the Industrial Legislation Commission, UG 62, 1951.

Report of the Select Committee on the Suppression of Communism Enquiry, SC 6—52, Parow, 1952.

Urban and Rural Population of South Africa, 1904—1960, Report No. 02-02-01, 1960.

Union Statistics for 50 Years: 1910—1960, 1960.

Unofficial reports and minutes

General Missionary Conference of South Africa: Reports of Proceedings of the Seventh Conference, Lovedale, 1928.

Carnegie Commission: The Poor White Problem of South Africa, Pro Ecclesia, Stellenbosch, 1932.

South African Institute of Race Relations, *Annual Report,* 1930—1936.

South African Trades and Labour Council, Reports of Annual Conferences, 1934—42.

Workers International League, *Internal Bulletins,* 1945.

Newspapers and journals

(published in Johannesburg unless otherwise indicated)

Africa!; Africa Perspective; Africa South (Cape Town); *African Advocate; The African Defender — Umvikeli Thebe; African Drum/Drum; Bantu Studies; Bantu World; The Call* (Durban); *Cape Standard* (Cape Town); *Chainbreaker; Common Sense; Discussion* (Cape Town); *Democrat/Democratic Monthly; Drum; Eastern Province Herald* (Port Elizabeth); *The Flame — Umlilo Mollo; Forum; Freedom; Friend* (Bloemfontein); *Garment Worker; Golden City Post; Guardian* (Cape Town); *Imvo Zabantsundu* (Kingwilliamstown); *Indian Opinion* (Verulam); *Inkululeko* (*see Transvaal Communist*); *Inkundla ya Bantu* (Durban) — incorporating *Territorial Magazine; Inyaniso; Journal of the South African Economic Society/South African Journal of Economics; Journal of Southern African Studies* (Oxford); *Militant* (New York); *Progressive Trade Union Bulletin; Race Relations; Race Relations News; Rand Daily Mail; Revolutionary Communist; Socialist Action; Socialist Review; South African Builder; South African Labour Bulletin* (Durban); *South African Outlook* (Lovedale); *South African Quarterly; Spark* 1935—39 (Cape Town); *Star; Sun* (Cape Town); *Sunday Times; Territorial Magazine* (later, *Inkundla ya Bantu*);

Torch (Cape Town); *Transvaal Communist/'Nkululeko/Inkululeko; Trek* (Cape Town); *Umsebenzi/South African Worker* (Cape Town); *Umteteli wa Bantu; The Voice* (Durban); *Workers Voice* (Cape Town); *Youth in Revolt.*

Interviews (in Britain, 1976—86, unless otherwise indicated)

By author
(Notes of conversations, tapes or transcripts, in author's possession. These will be deposited at the ICS.)
Nathan Adler; Hyman Basner; Miriam Basner; Myrtle and Monty Berman; E.J. Burford; Bettie du Toit; Gessie Gathercole; Ruth Heyman/Saffery/Lazar; Jack Hodgson; Eileen Jaff; Millie Kahn/Lee/Haston; Mary Klopper; Paul Kosten; Heaton Lee; Colin Legum; Saura Leslie/Joffe/Woolf; Julius Lewin; J.D. Nyoasa (Geneva, 1979); James Phillips; Vella Pillay; Pauline Podberry/Naidoo; Guy Routh; Lynn Saffery; Ray Sachs; Joan Schedrin; Julius Schochet; Errol Shanley; Nachum Sneh; Leon and Rolene Szur; Joe Urdang; Charles van Gelderen; Hilda Watts/Bernstein; Eli Weinberg; M.B. Yengwa

By others
Revd James Calata, by Gwendolen Carter; eastern Cape, CAMP, Reel 15a, 2:XC3:94 and 2:XC3:91/1.
J.B. Marks, by Tom Karis, Maseru, CAMP, Reel 12a, 2:XM65:94/2.
Edwin Mofutsanyana, interviewed by Bob Edgar, Maseru.
Josie Palmer, interviewed by Julia Wells, Johannesburg.

Secondary sources

Abrahams, Peter (1954), *Tell Freedom!* (Faber, London).
— (1968), *Mine Boy* (Heinemann, London).
Adler, T. (ed.) (1977), *Perspectives on South Africa: A Collection of Working Papers* (ASI).
Allen, V.L. (1954), *Power in Trade Unions* (Longman, London).
Anon. (c. 1948), 'Report on the split in the African trade union movement, Johannesburg' (mimeo).
Archer, Sean (1981), 'The South African industrialisation debate and the tariff in the inter-war years' (*SSAC*, Vol. 11).
Ballinger, Margaret (1969), *From Union to Apartheid. A Trek to Isolation* (Juta, Cape Town).
Ballinger, W.G. and M. (1938), 'Native wages and the cost of living' (mimeo).
Barry, M.E. (1943), 'Preliminary report on disease and health services in Alexandra Township, 1942—43' (NUSAS Health Research Department, mimeo).

Basner, Miriam (n.d.), 'Hyman Basner: a biography and sketch of twenty years of political life in South Africa' (typescript).

Beinart, William (1981), 'The family, youth organisation, gangs and politics in the Transkeian area', (Conference on the Family in Africa, London).

— (1984), 'Ethnic particularism, workers' consciousness and nationalism: the experience of a South African migrant, 1930—60' (*SSAC*, Vol. 13).

— and Bundy, Colin (1981b), 'The union, the nation, and the talking crow: the language and tactics of the independent ICU in East London' (*SSAC*, Vol. 12).

— Delius, Peter, and Trapido, Stanley (eds).(1986), *Putting a Plough to the Ground: Accumulation and Dispossession in Rural South Africa, 1850—1930* (Ravan, Johannesburg).

Benson, Mary (1966), *South Africa: The Struggle for a Birthright* (Penguin, Harmondsworth).

Blaxall, Arthur (1965), *Suspended Sentence* (Hodder and Stoughton, London).

Bonner, Phil (ed.) (1981), *Working Papers in Southern African Studies*, Vol. 2 (Ravan, Johannesburg).

Bowen, Walter (1954), *Colonial Trade Unions* (Fabian Publications, Research Series No. 167, London).

Bozzoli, Belinda (ed.) (1979), *Labour, Townships and Protest: Studies in the Social History of the Witwatersrand* (Ravan, Johannesburg).

— (1983), 'Marxism, feminism and South African studies' (*JSAS*, Vol. 9, No. 2, April).

— (ed.) (1987), *Class, Community and Conflict: South African Perspectives* (Ravan, Johannesburg).

Bradford, Helen (1985), 'The Industrial and Commercial Workers Union in the countryside, 1924—1930' (PhD thesis, Rand).

Bransky, D.M. (1973), 'Considerations of Man's concept of money and its application to the reproduction of money material: a prelude to the analysis of the South African gold mining industry' (B.Phil dissertation, University of York).

Brenner, Robert (1977), 'The origins of capitalist development: a critique of neo-Smithian Marxism' (*New Left Review*, No. 104, July—August).

Bridgman, F.B. (1926), 'Social conditions in Johannesburg' (*International Review of Missions*, July).

Bridgman, Mrs F.B. (1928), 'Social and medical work for native women and girls in urban areas' (in *Proceedings of the Seventh General Missionary Conference of South Africa*).

Brittain, Vera (1981), *Testament of Friendship* (Fontana, London).

Brooks, Alan K. (1967), 'From class struggle to national liberation: the Communist Party of South Africa, 1940 to 1950' (M.A. thesis, Sussex University).

Brookes, Edgar H. et al. (1930), *Coming of Age: Studies in South African Citizenship and Politics* (Maskew Miller, Cape Town).

Bryce, James (1899), *Impressions of South Africa* (Macmillan, London).

Bunting, Brian (1975), *Moses Kotane: South African Revolutionary* (Inkululeko Publications, London).

— (ed.) (1981), *South African Communists Speak: Documents from the History of the South African Communist Party, 1915–80* (Inkululeko Publications, London).

Burford, E.J. (1946), 'Organising the African mine workers' (*Democrat*, 2 March).

Burger, John [Leo Marquard] (1943), *Black Man's Burden* (Gollancz, London).

Burrows, Raymond (ed.) (1952), *Indian Life and Labour in Natal* (SAIRR, Johannesburg).

Christie, Renfrew (1984), *Electricity, Industry and Class in South Africa* (Macmillan, London).

Clack, Garfield (1962), 'The changing structure of industrial relations in South Africa' (PhD thesis, University of London).

Clarke, Tom and Clements, Laurie (eds) (1977), *Trade Unions Under Capitalism* (Fontana, Glasgow).

Cobb, Richard (1972), *The Police and the People* (OUP, London).

Coka, J. Gilbert (c. 1939), *Liberal or Nazi South Africa?* (publisher unknown, Johannesburg).

Cole, Monica (1966), *South Africa* (Methuen, London).

Communist Party of South Africa (c. 1936), *Communism and the Native Question: White and Black South Africa. The White Worker — and his Duty on the Race Issue* (Johannesburg).

— (c. 1937), *Vereeniging, Who is to Blame: The Communists? The Police? The Liquor Barons? The Government?* (Johannesburg).

— (c. 1941), *More Money* (Johannesburg).

— (1944), *Communists in Conference: The 1943–44 National Conference of the Communist Party of South Africa* (Cape Town).

— (c. 1945), *They Marched to Victory: The Story of the Alexandra Bus Boycott* (Johannesburg).

— (c. 1947), *The people overflow: the story of Johannesburg's shanty towns* (Johannesburg).

Connell, P.H. et al. (1939), *Native Housing: A Collective Thesis* (WUP, Johannesburg).

Cope, R.K. (c. 1943), *Comrade Bill: The Life and Time of W.H. Andrews, Worker's Leader* (Stewart Printers, Cape Town).

Coplan, David (1982), 'The emergence of an African working class culture' (in Marks and Rathbone).

Couzens, Tim (1982), 'Moralizing leisure time: the transatlantic connection and black Johannesburg, 1918–1936' (in Marks and Rathbone).

Cross, David (1946), 'Orlando squatters — and a Labour Council' (*Democrat*, 2 March).

Davenport, T.R.H. (1978), *South Africa: A Modern History* (Macmillan, London).

Davidson, Basil (1952), *Report on Southern Africa* (Cape, London).

Davies, Robert (1976), 'The class character of South Africa's industrial conciliation legislation' (*SALB*, Vol. 2, No. 6).
— (1979), *Capital, State and White Labour in South Africa: An Historical Materialist Analysis of Class Formation and Class Relations* (Harvester, London).
De Freitas, F. (1966), *Industrial Profile of South Africa* (Da Gama, Johannesburg).
De Kiewiet, C.W. (1950), *A History of South Africa: Social and Economic* (OUP, London).
De Kock, M.H. (1924), *Selected Subjects in the Economic History of South Africa* (Juta, Cape Town).
— (1936), *The Economic Development of South Africa* (King, London).
Deutscher, Isaac (1974), *Stalin* (Penguin, Harmondsworth).
Diamond, Charles R. (1969), 'African labour problems on the South African gold mines with special reference to the strike of 1946' (M.A. thesis, UCT).
Dikobe, Modikwe [Mark Ramitloa] (1973), *The Marabi Dance* (Heinemann, London).
— (1979a), 'The people overflow: a tribute to Schreiner' (in Bozzoli, 1979).
— (1979b), 'We shall walk' (ibid.).
Dixon, F.H.C. (*c.* 1946), 'Report on the final plan of Sharpe Native Township (Sharpeville)' (mimeo).
Eberhardt, Jacqueline (*c.* 1950), *A Survey of Family Conditions with Special Reference to Housing Needs, Orlando Township* (Johannesburg City Council).
Edwards, Iain (1986), 'The Durban Communist Party, 1940s' (*SALB*, Vol. 11, No. 4, February–March).
Edwards, Michael (1973), *Nehru: A Political Biography* (Penguin, Harmondsworth).
Engels, Frederick (1942), *Anti-Duhring* (Lawrence and Wishart, London).
— (1976), *The Conditions of the Working Class in England* (Panther, St Albans).
Fanon, Franz (1969), *The Wretched of the Earth* (Penguin, Harmondsworth).
Findlay, George (1944), 'Browderism' (Pretoria, mimeo).
First, Ruth (1961), 'The gold of migrant labour' (*Africa South in Exile*, Vol. 5, No. 3, April–June).
— (1983), *Black Gold: The Mozambican Miner, Proletarian and Peasant* (Harvester, Sussex).
Frankel, S. Herbert (1938), *Capital Investment in Africa: Its Course and Effects* (OUP, London).
Franklin, N.N. (1948), *Economics in South Africa* (OUP, Cape Town).
Gaitskell, Deborah Lyndall (1981), 'Female mission initiatives: black and white women in three Witwatersrand Churches 1903–1939' (PhD thesis, London University).
— (1982), ' "Wailing for purity": prayer unions, African mothers and

adolescent daughters, 1912—40' (in Marks and Rathbone).

— et. al. (1984), 'Class, race and gender: domestic workers in South Africa' (*Review of African Political Economy*, No. 27/28, February).

Gamble, Andrew and Walton, Paul (1976), *Capitalism in Crisis: Inflation and the State* (Macmillan, London).

Gann, L.H. and Duignan, Peter (eds) (1970), *Colonialism in Africa, 1870— 1960* Vol. 4 (CUP, Cambridge).

Glasser, Mona (1960), *King Kong: A Venture in the Theatre* (Norman Howell, Cape Town).

Good, Dorcas and Williams, Michael [pseuds] (1976), *South Africa: The Crisis in Britain and the Apartheid Economy* (Anti-Apartheid Movement, London).

Gordon, Max (*c.* 1938), 'The scope for native employment'. Saamwerk Papers, No. 2 (mimeo, *Rheinallt Jones Papers*).

Gordon, Suzanne (1985), *A Talent for Tomorrow: Life Stories of South African Servants* (Ravan, Johannesburg).

Green, Timothy (1973), *The World of Gold Today* (White Lion, London).

Gregory, Sir Theodore (1962), *Ernest Oppenheimer and the Economic Development of Southern Africa* (OUP, Cape Town).

Grundlingh, Louis (1984), 'The recruitment of South African blacks for participation in the Second World War' (conference on *Africa in the Second World War*, London).

Hahlo, H.R., and Kahn, Ellison (eds) (1960), *The Union of South Africa: The Development of its Laws and Constitution* (Juta, Cape Town).

Hailey, William Malcolm (1953), *Native Administration in the British African Territories*, Part 5 (HMSO, London).

Haines, Richard (1981), 'Resistance and Acquiescence in the Zoutpansberg, 1936—45: some random thoughts (Wits HW).

Hamerow, Theodore S. (1961), 'The German artisan movement, 1848—49' (*Journal of Central European Affairs*, Vol. 21, No. 2, July).

Harris, David [pseud.] (1981), 'Daniel Koza: a working class leader' (*Africa Perspective*, No. 19).

Haysom, Louise (n.d.), 'Mary Fitzgerald' (typescript).

Haywood, Harry (1978), *Black Bolshevik: Autobiography of an Afro-American Communist* (Liberator Press, Chicago).

Heaton, Herbert (1948), *Economic History of Europe* (Harper, New York).

Hellmann, Ellen (1939), 'Early school leaving and occupations of Native juveniles in Johannesburg' (PhD thesis, Rand).

— (1948), *Rooiyard: A Sociological Survey of an Urban Native Slum Yard* (OUP, Cape Town).

— (1953) *Sellgoods: A Sociological Survey of an African Commercial Labour Force* (SAIRR, Johannesburg).

— (1956), 'The development of social groupings among urban Africans in the Union of South Africa' (in UNESCO, *Social Implications of Industrialisation in Africa South of the Sahara*, United Nations, Paris).

— (1963), *The Impact of City Life on Africans* (ISMA Papers, No. 11, Johannesburg).

Hepple, Alex (1984), 'The South African Labour Party, 1908—1958. A Memoir' (typescript, London).

Hepple, B.A. (1960), 'Economic and racial legislation' (in Hahlo and Kahn).

Herd, Norman (1974), *Counter Attack: The Story of the South African Shopworkers* (National Union of Distributive Workers, Cape Town).

Hertslet, Jessie (1920), 'Native women and girls on the Reef' (*South African Quarterly*, June).

Hirson, Baruch (1977), 'The reorganisation of African trade unions in Johannesburg, 1936—42' (*SSAC*, Vol. 7). ·

— (1978), 'Rural revolt in South Africa: 1937—1951' (in Society of African Culture (ed.), *L'Afrique du Sud Aujourd'hui* (Presence Africaine, Paris).

— (1979), *Year of Fire, Year of Ash* (Zed, London).

— (1984), 'The Bloemfontein riots, 1925: a study in community culture and class consciousness' (*SSAC*, Vol. 13).

— 1986, 'The making of the African working class on the Witwatersrand: class and community struggles in an urban setting, 1932—47' (PhD thesis, Middlesex Polytechnic).

— (1989), 'A trade union organiser in Durban: M.B. Yengwa, 1944—46', ICS, London.

Hobsbawm, E.J. (1972), *Bandits* (Penguin, Harmondsworth).

Hoernlé, R.F. Alfred (1941), *South African Native Policy and the Liberal Spirit* (WUP, Johannesburg).

— (1945), *Race and Reason: Being Mainly a Selection of Contributions to the Race Problem in South Africa* (WUP, Johannesburg).

— et al. (1943), *The Future of Alexandra Township: Open Letter to the Citizens of Johannesburg by the Alexandra Health Committee* (publisher unknown, Johannesburg).

Hofmeyr, Isabel (1983), 'Building a nation from words: Afrikaans language, literature and "ethnic identity" ' (M.A. dissertation, London University).

Horwitz, Ralph (1967), *The Political Economy of South Africa* (Weidenfeld and Nicolson, London).

Houghton, D. Hobart (1971), 'Economic development, 1865—1965' (in Wilson and Thompson, Vol. 2).

— and Dagut, Jennifer (eds) (1973), *Source Material on the South African Economy, 1920—1970*, Vol. 3 (OUP, Cape Town).

— and Walton, Edith M. (1952), *The Economy of a Native Reserve* (Keiskammahoek Rural Survey, Vol. 2, Shuter and Shooter, Pietermaritzburg).

Huddleston, Trevor (1956), *Naught for Your Comfort* (Collins, London).

Innes, Duncan (1984), *Anglo American and the Rise of Modern South Africa* (Heinemann, London).

Jabavu, D.D.T. (1928a), 'Christianity and the Bantu' (in M. Stauffer).

— (1928b), *The Segregation Fallacy and Other Problems* (Lovedale Press, Lovedale).

Jacobsson, D. (1936), *Fifty Golden Years of the Rand, 1886—1936* (Faber, London).

— (1948), *Maize Turns to Gold* (Timmins, Cape Town).

Jaffe, Hosea (1943), 'Criticism of first manifesto issued by the African Democratic Party Provisional Committee' (Johannesburg).

Jingoes, Jason Stimela (1975), see Perry, J. and C.

Johannesburg Joint Council of Europeans and Natives (c. 1920), *Forced Labour in Africa* (Memorandum No. 6, Johannesburg).

Johns, Sheridan Waite (1965), 'Marxism-Leninism in a multi-racial environment: the origins and early history of the Communist Party of South Africa, 1914—1932' (PhD thesis, Harvard University).

Johnstone, Frederick A. (1976), *Class, Race and Gold: A Study of Class Relations and Racial Discrimination in South Africa* (Routledge and Kegan Paul, London).

Jones, J.D. Rheinallt (c. 1927), *The Native in Industry* (printed anon., Johannesburg Joint Council of Europeans and Natives).

— (1930a), 'The urban Native' (in I. Schapera).

— (1930b), 'The worker in industry' (in E.H. Brookes).

Kagan, Noreen (1978), 'African settlements in the Johannesburg area, 1903—1923' (M.A. dissertation, Rand).

Kaplan, David E. (1977), 'An analysis of the South African state in the "fusion" period, 1932—39' (*SSAC*, Vol. 7).

Karis, Tom and Carter, Gwendolen (eds) (1972—77), *From Protest to Challenge: Documents of African Politics in South Africa, 1882—1964* (Hoover Institution Press, Stanford, 4 volumes).

Katzen, Leo (1964), *Gold in the South African Economy* (Balkema, Cape Town).

Katzenellenbogen, Simon E. (1975), 'The miners' frontier, transport and general economic development' (in Gann and Duignan, Vol. 4).

Koch, Eddie (1981), 'Without visible means of subsistence: slumyard culture in Johannesburg, 1918—1940' (Wits HW).

— (1984), 'The destruction of Marabi culture — urban segregation in Johannesburg, 1923—1938' (Wits HW).

Kros, Cynthia (1978), 'Urban African women's organisation and protest on the Rand in the years 1939 to 1956' (B.A. (Hons) essay, Rand. Reprinted by *Africa Perspective*, 1980).

Kruger, D.W. (1971), *The Making of a Nation* (Macmillan, Johannesburg).

Kruger S. [pseud.] (1945), 'Prospects for secondary industries', *Revolutionary Communist*, August).

Krut, Riva (1980), 'The working class and the "housing shortage" in Johannesburg, 1890—1906' (unpublished paper based on M.A. thesis, Rand).

Lacey, Marian (1981), *Working for Boroko: The Origins of a Coercive Labour System in South Africa* (Ravan, Johannesburg).

La Hausse, Paul (1984), 'The struggle for the city: alcohol, the Ematsheni and popular culture in Durban, 1902—1936' (M.A. dissertation, UCT).

Lavis, S.W. (c. 1943), *Cape Town's Underworld* (Christian Council of South Africa, Lovedale).

Lawrence, Jeremy (1978), *Harry Lawrence* (David Philip, Cape Town).

Legassick, Martin and de Clerq, Francine (1984), 'Capitalism and migrant labour in Southern Africa: the origins and nature of the system' (in Marks and Richardson).

Leigh, Ramon Lewis (1968), *Vereeniging — South Africa* (Courier–Gazette, Johannesburg).

Lekhethoa, Herbert and Mbobo, Victor (1944), *Tears of the Black Folk* (no details given).

Lewis, Jonathan Peter (1981), 'The Germiston by-election of 1932: the state and the white working class during the depression' (in Bonner).

— (1982), 'Industrialisation and trade union organisation in South Africa, 1924–55' (PhD thesis, University of Cambridge).

Lewis, W. Arthur (1957), *Economic Survey, 1919–39* (Allen and Unwin, London).

Lodge, Tom (1983), *Black Politics in South Africa Since 1945* (Longman, London).

Lucas, F.A.W. (1927), 'Some aspects of the work of the wage board', address to the Economic Society, 21 November 1927 (printed in three instalments, *Star*, 24/26/28 November).

Lunn, Betty (1946), 'African adult education' (*Socialist Review*, Vol. 3, No. 1, January).

Macmillan, William Miller (1930), *Complex South Africa: An Economic Footnote to History* (Faber, London).

— (1948), *Africa Emergent* (Penguin, Harmondsworth).

Maliba, A.M. (*c.* 1938), *The Conditions of the Venda People* (CPSA, Johannesburg).

Mampuru, Self (1945), 'The African Democratic Party, and the Orlando Advisory Board Elections' (*Socialist Review*, Vol. 2, No. 6, December).

Mann, Michael (1973), *Consciousness and Action Among the Western Working Class* (Macmillan, London).

Mariotti, Amelia Marte (1980), 'The incorporation of African women into wage employment in South Africa, 1920–1970' (PhD thesis, University of Connecticut).

Marks, Shula (1985), 'Southern and Central Africa, 1886–1910' (in R. Oliver and G.N. Sanderson (eds), *The Cambridge History of Africa*, Vol. 6, CUP).

— and Rathbone, Richard (eds) (1982), *Industrialisation and Social Change in South Africa: African Class, Culture and Consciousness, 1870–1930* (Longman, London).

— and Richardson, Peter (eds) (1984), *International Labour Migration* (Temple Smith, London).

— and Trapido, Stanley (1979), 'Lord Milner and the South African state' (*History Workshop*, No. 8, Autumn; reprinted in Bonner).

Marx, Karl, *Capital: A Critique of Political Economy*, Vol. 1 (1976) (Penguin, Harmondsworth); Vol. 2 (1974) (Lawrence and Wishart, London); Vol. 3 (1959) (Lawrence and Wishart, London).

— (1973), *Grundrisse* (Penguin, Harmondsworth).

Matthews, Z.K. (1946), 'Reasons why the Native Representative Council in the Union of South Africa adjourned' (Karis and Carter, Vol. 2, p.232).

Maud, John (1938), *City Government: The Johannesburg Experiment* (Clarendon, Oxford).

Mayer, Philip (ed.) (1980), *Black Villagers in an Industrial Society: Anthropological Perspectives in Labour Migration in South Africa* (OUP, Cape Town).

Mdatyualwa, J.Z. (1946), 'Report to the Annual Business Meeting of the Johannesburg Joint Council of Europeans and Africans' (13 May, *Xuma Papers*, ABX 460521a).

Millin, Sarah Gertrude (1934), *The South Africans* (Constable, new edition, London).

Mkele, Nimrod (1961), *The African Middle Class* (*ISMA Papers*, No. 4, Johannesburg).

Modisane, Bloke (1963), *Blame Me on History* (Thames and Hudson, London).

Mokgatle, Naboth (1971), *The Autobiography of an Unknown South African* (University of California Press, California).

Moodie, T. Dunbar (c. 1984a), 'The role of the state in industrial conflict: the 1940s war years' (typescript).

— (c. 1984b), 'The moral economy of the mine and the African Mine Workers Union: 1940s mine disturbances' (typescript).

— (c. 1984c), 'The black miners' strike of 1946' (typescript).

Mphahlele, Ezekiel (1962), *Down Second Avenue* (Seven Seas, Berlin).

Mutwa, Credo (1964), *My People* (Anthony Blond, London).

Neumark, S.D. (1934), 'The world agricultural crisis' (*South African Journal of Economics*, Vol. 2, No. 1, March).

Nkosi, Lewis (1965), *Home and Exile* (Longman, Green, London).

Norval, A.J. (1962), *A Quarter of a Century of Industrial Progress in South Africa* (Juta, Cape Town).

Ntantala, Phyllis (1957), 'African tragedy' (*Africa South*, Vol. 1, No. 3, April–June).

— (1958), 'The widows of the Reserves' (*Africa South*, Vol. 2, No. 3, April–June).

O'Brien, B. [pseud.] (1946), 'Should communists contest municipal elections' (*Freedom*, Vol. 5, No. 1, February).

O'Connell, M.C. (1980), 'Xesibe reds, rascals and gentlemen at home and at work' (in P. Mayer).

Oliver, Roland and Sanderson, G.N. (eds) (1985), *The Cambridge History of Africa*, Vol. 6 (CUP, Cambridge).

O'Meara, Dan (1975), 'The 1946 African mine workers' strike and the political economy of South Africa' (*Journal of Commonwealth and Comparative Politics*, Vol. 13, No. 2, July).

— (1983), *Volkskapitalisme: Class, Capital and Ideology in the Development of Afrikaner Nationalism, 1924–1948* (Ravan, Johannesburg).

Padayachee, Vishnu, Vawda, Shahid, and Tichman, Paul (1985), *Indian Workers and Trades Unions in Durban: 1930–1950* (The Institute for Social and Economic Research, University of Durban-Westville).

Palmer, Robin and Parsons, Neil (eds) (1977), *The Roots of Rural Poverty in Central and Southern Africa* (Heinemann, London).

Patel, Essop (ed.) (1975), *The World of Nat Nakasa: Selected Writings of the Late Nat Nakasa* (Ravan, Johannesburg).

Perry, John and Cassandra (eds) (1975), *A Chief is a Chief by the People: The Autobiography of Stimela Jason Jingoes* (OUP, London).

Peteni, R.L. (1979), *Towards Tomorrow: The Story of the African Teachers Association of South Africa* (Reference Publications, Michigan).

Phillips, Ray E. (1930), *The Bantu are Coming: Phases of South Africa's Race Problem* (SCM Press, London).

— (1938), *The Bantu in the City: A Study of Cultural Adjustment on the Witwatersrand* (SCM, Lovedale).

— (1940), 'The rising tide of native crime: an address to the Rotary Club of Johannesburg, Tuesday 7 May'.

Piven, Frances Fox, and Cloward, Richard A. (1979), *Poor People's Movements: Why They Succeed, How They Fail* (Vintage, New York).

Proctor, André (1979), 'Class struggle, segregation and the city: a history of Sophiatown, 1905–1940' (in Bozzoli, 1979).

Richards, C.S. (1940), *The Iron and Steel Industry in South Africa* (WUP, Johannesburg).

— et al. (1948), *A Study of Johannesburg Employment Records* (Industrial Research Section of the Department of Commerce, Rand).

Richardson, Peter, and Van Helten, Jean Jacques (1982), 'Labour in the South African gold mining industry, 1886–1914' (in Marks and Rathbone).

Roberts, Michael and Trollip, A.E.G. (1947), *The South African Opposition, 1939–1945* (Longman, Green, Cape Town).

Roth, M. (1983), 'Domination by consent: elections under the Representation of Natives' Act, 1937–1948', mimeo, ASI).

Roux, Edward (1944), *S.P. Bunting, A Political Biography* (Cape Town).

— (1949), *Time Longer Than Rope: A History of the Black Man's Struggle for Freedom in South Africa* (Gollancz, London).

— and Roux, Winifred (1972), *Rebel Pity: The Life of Eddie Roux* (Penguin, Harmondsworth).

Rudé, George (1980), *Ideology and Popular Protest* (Lawrence and Wishart, London).

Sachs, E.S. (1952), *The Choice Before South Africa* (Turnstile, London).

— (1957), *Rebels' Daughters* (McGibbon and Kee, London).

Saffery, A. Lynn (1941a), 'African trade unions and the institute' (*Race Relations*, Vol. 8, No. 2).

— (1941b), *How to Get Higher Wages* (SAIRR, Johannesburg).

Sapire, Hilary (1987), 'The stay-away of the Brakpan Location, 1944' (in Bozzoli, 1987).

Scott, Michael (1946), 'Strike of African gold miners, Johannesburg' (typescript, 7 November; together with statements by mineworkers, collected by Scott).

— (1958), *A Time to Speak* (Faber, London).

Schapera, I. (ed.) (1930), *Western Civilization and the Native in South Africa* (Routledge, London).

Sewell, W.H. (1974), 'Social change and the rise of working-class politics in nineteenth-century Marseilles' (*Past and Present*, No. 65, November).

Simons, H.J. (1936), 'The Criminal Law and its administration in South Africa, Southern Rhodesia, and Kenya' (PhD thesis, University of London).

— (1961), 'Death in South African mines' (*Africa South in Exile*, Vol. 5, No. 4, July–September).

Simons H.J., and Simons R.E. (1969), *Colour and Class in South Africa, 1850–1950* (Penguin, Harmondsworth).

Smith, R.H. (1950), *Labour Resources of Natal* (OUP, Cape Town).

Smuts, J.C. (1952), *Jan Christian Smuts* (Cassell, London).

Stadler, A.W. (1979), 'Birds in the cornfields: squatter movements in Johannesburg, 1944–47' (in Bozzoli, 1979).

— (1981), 'A long way to walk: bus boycotts in Alexandra, 1940–1945' (in P. Bonner).

Stauffer, Milton (ed.) (1928), *Thinking with Africa: Chapters by a Group of Nationals Interpreting the Christian Movement* (SCM, London).

Stein, Mark (1977a), 'African trade unionism on the Witwatersrand, 1928–1940' (B.A. (Hons) essay, Rand).

— (1977b), 'The Non-European Iron and Steel Workers Union, 1942–50' (seminar paper, University of Warwick).

— (1981), 'Black trade unionism during the Second World War: the Witwatersrand strikes of December 1942' (*SSAC*, Vol. 10).

Storman, L. [Szur] (1943), *Whose Tomorrow? The Choice Before the Labour Movement* (Johannesburg).

Sundkler, Bengt G.M. (1958), *The Concept of Christianity in the African Independent Church* (University of Natal Institute for Social Research).

— (1964), *Bantu Prophets in South Africa* (OUP, London).

Susser, Ida (1982), *Norman Street: Poverty and Politics in an Urban Neighborhood* (OUP, New York).

Tabata, I.B. (1950), *The All African Convention: The Awakening of a People* (People's Press, Johannesburg).

Tayal, Maureen (1984), 'The 1913 Natal Indian strike' (*JSAS*, Vol. 10, No. 2, April).

Thompson, E.P. (1968), *The Making of the English Working Class* (Penguin, Harmondsworth).

— (1978), 'Eighteenth-century English society: class struggle without class?' (*Social History*, Vol. 3, No. 2).

Thorne, Athol (1977), 'Tribute to Max Gordon', at the graveside, 18 May.

Tinley, J.M. (1942), *The Native Labour Problem of South Africa*

(University of North Carolina Press, Chapel Hill).

Trapido, Stanley (1971), 'South Africa in a comparative study of industrialisation' (*Journal of Development Studies*, No. 7).

— (1986), 'Putting a plough to the ground: a history of tenant production on the Vereeniging Estates, 1896—1920' (in Beinart, Delius and Trapido).

Trewhela, P.H. (1970), 'The development of the world economy and the war in South Africa' (M.A. dissertation, University of Sussex).

Trotsky, Leon (1938), 'Trade unions in the transitional epoch' (in Clarke and Clements).

— (1940), 'Trade unions in the epoch of imperialist decay' (Workers International League, London).

Turrell, Rob (1982), 'Kimberley: labour and closed compounds, 1871—1888' (in Marks and Rathbone).

UNESCO (1956), *Social Implications of Industrialisation in Africa South of the Sahara* (United Nations, Paris).

Van der Horst, Sheila (1942), *Native Labour in South Africa* (OUP, London).

— (1971), *African Workers in Town* (Cass, London).

Van der Poel, Jean (ed.) (1973), *Selections From the Smuts Papers*, Vols. 5—7 (CUP, Cambridge).

Van-Helten, Jean Jacques (1977), 'British Capital, the British state and economic investment in South Africa, 1886—1914' (*SSAC*, Vol. 9).

— (1982), 'Empire and high finance: South Africa and the international gold standard 1890—1914' (*Journal of African History*, Vol. 23, No. 4).

Van Onselen, Charles (1982), *Studies in the Economic History of the Witwatersrand, 1886—1914* (2 Vols) (Longman, London).

Vucinich, Wayne S. (ed.) (1968), *The Peasant in Nineteenth Century Russia* (Stanford University Press, Stanford).

Walkin, Jacob (1954), 'The attitude of the Czarist government towards the labour problem' (*American Slavonic and East European Review*).

Walshe, Peter (1970), *The Rise of African Nationalism in South Africa: The African National Congress, 1912—1952* (Hurst, London).

Webb, Sidney and Beatrice (1907), *A History of Trade Unionism* (Longman, Green, London).

Webster, Eddie (ed.), (1981), *Essays in Southern African Labour History* (Ravan, Johannesburg).

Weinberg, Eli (1944), 'The African miner' (*Freedom*, May).

Weiss, Herbert (1967), *Political Protest in the Congo. The Parti Solidaire Africaine During the Independence Struggle* (Princeton University Press, New Jersey).

Wells, Julia C. (1982), 'The history of black women's struggle against pass laws in South Africa' (PhD thesis, Columbia University, New York).

Welsh, David (1971), 'The growth of towns' (in Wilson and Thompson).

Willan, Brian Peel (1979), 'The role of Solomon T. Plaatje (1876—1932) in South African society' (PhD thesis, University of London).

Williams, J. Greenfel and May, John Henry (1936), *I Am Black* (Cassell, London).

Williams, M. [D. Bransky] (1975), 'An analysis of South African capitalism — neo-Ricardianism or Marxism?' (*Bulletin of the Conference of Socialist Economists*, February).

Williams, M.C. (n.d.), 'An account of the Diocesan Training College' (Grace Dieu, Pietersburg).

Williams, Raymond (1976), *Keywords: A Vocabulary of Culture and Society* (Fontana, Glasgow).

Wilson, Francis (1971), 'Farming 1866—1961' (in Wilson and Thompson).

— (1972a), *Migrant Labour in South Africa* (Spro-Cas, Johannesburg).

— (1972b), *Labour in the South African Gold Mines, 1911—1969* (CUP, Cambridge).

— and Perrot, Dominique (eds) (1973), *Outlook on a Century: South Africa, 1870—1970* (Lovedale Press, Johannesburg).

Wilson, Monica, and Thompson, Leonard (eds) (1971), *The Oxford History of South Africa*, Vol. 2 (Clarendon, Oxford).

Witz, Leslie (1987), 'A case of schizophrenia: the rise and fall of the Independent Labour Party' (in Bozzoli, 1987).

Xuma, A.B. (1943), 'The art of making criminals' (*Common Sense*, March).

Zelnik, Reginald E. (1968), 'The peasant and the factory' (in Vucinich).

Index

www.ingramcontent.com/pod-product-compliance
Ingram Content Group UK Ltd.
Pitfield, Milton Keynes, MK11 3LW, UK
UKHW031249020325
455689UK00008B/151